Experimental Social Programs and Analytic Methods
AN EVALUATION OF THE U.S. INCOME MAINTENANCE PROJECTS

QUANTITATIVE STUDIES IN SOCIAL RELATIONS

Consulting Editor: Peter H. Rossi

UNIVERSITY OF MASSACHUSETTS
AMHERST, MASSACHUSETTS

The list of titles in this series continues on the last page of this volume

Experimental Social Programs and Analytic Methods

AN EVALUATION
OF THE U.S. INCOME MAINTENANCE PROJECTS

ALEXANDER BASILEVSKY

Department of Mathematics and Statistics
University of Winnipeg
Winnipeg, Canada

DEREK HUM

Department of Economics
St. John's College
University of Manitoba
Winnipeg, Canada

1984

ACADEMIC PRESS

(Harcourt Brace Jovanovich, Publishers)

Orlando   San Diego   San Francisco   New York   London
Toronto   Montreal   Sydney   Tokyo   São Paulo

c.,

ACADEMIC PRESS, INC.
Orlando, Florida 32887

United Kingdom Edition published by
ACADEMIC PRESS, INC. (LONDON) LTD.
24/28 Oval Road, London NW1 7DX

Basilevsky, Alexander.
    Experimental social programs and analytic methods.

    (Quantitative studies in social relations)
    Includes bibliographical references and index.
    1. Labor supply--United States--Statistical methods.
2. Income maintenance programs--United State.
I. Hum, Derek. II. Title. III. Series.
HD724.B345 1983   362.5'82   83-11846
ISBN 0-12-080280-5

To our wives, Annick and Mary

Contents

3. The Sample Design and Assignment Model of the Guaranteed Income Experiments

4. Methodological Issues and Experimental Data

5. The New Jersey Graduated Work Incentive Experiment

6. The Rural Income Maintenance Experiment

7. The Seattle–Denver Income Maintenance Experiment (SIME–DIME)

8. The Gary Income Maintenance Experiment

9. Conclusions   212

Preface

During the late 1960s and 1970s the United States embarked on a series of social experiments to explore the economic and social consequences of a guaranteed income program. The experiments required millions of dollars, lasted many years, and focused on the negative income tax method of delivering cash benefits. At the forefront of policy discussion were a number of issues, including the estimated cost to the United States of a guaranteed income and general matters concerning welfare reform. But the heart of the controversy was the question of work disincentives; that is, whether a guaranteed income would cause low-income able-bodied individuals to work less. This was a key concern for policy makers and required careful empirical research together with precise measurement to provide the necessary answers.

Most of the experiments on guaranteed incomes are now complete and findings on the work disincentive effects have appeared. However, there is still controversy as to the significance and confidence of estimates. Because this research is scattered throughout monographs, limited-circulation reports, journal articles, unpublished manuscripts, and other sources not readily accessible to many, knowledge and appreciation of this research is quite limited. Consequently many academics, policy makers, and concerned citizens are less than fully informed. Furthermore, there is a widespread tendency to recall the *first numbers* associated with the preliminary results from the experiments as *the truth* or, alternatively, to regard the *latest numbers* as *the final word*. There has been neither a conveniently accessible description of the total research findings nor a systematic critical appraisal of methodology and results. This book therefore examines in a thorough fashion the statistical and econometric research on work disincentive effects reported by these unique social experiments. In addition to providing a comparative description of the several experimental designs and labor supply results, we include a general discussion of methodological issues common to all the experiments. We also include a detailed presentation of the Conlisk–Watts model for sample assignment and discuss the labor supply findings from both an econometric as well as a statistical perspective. We attempt to discuss how the methods and models vary for each of the experiments and how the results might be sensitive to the model specified.

The American experiments were unique in applying, for the first time, large-scale experimental design techniques to estimate labor supply responses for policy goals. Econometricians had little previous experience with experimental design issues, survey research, and the like. The fact that data of an apparently experimental nature were generated created an opportunity and challenge for labor economists and econometricians, but they also posed a new problem. How should the experimentally induced *treatment* be incorporated? Because this unique feature characterized the experiments and represented unfamiliar terrain for labor supply economists and econometricians, we focus on this aspect: namely, how did each of the researchers specify the *treatment*, and how successful was each researcher in exploiting the experimental nature of the data? At the same time, the income maintenance experiments posed special problems for statistical experimental design because they could be interpreted not only as experiments but also as social programs provided with a convenient control group. This second viewpoint was not always taken by researchers performing the *first*-round analysis, so the first stage of the analysis was characterized by more-or-less classical experimental methodology, whereas in the second stage (for example, the Gary analysis and the reworking of the New Jersey data) there was a conscious effort to take into account nonparticipation, sample attrition, and other aspects of nonrandomly missing data.

Our book is aimed at two groups of readers, not necessarily mutually exclusive. It will be of interest to professionals and students in econometrics, labor economics, statistics, and quantitative research. At the same time, it should prove useful to policy analysts and others concerned with social welfare reform, public administration, and the like. As a summary document of all the experiments and a critical survey of the work response findings, the book should provide much general information. Furthermore, separate chapters on experimental design, on methodological issues, and on each separate experiment should be welcomed by professional researchers or those who wish a more technical discussion of individual report findings. The purpose of this book then is to give both professional researchers and policy analysts an up-to-date survey of the work response findings from the American negative income tax experiments. There is a need for a book such as the present one—if only to gather in one place the voluminous scattered literature. Our book is an attempt to integrate and appraise this literature from a combined statistical and econometric viewpoint.

The technical level of this book varies from chapter to chapter. Although we assume a basic knowledge of economics and statistics, the material in Chapters 1, 2, and 9 require little technical training to understand. These chapters describe the background to the experiments and the research and policy issues, summarize (without criticism) the work response findings, and attempt to provide an appraisal of the scientific validity of the labor supply response estimates made by the various experiments. This discussion may be read by anyone with a general interest in the issues involved and in the major findings, although a grasp of statistical methodology is clearly helpful when it comes to the interpretation of results and the weighing of evidence. Chapters 3 and 4 are more technical. These chapters discuss the experimental and sample design issues and present an analytic framework that encompasses both the statistics and econometrics disciplines. Readers with a general interest in statistical methodology or quantitative research, but a less particular interest in labor supply issues per se, will find these chapters relatively autonomous. That is, issues are raised that are not peculiar to estimation of labor supply but are pertinent to quantitative research in general and would have arisen in any other major socioeconomic project. Chapters 5–8 deal with the labor supply models and estimates of work disincentive from each of the four experiments. These are written mainly for labor supply economists and econometricians, but parts of these chapters may be read by the general reader having an elementary statistical background.

This book had its intellectual origin as early as 1973 when both authors were employed by the Manitoba Guaranteed Annual Income Project (Mincome Manitoba) in capacity as director of research (D.H.) and senior researcher (A.B.). However, it was not until 1978, in preparation for the analysis stage of the Canadian project, that initial research was undertaken on the U.S. guaranteed income projects. When it became clear that government agencies would not fund analysis of the Canadian labor supply data, both authors turned to the U.S. results, which were then beginning to appear with increasing frequency, as a full-time research project. There were long stretches of "downtime" as we located inaccessible material, corresponded with individual authors, sought clarification, and in some instances discussed matters with individuals directly or indirectly involved with the various experiments. Although written over a period of several years, the book has been expanded and updated during 1981–1982 to incorporate new results, which have begun to appear in increasing numbers and which no doubt will continue to appear.

The authors would like to thank the Social Sciences and Humanities Research Council of Canada for partial support of one author's (D.H.) sabbatical leave, which permitted him to devote more time to the book than would have been otherwise possible. We must also acknowledge our respective universities, the

University of Winnipeg and the University of Manitoba, for financial aid toward the preparation of the manuscript. We would also like to thank Andy Anderson of the University of Massachusetts and Don Sabourin of the Institute for Social and Economic Research, University of Manitoba for numerous suggestions on portions of previous drafts that greatly improved the manuscript, as well as for his constant encouragement. We are also indebted to our editor, whose diligent efforts also greatly improved our book. Finally, our families deserve our appreciation and gratitude for their patience and support. We are alone responsible, of course, for any error of fact or interpretation that may have made its way into the manuscript. Although each author took responsibility for the first draft of various chapters the final manuscript, after much rewriting, is the indivisible result of an equal collaboration, and authorship order is alphabetical.

1 Poverty and Experiments — The Background

I. INTRODUCTION

The United States is an affluent society. At the same time it is also a society that has a great deal of poverty. Although discussion on the causes of poverty appears unending, it is doubtlessly true that measuring the extent of poverty by income levels has become common.[1] In fact, the construction of poverty lines and periodic counting of the poor is now a fairly standard, replicable exercise carried out by government officials and academics alike. Consequently, one is often tempted to define the issue of poverty rather narrowly in terms of either low or inadequate incomes and to phrase policy concerns in terms of either income maintenance or cash transfer programs. Although such an approach is unnecessarily restrictive, it does serve to focus attention on income support measures and their associated problems. And among the most contentious and controversial antipoverty strategies advanced is the program of guaranteed incomes.

Proposals to alleviate poverty based on a government guarantee of a certain minimum level of income to every individual or family are no longer new. These proposals have a moderately long history of intellectual advocacy, policy discussion, and program proposals. When one views the poverty problem primarily as a matter of insufficient income in a market-oriented society, as do most economists, it is natural to look to tax transfer measures to redistribute income. Simultaneously the tax transfer system is seen as the vehicle for administering the welfare system, financing the transfer costs, and integrating the able-bodied poor into the labor market. Friedman (1963) was among the first to suggest a "negative income tax" (NIT) by means of which a portion of the unused tax exemptions and deductions allowable under the personal income tax system would be actually paid to individuals by the government. Lampman's (1965a, b) various proposals specified that different rates of subsidy be added to earnings in order to bring an individual's income up to some predetermined level. Tobin (1965, 1966) advocated a system of income allowances in which those with no earnings would receive a certain minimum amount. All of these proposals are related to the income tax system; hence a NIT generally means any form of income maintenance or supplementation based on the mechanism of the personal income tax. Specifically, it involves the payment of cash transfers by the government to households having income below a prespecified amount; it is the technical inverse of taxes paid to the government by households with incomes above a certain exemption level.[2] The combination of three elements, namely, the view that poverty can be largely defined in terms of income, the belief that the tax transfer mechanism is an appropriate instrument for welfare reform objectives, and the economist's fascination (or infatuation) with the logical symmetry of the income tax system, influenced much of the design and basic language of NIT schemes. The NIT proposal has had its share of advocates (e.g., Rolph, 1967; Tobin *et al.,* 1967), detractors (e.g., Schorr, 1966; Hitch, 1966; Vadakin, 1968), and skeptics (e.g., Hildebrand, 1967).

Almost all variants of income maintenance schemes embody a basic support level, to which families are entitled if they have no earnings or other income, and some rate of taxation by which this support amount is reduced or "offset" for each dollar earned. Consequently, a NIT scheme may be characterized by the combination of its guaranteed minimum income level *G* and its offset taxation rate *t*. A breakeven level of income *B* can then be defined in terms of *G* and *t*, and it is that level of income at which cash transfers or negative taxes to the family are no longer paid. The higher the level of the minimum income guarantee and/or the lower the tax rate, the higher is the level of income below which negative taxes will be paid and consequently the greater will be the proportion of the population that receives negative taxes. The costs of such NIT transfers are therefore greater with higher guarantee levels and lower tax rates. At the same time a NIT offers able-bodied, low-income individuals a certain lump sum amount of income unconditionally; that is, without reference to work performance. Operating in conjunction with a tax on earned income, the guaranteed income will tend to lessen work incentives according to standard economic theory. Again, the higher the degree of work disincentive, the higher will be the transfer costs associated with the NIT and, as well, the less likely it will be that public support or political initiative would be forthcoming. So the crucial policy questions concerning the NIT are How much work disincentive is there likely to be, and what will be the costs associated with different levels of support and taxation rates?[3]

Unfortunately, precise and reliable estimates of work response to non-work-conditioned income receipts were not available and, in the opinion of most econometric researchers, were unlikely to be forthcoming from non-experimental data alone. Also it was not clear whether general research results on work behavior could be applied to the low-income working poor, and it is upon this group that NIT policy concerns were focused and about which, perhaps, the least was known concerning work habits and responses. Consequently, the stage was set for a series of large-scale social experiments in the United States to address this important issue of income guarantees and work incentives. These experiments were conducted in a variety of locations, cost millions of dollars each, took place over a number of years, and required vast amounts of resources in terms of research and scientific talent, operational and administrative effort, data processing, and field survey and other professional personnel. Taken as a whole the experiments were audacious and innovative. As a research endeavor they established a precedent in introducing large-scale randomized controlled experimental designs to the social sciences and resulted in methodological advances in many areas. At the same time, they produced new policy-relevant information and novel administrative techniques. Their total impact has been to change, substantially and irrevocably, the nature of the debate concerning welfare reform, work incentives, and the NIT.

Although small-scale policy experiments can be traced back to the early 1960s in the United States, the character and consequences of the more recent large-scale social experiments are entirely different. These experiments pose a distinct set of advantages, difficulties, and issues for policy makers and researchers alike. The remainder of this chapter will provide an overview of some income maintenance policy issues and a chronology of the events leading to social experimentation in the United States. It is concerned primarily with the decade of the 1970s. Section II describes the central issue underlying income maintenance experimentation by juxtaposing both the policy and research viewpoints that eventually converged to make the work incentives question the prime issue. Section III provides some historical background to the NIT experiments; Section IV gives a brief statement of the theoretical effect of a NIT on work response.

II. WORK INCENTIVES, COST, AND EXPERIMENTATION

The design parameters of a guaranteed income program can be described in terms of a basic support level or guarantee G to which the family is entitled if it has no other income, and some provision for a taxation rate by which the guaranteed amount is reduced for each dollar of earned income. The NIT is no exception and can also be characterized in this fashion as, indeed, almost any income maintenance scheme can be. Supporters of the NIT concept at various times have stressed the mechanism's equity, objectivity, cost effectiveness, social advantages, and simplicity. Its critics draw attention to the scheme's high cost, impracticality, social disintegration tendencies, cumbersome bureaucratic demands, and damaging effects on work effort. Central to both the political acceptability and economic feasibility of the NIT idea was the controversy concerning the labor supply disincentive effect of a guaranteed minimum income.

It is clear that the more generous the program, as measured by high support levels and low taxation rates, the larger will be the total program costs of a guaranteed annual income (GAI). This results because nonworkers would receive larger amounts, low-income workers would keep a larger proportion of their earnings, and a larger proportion of the population would be recipients since high guarantees and low tax rates have the effect of raising the income level (called the breakeven point) below which NIT payments are made by the government. Consequently, attempting to eliminate poverty by providing income payments to the poor through a GAI can be very costly, depending on the support level and tax rate chosen. At the same time attitudes toward income support in general, and toward the poor in particular, are strongly conditioned by the work ethic and the institutional fact of labor markets. A guaranteed income could lessen work incentives, perhaps to the point of net social detriment. Just how much less people would work in response to a guaranteed income no one can confidently say. And it is not clear that nonexperimental data can provide answers to this very important question.

The idea of an experimental test was the next logical step. In addition to the many tangible benefits for policy makers of having answers to the work disincentive question, and cost estimates for a GAI, an explicit policy experiment also held tremendous appeal for researchers. Frustrated with more conventional research approaches using ex post facto data, researchers saw the immense potential of a social experiment in NIT. Such an experiment would permit researchers to select the sample size required, the composition of the sample, and to induce a measurable response.[4] A NIT experiment could also provide guarantee levels and tax rate combinations not possible in any real-life public program. A true experiment would then allow superior inferences concerning the causal effect of a guaranteed income on work behavior.

In sum, policy concerns and research interests collided favorably in a happy combination of need and opportunity. These circumstances led to the mutual identification of the issue of labor supply response to a guaranteed income as all important.

III. HISTORICAL ORIGINS OF THE AMERICAN EXPERIMENTS

No one looking back at the experience of the income maintenance experiments — be they researchers or policy makers — can fail to be impressed by the sense of historical occasion. Some sympathy for those "best of times and worst of times" is necessary. The mid-1960s is a convenient place to start. President Lyndon Johnson had called for a War on Poverty in his State of the Union address in 1964. In that same year the U.S. Congress passed the Economic Opportunity Act, establishing the Office of Economic Opportunity (OEO) as the headquarters and vanguard for the antipoverty effort. The set of programs discussed by the research planners of the OEO aimed at eliminating poverty comprised three major components: public employment strategies, community action programs, and income maintenance. Although the crucial role of income maintenance in combating poverty was recognized and readily accepted, a NIT approach to delivering cash transfers to the low-income groups was more controversial.

The NIT idea was reasonably novel and initially met both opposition and neglect. For example, some, like Alvin Schorr, deputy director of research for OEO, favored an alternative proposal based on children's allowances payable to all families with children regardless of income. On the other hand, Joseph Kershaw, director of the research office of OEO, stressed the distributional efficacy of income-conditioned payments and recommended the NIT proposal to Sargent Shriver, director of the OEO. Shriver was won over by the strong advocacy of the OEO research group and the antipoverty plan that was submitted to the White House in September 1965 contained the NIT as a component. The OEO also forwarded in October 1965 to the Bureau of the Budget an NIT proposal costing $4.7 billion as the centerpiece of its antipoverty plan. The White House, however, being preoccupied with the Vietnam War and the falling popularity of some of the OEO's social programs, did not take the NIT proposal seriously (Levine, 1975) and the only response from the President was to appoint a commission on income maintenance programs (Lampman, 1974).

Despite the lack of political and general government support, the NIT did not die. Partly because of the OEO's unwavering faith and strong support, and partly because of the continuing war on poverty, the NIT was regarded by its proponents as an idea whose time had come. A slight unscheduled delay was tolerable. Besides OEO's support, additional factors contributed to the eventual success in launching the series of NIT experiments in the United States.

The OEO continued to single out the NIT for attention as part of its mandate concerning antipoverty strategies. Additionally, the research staff and OEO bureaucrats were very heavily influenced by what Lampman (1974) has called the "ascending discipline of the Program Planning Budget System" (PPBS). Prominent within the OEO were a key group of individuals—many recruited from RAND or the Pentagon, new to social welfare, and without sharply defined loyalties to specific agencies or proposals. These individuals accepted the application of formal evaluation techniques. Accordingly, the goal of eliminating poverty was stated in income maintenance terms, alternative proposals were arrayed, and cost effectiveness scores were assigned to different schemes on the basis of the "most bang for a billion bucks." Under this exercise the NIT received high marks and consequently had the effect of focusing further discussion on particular aspects of the NIT approach such as the cost sensitivity and work disincentive effect of guaranteed amounts and tax rates. The effect of general cash transfer mechanisms on the work effect of the non-aged, able-bodied individual therefore emerged as the (now clarified) prime empirical issue.

Although many felt that the negative income tax would cost more than existing welfare programs because the objective of the NIT was to extend cash transfers to the working poor—a group largely ineligible for most other programs—the proponents of the NIT perceived that the major stumbling block was political. The belief, on the part of politicians as well as the general public, that a NIT would increase idleness among the able-bodied poor was strongly held and no amount of argument "without hard facts" was likely to dispel such beliefs. This then became the dominant issue, pushing into the background all other disagreements concerning the cost of the NIT, the administrative practicality and mechanics of the scheme, the lack or otherwise of stigmatizing effects, and other issues.

Perception of the central problem of the NIT as one of potential work disincentive effectively translated the issue into one for which economists could claim special competence. In the jargon of the economics discipline, the NIT was restated as a controversy concerning evidence regarding wage rate (price) and income elasticities pertinent to labor–leisure choice. The economics discipline provided a theory, and economists themselves readily demonstrated that existing data sources could not answer the incentives issue with confidence. However, the necessary information and evidence could be gained with an experiment. The proposition seemed breathtakingly simple. If you want to find out something new about which present knowledge is wholly inadequate, *try it out!* The credit for the initial idea and proposal goes to Heather Ross, a graduate student in economics with the Council of Economic Advisors during the summer of 1965. Although Heather Ross' specific proposal was not accepted, it received wide circulation within the OEO and many econometricians strongly endorsed the idea of an experiment (Orcutt and Orcutt, 1968). Proposal for an experiment received strong support from OEO, which initiated work and serious planning on the design for an experiment in 1966. The final proposals were also endorsed by the OEO research staff as well, and Sargent Shriver added his approval in 1967. Shriver was able to counteract political opposition[5] and by the fall of the next year families had been selected for enrollment in a negative income tax experiment, payments were being made, and the first of the large-scale social experiments in North America—the New Jersey Graduated Work Incentive Experiment—had begun. The undertaking was not called a negative income tax experiment but instead, for political purposes, a "work incentive experiment," connoting a happy rather than unhappy anticipated outcome. As well, the experiment now emphasized the purely scientific dimensions of the project, as evidenced by the (deliberate) funding of the experiment through the Institute for Research on Poverty in Wisconsin.

The first negative tax experiment in the United States was therefore forged out of sharply different motivations and interests. Undoubtedly, the antipoverty program was a major stimulus and factor in setting the climate for political discussion and policy debate. Equally, the cost effectiveness apparatus of the PPBS and the strong advocacy of OEO's research staff for the NIT were also ingredients. Further, academic econometricians "raring to take social science over the threshold into the realm of controlled experimentation" played an influential role (Lampman, 1974). It remains that no single statement can fully capture the subtleties of how and why the New Jersey experiment came to be. Neither did the matter end with the birth of an experiment, as Haveman and Watts (1976) observed:

> [The] tension between the motivations of those who supported the experiment for "general-political-demonstration" reasons and those who desired it for "technical-economic-experimental" reasons persisted throughout the [New Jersey] experiment. It affected all of its primary characteristics from technical design to duration to selection of sites and finally to interpretation of results [p. 427].

Other income maintenance experiments in the United States rapidly followed. The OEO awarded a further grant to the Institute for Research on Poverty for a negative tax experiment in rural areas. The Department of

Health, Education and Welfare (HEW) also funded one in Gary, Indiana, and others in Seattle, Washington, and Denver, Colorado.   Each of these other experiments had slightly different foci and often incorporated additional research objectives but the New Jersey experiment remains distinctive in setting the precedent for the series of carefully controlled, scientific field tests of different negative income tax or benefit formulas on work behavior.[6]

IV.   THE EFFECT OF NIT ON WORK RESPONSE: A BRIEF STATEMENT OF THE THEORY

The research design of the experiments was heavily influenced by economic theory relating the effect of income maintenance to the labor–leisure choice.   Although models of the labor supply decision can differ in many details, nonetheless a "representative" model can be illustrated as a standard application of static consumer choice theory to the problem of labor supply.   It is important to understand that it was this "representative" economic model that determined, more or less, which aspects would be experimentally varied in the guaranteed income projects.

The individual is assumed to maximize a well-behaved utility function characterizing his preferences subject to a budget constraint.   The basic resource of the individual is the total amount of available time T, which may be allocated to either work for pay or nonmarket activities.   Time allocated to work H provides earnings used to purchase a "composite commodity" X, having price p.   Aggregated nonmarket uses of time is called leisure L, with price w, the opportunity cost of leisure measured in wage units.   Assuming the consumer-worker has unearned income of Y, the budget constraint is

$$pX = w(T - L) + Y = wH + Y, \tag{1.1}$$

where $H \equiv T - L$ is hours worked.   Faced with a fixed set of values for p, w, and Y, the individual chooses values of L and X so as to maximize his preference function: $U = U(X, L)$.   Formally, the problem may be written:

$$\text{Maximize} \quad U = U(X, L)$$
$$\text{subject to} \quad pX - w(T - L) - Y = 0.$$

Introducing a Lagrangian multiplier λ, we may maximize

$$U(X, L) + \lambda[pX - w(T - L) - Y]. \tag{1.2}$$

The necessary conditions are

$$\frac{\partial U}{\partial X} - \lambda p = 0,$$

$$\frac{\partial U}{\partial L} - \lambda w = 0, \tag{1.3}$$

$$pX - w(T - L) - Y = 0$$

The first-order conditions for work–leisure equilibrium may be viewed as a set of three equations in the three unknowns, L, X, and λ, where λ is interpreted as the marginal utility of income. For given values of p, w, and Y, the unknowns may be solved as functions of p, w, and Y. In particular, we have

$$L = L(w, p, Y) \tag{1.4}$$

as the demand function for leisure. Since $T - L = H$, the equation that defines the demand function for leisure also gives the supply function for labor

$$H = H(w, p, Y). \tag{1.5}$$

Consider now the effect of income maintenance on the supply of work effort. Availability of the NIT program changes the effective budget constraint to

$$pX = G + (1 - t)(wH + Y), \tag{1.6}$$

where, as before, G is the support level or basic guarantee amount for period T, and t is the offset tax rate of the program. The preceding budget constraint applies only to families with $wH + Y < G/t = B$; that is, to families with income levels below the breakeven point. Because $(wH + Y)$ and $G + (1 - t)(wH + Y)$ are respectively the amounts of income available before and after the NIT subsidy, it is easy to see that the NIT payment is $G - t(wH + Y)$. Clearly, (1.6) is formally equivalent to (1.1) except that Y is replaced by $G + (1 - t)Y$ and w is replaced by $w(1 - t)$. Accordingly, the change in work effort consequent upon introduction of a NIT program is[7]

$$\Delta H = H[w(1 - t), p, G + (1 - t)Y] - H(w, p, Y)$$

$$= F(G, t). \tag{1.7}$$

Consequently, the crucial problem for public policy concerns the magnitude of the work response for alternative values of the support level and offset tax rate since combinations of G and t determine the overall program coverage, as well as the amount of work disincentive and costs.

The standard theory of consumer choice allows the decomposition of the effect of a change in the wage rate on hours of work, $\partial H/\partial w$, into two components: a substitution effect S and an income effect $(\partial H/\partial Y)H$, such that

$$\partial H/\partial w = S + H(\partial H/\partial Y). \qquad (1.8)$$

Differentiating totally (1.5) and substituting (1.8) we may write

$$dH = S\,dw + \partial H/\partial Y[H\,dw + dY] \qquad (1.9)$$

where we assume that $dp = 0$. Consumer theory derives the result $S > 0$. We also assume that leisure is a normal good, $\partial H/\partial Y < 0$; and that p, S, and $\partial H/\partial Y$ are constant over the range of variation in Y and w considered. Under these conditions the impact of the NIT program is given by:

$$dw = -tw \quad \text{and} \quad dY = G - tY.$$

Consequently, we have

$$dH = -twS + (\partial H/\partial Y)[G - t(wH + Y)] < 0 \qquad (1.10)$$

Equation (1.10) summarizes the theoretical effect of income maintenance on work response. With leisure not being an inferior good, a negative income tax is seen to reduce the work effort of those individuals having incomes less than the breakeven level not previously participating in such a program.[8]

A diagrammatic presentation of the effect of G and t on the supply of work effort is presented in Figure 1.1. The vertical axis measures income per unit time period T, the horizontal axis measures hours of leisure up to the maximum time available T. The difference between T and the number of hours of leisure L is the number of hours worked, H. Equally satisfactory combinations of income and leisure are represented by indifference curves I_0 and I_1 with I_1 depicting a higher level of satisfaction than I_0. The budget constraint is depicted by YT, the slope of which represents the constant wage rate facing the individual. In the absence of income maintenance the consumer-worker is in equilibrium at E on indifference curve I_0, working H_0 hours and earning W_0.

The negative income tax program provides a basic support of G and an offset tax rate represented by the slope of BG. The new budget line is now GBY. The consumer-worker equilibrium is now at J, which is on a higher indifference curve I_1, with fewer hours worked, H_1, and a higher level of total income, W_1, composed of both wage earnings and income maintenance payments. Consequently, the effect of income maintenance is seen to reduce hours of work and earned income but to increase satisfaction and total income.

Decomposition of the reduction in hours worked may be illustrated by

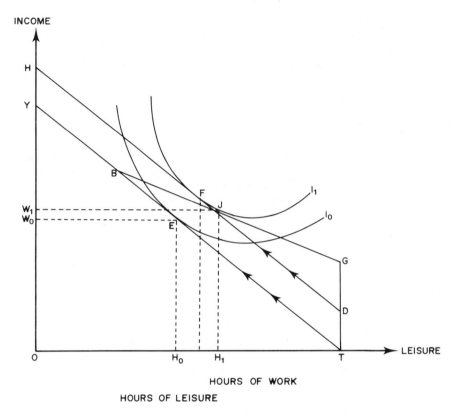

Fig. 1.1. *Work response under a constant negative income tax program.*

drawing HD parallel to YT. The total reduction in hours worked is H_0H_1. The horizontal distance EF represents the income effect since the wage rate is identical at both points. The horizontal distance FJ is the substitution effect since the level of satisfaction is the same at both points. Finally, it should be noted that the income effect refers to the combined effects of the support level and the offset tax rate on the level of satisfaction, and not that of the guarantee alone.

The preceding discussion outlines how alternative values of the support level and offset tax rate are significant in determining the level of payments a family will receive and therefore influencing the extent of the work response. These two parameters, the support level and the offset rate, are significant for policy since combinations of G and t selected will largely determine labor supply effort and overall program costs. Because of their theoretical importance, the guarantee level and the offset tax rate were the only two program parameters selected as experimental variables in all the NIT experiments.

NOTES

1. See, for example, *The Measure of Poverty* (U.S. Department of Health, Education and Welfare, 1976).

2. The proposals of Friedman, Lampman, and Tobin being emphasized are all based on considerations of fiscal efficiency and tax equity. Robert Theobald (1963) was also among the first to argue for a guaranteed income based on the view that new technology and automation will increasingly displace human beings in the productive process. He therefore advocated a guaranteed income as an absolute and constitutional right, not because of anything to do with personal income tax mechanics. In a similar vein, Schwartz (1964) also advocated a guaranteed income based on his social work philosophy. The income allowance approach of Tobin's can be traced back to Lady Rhys-Williams (1942, 1953), who proposed weekly cash dividends together with a work test.

3. There are dozens of other policy issues. For example, what is the role of in-kind transfers? How should social services be regarded? How should income (or wealth) be defined or treated? What should be the relationship of a NIT to other forms of social security, either work related or not? Another important issue is how the NIT would be integrated with the positive income tax (PIT) system and with other income maintenance programs. Our purpose here is merely to highlight the importance of the work disincentive and cost sensitivity issues as items of major political and policy concern that led eventually to the experiments.

4. A simple illustration can make these points more concretely. Consider the standard linear regression model $Y = \alpha + \beta X + e$ estimated by OLS with a data set of n observations. Whether or not some public policy X has a causal effect on behavior Y may be posed in terms of the estimated parameter for β. The objective for research and public policy is to draw "correct" (unbiased) and "reliable" (consistent, precise) conclusions about the program in question. Experimentation accomplishes this. It is well known that $\hat{\beta}$ is unbiased if $Cov(X,e) = 0$, which is certainly possible since X can be fixed. Additionally, where $E(e^2) = \sigma^2$, Var $(\hat{\beta}) = \sigma^2/\Sigma_{i=1}^{n} (x_i - \bar{X}_n)^2$. Because an experiment can control both n and X it follows that an adequate degree of precision can be obtained by choosing n large enough and the range of variation in X sufficiently wide. Note also that precision increases proportionally with sample size but with the square of the treatment intensity (placement of X), so that a doubling of the treatment intensity is equivalent to increasing the sample size fourfold.

5. For a description by an "insider" of some of the politics and institutional involvements in the development of the New Jersey experiment, see Levine (1975), who views the experiment as part of OEO's strategy for congressional approval. Skidmore (1975) provides an account of the decision-making setting regarding the experiment's actual design. The role of the noneconomist and the internal politics of the experiment are discussed briefly by Rossi (1975) and Rossi and Lyall (1976).

6. A series of income maintenance experiments, each focusing on different subpopulations, was more or less assumed in the planning discussions in 1967 on the New Jersey experiment.

7. The notation ΔH is used to denote the difference in equilibrium work effort after and before the introduction of the NIT program. For simplicity, the tax rate on earnings before the NIT is assumed to be zero. Alternatively, t may be interpreted as the change in tax rate resulting from the introduction of the NIT program.

8. The wage rate before and after introduction of the NIT are w and $(1 - t)w$, respectively. Hence the impact of the NIT program on the wage rate is to change the wage rate (dw) by $(1 - t)w$ minus w, hence $dw = -tw$. A similar argument holds for $dY = G - tY$. In (1.10) $w > 0$, $S > 0$, hence the first term, $-twS$, is negative. Since $\partial H/\partial Y$ is negative and $G - t(wH + Y)$ is positive for families below breakeven, the second term of (1.10) is negative and hence the entire expression (1.10) is negative.

2 Overview of Initial Work Response Findings

I. INTRODUCTION

The previous chapter described the policy setting and historical origins of the American negative income tax experiments. Before proceeding to more technical issues of methodology and a detailed consideration of each income maintenance experiment separately, a broad overview of the initial work response findings is appropriate at this point. This is so for several reasons. First of all, a general appreciation of the range of findings should help to direct attention to the question whether or not the results of the separate experiments are sensitive to the methodology or research approach adopted. Some general outline of the forest before us is necessary before a more detailed description of the trees can be usefully undertaken. Two other reasons concern the ongoing nature of much research and the level of information required for policy-making purposes. The research and academic community will certainly wish to consider the various findings in great detail; however, even where experiments have released an official final report, the research results should still be regarded as "first-round" explorations. Future research may well amend initial findings and add to our knowledge. At the same time a case can be made that policy makers cannot always wait for an authoritative consensus to emerge. Their requirements for information often differ from those of academic researchers and may well be satisfied by a broad survey of findings gathered from initial reports. Accordingly, it is hoped that a review of initial work response findings provided in this chapter will serve those who do not need to consider the technical peculiarities of each individual experiment. In any case a summary of the initial findings provides the necessary introduction to subsequent chapters that examine the results of each experiment separately.

The next section describes specific features of the design of each experiment. It includes a description of the Canadian income maintenance experiment for completeness. The following section summarizes the initial work response findings, focusing primarily on family earnings.

II. THE DESIGN OF THE NEGATIVE INCOME TAX EXPERIMENTS

There have been five negative income tax experiments in North America, four in the United States and one in Canada. In chronological sequence they are: (1) The New Jersey Graduated Work Incentive Experiment (hereafter New Jersey experiment), (2) The Rural Income Maintenance Experiment (RIME), (3) The Seattle–Denver Income Maintenance Experiment (SIME-DIME), (4) The Gary Income Maintenance Project (G-X), and (5) The Manitoba Basic Annual Income Experiment (Mincome Manitoba). This section outlines, in turn, salient design features of each of the experiments, focusing on their "policy design space," that is, the set and range of relevant parameters deemed of policy interest.[1]

The Design of the New Jersey Experiment

The New Jersey experiment was the first of the income maintenance experiments. Its very remarkable achievement in design, data collection, and analysis is all the more significant because many of its features were subsequently adopted by other negative income tax projects. The New Jersey experiment started its initial enrollment of families in 1968 in three urban sites in New Jersey, a state chosen partly because it had no welfare program covering families with unemployed fathers (AFDC-UP) and partly because of research administrative convenience and sympathetic state welfare officials. As well, the sites in New Jersey represented a substantial low-income population in central cities. Later, a fourth site in Scranton, Pennsylvania, was included to increase the number of non-Spanish-speaking whites in the experiment. The experiment's paramount interest in the labor supply reponse of the "working poor"—a group for whom the NIT work disincentive issue was thought most relevant and about which the least was known concerning the behavioral effects of extending cash assistance —

motivated certain eligibility restrictions in defining the relevant target population for the experiment. Participation in the experiment was therefore limited to (randomly) selected low-income, male-headed, able-bodied family units; that is, eligible families had to contain a male between the ages of 18 and 58, not enrolled in school, the armed forces, or an institution, and receiving a normal income not greater than 150% of the official poverty line.[2] A sample of 1357 families, stratified primarily by normal income range, ethnicity, and race, was eventually enrolled in the experiment for a three-year period. Families selected were randomly assigned either to a control group, which did not receive NIT payments, or alternatively, to one of several treatment programs paying benefits according to a specified guarantee level and tax rate combination *(G,t)*. Three constant tax rates (.3, .5, .7) were used to offset earned income and four support levels (50%, 75%, 100%, 125%) expressed in terms of percentages of the official poverty line were employed. These were combined into eight separate NIT treatment plans to be tested.[3] The resulting sample of the New Jersey experiment assigned to the various NIT plans, it must be stressed, was not a nationally representative segment of the American low-income population. In fact, the experimental sample contained a higher proportion of nonwhites, large families, and young family heads when compared to the national population of the non-aged, male-headed, low-income families. In addition, the sample represented sites characterizing the non-South urban United States at most. In keeping with the central interest of the experiment to focus on the labor supply effects of a guaranteed income, the experimental treatments in the New Jersey experiment were strictly financial.[4]

The Design of the RIME Experiment

The Rural Income Maintenance Experiment (RIME) was the second of the American NIT experiments and focused on the work efforts of rural low-income families. Because of differences in labor markets and the proportion of self-employed individuals, the work response of rural low-income families was expected to be different from that of the urban work-eligible poor. The rural experiment was conducted in North Carolina and Iowa and its design had many of the same features as the New Jersey experiment. Families were randomly assigned to either a control group or a variety of guarantee and tax treatments. The NIT program was to last three years; three distinct tax rates (.3, .5, .7) were employed in combination with four guarantee levels (50%, 75%, 100%, 125% of official poverty level). Originally, only five experimental treatments were specified but because AFDC benefit levels in Iowa were more generous than all but the most generous

NIT plan, three new treatments were established for Iowa alone. A distinctive feature of RIME was the inclusion, at the insistence of the OEO, of female-headed families as well as aged-headed (either sex) families in addition to non-aged male-headed families in the sample. The RIME experimental sample was therefore stratified by sex, age of head, and site as well as three normal income strata. Again, as in the New Jersey experiment, the RIME sample was truncated to exclude families with income levels in excess of 150% of the poverty line. Final enrollment numbered 809 families of whom 729 remained in the program for the entire three-year period. The RIME sample is relatively small, as the 809 sample households must "represent" the approximately 35.5% of the U.S. poverty population residing in rural areas. Of the 809 sample families, 587 were headed by a non-aged male, 108 by a non-aged female, and 114 by an older family head of either sex. Blacks comprised 56% of the North Carolina sample, and there were no blacks in the Iowa segment. In general, the North Carolina and Iowa samples differed substantially with respect to race composition, education level, and occupational mix as well as other demographic differences. The RIME sites are representative of groups of states in the Midwest (Illinois, Iowa, and Wisconsin) and the South (Alabama, Georgia, Mississippi, North Carolina, and South Carolina) rather than all of American rural poverty. The Midwest typifies the condition of scattered poverty within a prosperous agricultural region and the South represents area-wide poverty or a depressed region.

Although the RIME experiment continues the central emphasis on investigating the labor supply response to a guaranteed income, RIME is distinctive in focusing on the rural poor and farm operators, extending the sample to include female-headed and aged-headed family units, broadening the research interest to include some noneconomic topics, and providing some provision for administrative experimentation by placing families on either a 3-month or 1-month accounting plan. The payments system of RIME was also a major innovation from that of the New Jersey experiment and provided valuable insights into the administration of an income maintenance plan.

The Design of the SIME-DIME Experiment

The Seattle–Denver Income Maintenance Experiment (SIME-DIME) is the largest and most elaborately designed of the American experiments. The major research objective of SIME-DIME is the work effort and family stability responses of families to a variety of negative income tax plans in combination with manpower programs and training subsidies. The manpower component is intended to counteract any negative effects on work responses resulting from the negative income tax program. The intent of SIME-DIME is to measure both the separate and combined effects of these programs. A variant of the Conlisk–Watts model (see next chapter) was used to generate the sample requirements. The sample was stratified by race (whites, blacks, Mexican-Americans), number of family heads, and normal income (six levels), and truncated to exclude families with incomes exceeding a given level (approximately $11,000).

The policy design space of SIME-DIME is elaborate. Three support levels are employed: $3800, $4800, and $5600 (1970–1971 prices) per annum for a family of size four. Unique to the SIME-DIME design is the fact that a variety of constant and declining tax rates are specified.[5] In essence, two types of tax systems were employed. The tax function may be represented in general terms as $(tY) = t - rY$ where t is an initial tax rate, r is the rate of decline, and Y is income. When $r = 0$, the tax rate is constant. In SIME-DIME two tax rates are constant at .5 and .7 and two others begin at either .7 or .8 and decline at the rate of 2.5% per $1000 increment in income. Altogether 11 financial treatments are given. The two constant tax rates are combined with each of the three support levels; the two declining rates are used with the low and middle support levels, and the declining rate with the higher initial value (i.e., $t = .8$, $r = .025$) is used with the high support level ($5600).

A manpower component also distinguishes the SIME-DIME policy design space. Treatments consist of manpower counseling as well as counseling together with training subsidies. Direct costs of training in programs not longer than two years are reimbursed at the rate of either 50% or 100%. Actual training programs were not feasible as it would not have been possible to design a set of experimental training and educational options comparable to those available from the existing manpower system in Seattle and elsewhere. However, the manpower treatments of SIME-DIME are consistent with the general spirit of the NIT approach. In terms of the human capital accumulation framework, the cash support of the NIT can be viewed as replacing the foregone income costs of seeking training. The cost reimbursement component of the manpower experiment may be viewed as changing the effective price of increasing human capital, in much the same manner as negative taxes change the effective price of leisure (Kurz and Spiegelman, 1971).

Another distinctive design feature of SIME-DIME is its treatment of program duration as an experimental variable. In order to isolate short-run responses from longer-term behavior, experimental families are assigned to financial treatments for a 3-year, 5-year, or 20-year duration. Accordingly

SIME-DIME is the only experiment that will allow some evaluation of the validity of limited duration experiments.

The experimental sample of SIME-DIME is the largest of all the income maintenance experiments, having an original sample of about 4800 urban families representative of the western United States. A greater proportion of experimental families are in low-income groups, compared to the total U.S. population. Finally, because of Seattle's highly volatile unemployment rate (3% in 1969 to 10.5% in 1971), it is possible that estimates of effects can be made for varying levels of unemployment.[6]

The Design of the G-X Project Experiment

The fourth American NIT experiment was the Gary Income Maintenance Project (G-X), which commenced payments in 1971 for a three-year period. Distinguishing the G-X from its predecessors is the fact that its target population represents segments not prominently treated in other experiments, namely black, female-headed families in a ghetto setting. The G-X experimental sample has a size of approximately 1800 units, composed entirely of black families and structured so that a large portion (60%) are headed by females. The G-X sample was also allocated by a version of the Conlisk – Watts model and was stratified by normal income level (four strata), sex of head, and place of residence (model city or nonmodel city).

The principal focus of the Gary experiment was directed toward economic responses such as labor supply, consumption, investment in human capital (education), etc., resulting from financial NIT programs. In addition, interest was expressed in examining income maintenance in conjunction with various social services treatments. In other words, G-X sought to determine the amount of social services demanded with and without income maintenance, and whether there exists an interaction between the receipt of social services and the receipt of cash transfers such that the social benefits deriving from the programs in combination exceed the sum of individual programs alone. The G-X project was intended, therefore, to have a slightly more sociological orientation than previous income maintenance experiments.

The financial treatments of G-X constitute a straightforward two-by-two design; that is, support levels of $3300 and $4300 are each combined with tax rates of .4 and .6 to yield four NIT plans. The G-X project also included social services and day care components in its design space. Social services treatment was given by an access worker who provided information on a mix of services available from existing agencies. The day care component of the experiment comprised subsidies of varying amounts (35%, 60%, 80%, 100% of cost) together with an eligibility requirement; that is, for some families the subsidies were also contingent on working. In sum, the G-X experiment is distinctive for its reemphasis of the interest in the economic effects of a NIT program, the addition to this policy concern of an investigation of the relationship between income maintenance and social services, and the fact that its sample is composed entirely of black families, 60% female-headed.

Addendum on the Canadian Design

The first large-scale social experiment ever undertaken in Canada was jointly funded by Canada and Manitoba and had as its objective the evaluation of the economic and social consequences of a NIT. Similar to the design of the American experiments, the Manitoba Basic Annual Income Experiment (Mincome) also focused on the issue of labor supply response to a guaranteed income. As well, attention was paid to a range of administrative issues relating to program participation and operation.

The design of Mincome involved selecting participants employing a modified Conlisk–Watts model and assigning families to alternative NIT programs for a 3-year duration. The experimental sample was drawn from three sites: the urban center of Winnipeg, the community of Dauphin, and a number of small rural communities collectively referred to as the "rural dispersed sites." The sample was stratified by family structure type (number of heads, one or two earners, single individuals) and normal income (four or five levels), and truncated at a prespecified income level (approximately $13,000 for a double-headed family of size four). Since the primary research objective influencing the design of the experiment was work response, the experiment also excluded the aged, the disabled, and the institutionalized from the sample.

Payments to an initially enrolled sample (approximately 1000) began in 1975. A supplementary sample (approximately 300) was subsequently enrolled and received payments also for a three-year period, but commencing one calendar year after the originally enrolled sample. Three support levels were used: $3800, $4800, and $5800 (1975 prices) for a family of four, composed of two adults and two children.[7] The support levels are adjusted for differing family sizes and structure, and increased periodically to maintain approximately constant real value. Three constant-offset tax rates were specified: .35, .50, and .75. The three support levels and three tax rates yield nine possible combinations. The combination of the highest guarantee and the lowest tax rate was not employed, nor was the combination of the lowest support level with the highest tax rate. Inclusion of a control group resulted in the design space comprising eight distinct NIT plans.

The outstanding feature of the Mincome design was its inclusion of Dauphin as a "saturation" site in the sense that every resident was eligible to participate in a single NIT program ($3800, .50). Previous American experiments had all used randomly drawn dispersed samples in their design. The essential methodological advantage of a dispersed sample lies in isolating treatment families within a given area, thereby making it possible to vary experimentally the NIT program parameters. However, this very isolation placed treatment families in a highly artificial environment— quite unlike the circumstances that would exist under a national NIT whereby all eligible families could benefit from receiving cash transfers. In recognition of this, Mincome included in its overall design a single saturation site (Dauphin) wherein everyone was eligible for payments.[8] By so doing, Mincome hopes to improve the extent to which results of dispersed experiments can be generalized and to answer questions about administrative, operational, and community issues resulting from a less artificial environment.

III. INCOME AND WORK RESPONSE: INITIAL FINDINGS

The negative income tax experiments were extremely complex research undertakings. All were elaborately designed, produced massive amounts of data, and resulted (and continue to result) in an enormous amount of research. The findings are not easy to summarize. Similarly, because each experiment differed in design, sample composition, payment delivery mechanism, statistical methodology, as well as specific research focus, the results of different experiments are also not directly comparable. Nevertheless, some overall indication of the "first-round" evidence being generated by the various income maintenance experiments can be given.

On Interpreting Experimental Responses

In this chapter we will restrict our attention to describing broad results, paying particular attention to income (total earnings) and work incentives (hours worked). We shall focus principally on one particular unit (the family) and concentrate almost exclusively on one particular experimental effect measure (the mean difference between treatment families and control families). Many measures of work incentives are possible. Commonly used measures of labor supply response include: labor force participation, employment, hours worked, and earned income. Labor force participation rates include unemployed individuals without earnings, and employment measures reflect changes in both participation and unemployment. Hours worked includes changes in participation, unemployment, as well as variations in work intensity (i.e., hours per week of persons at work). Since hours worked is the more comprehensive and understandable of these measures, we will concentrate on describing work incentives using this response. At the same time, total earned income is the most inclusive of all measures. In addition, it is (family) earnings that is the relevant magnitude for calculating payments, and hence in determining the overall costs of NIT plans. Hence the effect of a NIT on earnings is of direct interest to policy.[9]

Response to a NIT by the family as a whole will undoubtedly mask interesting income responses and work efforts by individual members. But again, it is usually in the context of the family unit rather than the individual that policy concerns are focused when considering income maintenance and NIT proposals. Finally, by focusing on the "experimental" response, that is, the difference in response between families eligible for NIT payments (treatment families) and those not eligible to receive payments (control families), we can simultaneously highlight the "experimentally induced" dimension of the research result as well as avoid the more complicated and qualified findings associated with different experimental plans, modes of administration, econometric models, etc.

In other words, we are reporting only whether or not experimental families (those eligible for payments) behaved differently from control families as a result of merely being in the experiment, and if so, by how much. Two more points need to be noted for interpretation. First, assignment of treated families to specific NIT plans is neglected; hence, any response is generally an overall "single-number" measure typifying reaction to an "average" NIT program in the experiment. Second, in most cases differences in age, education, family size, etc., between the treatment and control sample groups were "controlled for" statistically; accordingly, the response may be viewed as representing solely the net experimental effect of being given a guaranteed income. Finally, it is useful to express the results in terms of an "experimental percentage differential," that is, the difference in response (hours worked or income) between similarly composed treatment and control families as a percentage of the control group. In sum, the behavior of the control families is taken as the benchmark.

Work Response Results from the New Jersey Experiment

The New Jersey experiment was the first of the experiments to publish its research results.[10]   Based on a sample of 693 "continuous husband–wife families" who completed at least eight of the quarterly interviews, the New Jersey experiment findings were in accord with general theoretical expecta- tions.   The overall labor supply effect for the experimental group as a whole was negative, small, and of mixed statistical significance.   More specifically, small, statistically insignificant, absolute and relative experimental differen- tials were reported for husbands, 95% of whom worked full time during the experiment.   For white and Spanish-speaking husbands the percentage differential measured by hours worked per week was negative; approxi- mately −6% and −1%, respectively.   For black husbands the percentage differential was positive, 2.3%, contrary to theoretical expectations.   In- deed, the behavior of the black families defies plausible explanations.   In terms of earnings[11] per week the percentage differentials for white (.1%), black (9.3%), and Spanish (6.4%) husbands were all positive and insignifi- cant.

The results for wives indicate predominantly negative labor supply differ- entials.   Because of the generally low levels of market work effort by wives, a fairly small absolute magnitude translates into a large percentage experi- mental differential.   At the same time, the very small number of working wives in the sample made such estimated effects highly unreliable.   The estimated percentage differentials in hours worked per week for wives were −30.6% for whites, −2.2% for blacks, and −55.4% for the Spanish-speaking females.   The percentage differentials in earnings per week between treat- ment and control groups were −33.2% for whites, 7.8% for blacks, and −54.7% for the Spanish.   All the preceding results were statistically insignif- icant; that is, these differentials could have occurred purely by chance.

The prime interest is in the mean labor supply response and earnings for the family as a whole, that is, including husbands, wives, and all other members of the household 16 years of age or older.   The reported experi- mental effects were again predominantly negative, generally insignificant, and relatively small.   Most of the estimated experimental differentials were less than 10%.   Measured in terms of percentage differences in hours worked per week between treatment and control families of identical com- position, white families worked approximately 13% less, black families worked 5% less, and Spanish-speaking families 1% less.   With respect to total earnings of all members of the household, white experimental families received 8% less, black treatment families enjoyed approximately 4% more, and Spanish families 5% more earnings than their control counterparts.

Of all the preceding experimental responses for the family, only the hours per week measure for white families was statistically significant (.99 level, two-tailed test). In general then — based on the simplest summary measure of experimental effects, the mere presence of cash payments without regard to distinction among the different NIT programs — the New Jersey findings present a picture of generally small labor supply differentials between treatment and control groups as a whole. Total family earnings seem little affected; hence the impact on earnings of a NIT with benefit structures of the levels approximately those of the New Jersey experiment for double-headed intact families was not dramatic. Although more detailed and refined technical analyses were performed and added to the overall understanding, certain ambiguities remain. The New Jersey experiment could not detect consistently significant effects in response to variations in either the support level or the tax rate, failed to find significant results or explanations for the "unusual behavior" of the black families, and remains "puzzled" by the perplexities of ethnic differences. These and other results of the New Jersey experiment are continually subject to challenge, reinterpretation (Aaron, 1975; Hall, 1975; Cogan, 1978), and extension (Hauseman and Wise, 1976).

Work Response Results from the RIME Experiment

The Rural Income Maintenance Experiment[12] was designed to include rural families in its test of response to a NIT. Accordingly, interest was high in examining the work and income responses of rural wage earners as well as those families whose major source of income derived from self-employed farming. Significantly different response patterns were found to vary by site and race; hence results were separately reported for North Carolina whites, North Carolina blacks, and Iowa families (all white). We shall again focus narrowly on the average experimental response, that is, the behavior of those who received cash payments compared to a control group of families having similar characteristics who received no benefits. Because of the different experimental NIT benefit structures, the experimental differential can be best interpreted in terms of an estimated response to a "standardized" combination of a 45% tax rate and 80% basic guarantee level. Similarly, because the experimental sites were chosen to represent the low-income rural population of an eight-state region, the result is more meaningful if stated in terms of a weighted eight-state aggregate response.

For families in which wages constitute the major source of income, the relative experimental differential measured by total income was − 13% for the eight-state aggregate. This means that experimental families were estimated to have 13% less total income (excluding general assistance payments and transfers conditional on experimental payments such as food stamps and free school meals) than similar control families as a result of being given the "standardized" NIT treatment. The estimated experimental differential for North Carolina black families, North Carolina white families, and Iowa families were − 14%, − 9%, − 18%, respectively. The experimental response of families measured by hours worked for wages were − 10%, − 18%, − 5%, and − 13%, respectively, for North Carolina black families, North Carolina white families, Iowa families, and the eight-state aggregate.

The preceding results unavoidably conceal great variations in response among individual family members. Husbands in particular responded very little to the experiment. For the eight-state aggregate, the estimated experimental differential for husbands was − 4% in wage income and − 1% in hours worked. Only the result for Iowa husbands, who had an experimental differential of 11 – 13%, was statistically significant (.95 level). Large negative responses were noted for wives, however. These differentials averaged about − 25% for the eight-state aggregate, whether measured in terms of wage income or hours of wage work. Of the three subpopulations, only North Carolina black wives revealed a statistically significant response (.95 level). Among dependents—defined to be those living at home, unmarried, and under 21 or married and under 18—large average negative experimental differentials in both earnings and hours worked were also reported, approximately 55 – 65%. The response was statistically significant (.95 level) only for North Carolina white dependents (− 56.3% differential). Again, it should be noted that although the experimental responses seem quite large in percentage terms for wives and dependents, the absolute effect on family income is very much smaller because of the small contribution to total family income of this group. Finally, the experimental effect appeared to be insensitive to the guarantee level but slightly positive in response to the implicit tax rate.

The response to a NIT by self-employed farm operators was a major research interest of RIME. Since self-employed farmers do not receive a well-defined hourly wage rate, the most appropriate measure of farm earnings is profits, defined as gross revenue minus current variable costs. This magnitude will include a return to land and capital as well as to operators' labor. Adopting such a measure, the average experimental differential was approximately − 25% for North Carolina farmers and − 8% for Iowa farmers, both marginally significant (.80 level and .85 level, respectively). It is clear that farm work cannot be viewed in isolation of wage work opportunities. In fact, 78% of North Carolina families and 50% of Iowa families had one or more members also in the wage work force. Hours of wage work declined for farm families. The experimental differential for farm operators was about −31% for North Carolina and −10% for Iowa, and a quite substantial −63% (North Carolina) and −54% (Iowa) for farm wives. Accompanying this was a positive farm operator experimental differential of approximately 11% for farm work. In sum, because of the intricate interaction of wage work and self-employed endeavor, there seemed to be a substitution of wage work toward farm work. This simultaneous pattern of lower profits and increased farm work effort implies a declining efficiency of farm operations. Farms operated by experimental families were found to be less technically efficient in terms of output produced per given amount of inputs. Why this should occur remains unclear although it is suggested that experimental farm families might have deferred sales of output, invested in activities with a longer-run payoff, shifted production from market to own-consumption activities, or simply underreported income. In summary, the work response of RIME wage earners resembles the New Jersey results. Total income of experimental families declined modestly relative to their control counterparts. Hours of farm work increased, however, whereas both profits, efficiency, and hours of wage work declined. The RIME findings have also been subject to review and some reanalysis (Ashenfelter, 1978, Welch, 1978).

Work Response Results from the G-X Project

The Gary Income Maintenance Project (G-X) released a final report in 1979. Preliminary findings were reported in 1976 and 1978.[13] Although a number of nonwork responses were reported in a special issue of *The Journal of Human Resources* (1979, **XIV**, 4), the initial analysis of G-X focused on the work response of the experimental participants. We again conveniently summarize findings in terms of the average experimental differential, that is, by comparing treatment families to their control counterparts without regard to assignment to specific NIT treatment plans. The G-X project has not published experimental responses in terms of family labor supply or total earnings directly. Employing hours worked per month as the measure of experimental response, the findings by G-X reveal a modest disincentive effect. In intact families the treatment husbands reduced their work effort by an average of 2.9–6.5% relative to control husbands, after statistically taking into account age, education, family income, preexperimental work effort, and other factors. The labor supply responses of husbands detected by G-X are roughly of the same order of magnitude as that found by the New Jersey experiment generally. One interesting difference is worth highlighting, however. Although the decline in work effort on the part of husbands in New Jersey and RIME was attributed to a small deduction in hours worked by many husbands, the G-X response resulted from a complete withdrawal from the labor force on the part of a few husbands, suggesting that for institutional reasons small adjustments to work effort may not always be possible in some labor markets.

For wives of husband–wife families, the percentage experimental differential in terms of hours worked per month was approximately 1.0–5.0%. Again, this percentage differential found for wives constitutes a small overall impact on either family labor supply or total earnings since wives had low levels of work effort initially. The wives in the G-X Project had a very low employment rate, about 15%.

One of the more interesting aspects of the G-X sample population was the fact that approximately 60% of the participating families were female-headed, that is, families without a male head of household present. The work response of female heads of households is especially relevant in NIT policy discussions. Among female heads a significant and high work reduction was found. For female heads the experimental differential ranged between 26 and 30%. In addition, these responses seem to be primarily due to the guarantee level rather than to the tax rate. In addition to the results presented in the Final Report of the G-X Project, there have also been a number of papers estimating the work response by Burtless and Hausman (1978), Hausman and Wise (1979), and others.

Work Response Results from SIME-DIME

The Seattle–Denver Income Maintenance Experiment (SIME-DIME) released interim reports in 1977 on the work effort effects based on data from the second year of the experiment.[14] The sample analyzed included black and white (but no Mexican-American) families from both sites and from both the three-year and the five-year plans. Separate responses were reported for husbands (sample size 1593) and wives (sample size 1698) in two-headed households and for female heads of single-parent families (sample size 1358).

Before considering the results reported by SIME-DIME, several remarks are necessary in order to interpret the findings. Unlike the New Jersey, RIME, and G-X experiments, SIME-DIME did not calculate an overall "experimental differential," that is, the average response of those receiving payments regardless of benefit structure compared to the response of similar control families. Instead, SIME-DIME attempted to estimate directly the "substitution" and "income" effects employing models that incorporate the benefits of participation in the experiment in terms of individual inducements to change behavior. Very briefly, SIME-DIME calculated by how much an individual's wage rate and disposable income would have been changed as a result of the combination of particular NIT opportunities offered him (her) and his (her) initial situation. For control families, the inducements to alter behavior are defined to be zero. The subsequent work effort response is then measured in terms of a separate substitution effect (due to the change in net wage rate) and the income effect (the change in disposable income evaluated at the initial hours of work). Within the context of this viewpoint, the total work response effect comprises both these effects and applies only to workers and families below breakeven. Because nonworkers and families with incomes above breakeven are excluded, the reported mean effects are larger than those of the experimental sample as a whole since the excluded individuals would have smaller responses.

Based on the second year of data and measured in terms of annual hours worked, the estimated mean total effects found by SIME-DIME were quite large. In percentage terms the average work disincentive is −5.4% for husbands, −22% for wives, and −11.2% for female heads.[15] Tests for different responses by race, site, or duration of experimental program were not statistically significant. SIME-DIME was also able to distinguish the effects of different program levels on response; specifically, higher payments and higher marginal tax rates caused greater work effort reductions. This latter point is particularly relevant in the design and costing of income maintenance options (e.g., Keeley *et al.*, 1977b).

The results of the SIME-DIME experiment were subsequently published as a journal article in the *American Economic Review* in 1978 (Keely *et al.*, 1978). Though less detailed than the original reports, the journal article is more accessible.

NOTES

1. A comment on sources is required. Every attempt has been made to ensure that the information provided is accurate. However, changes in design were often made during the experiments and published documents often do not reflect these alterations. As well, some design features were not fully documented. Accordingly, we have relied on a combination of public documents, where available, unpublished material in some cases, personal conversations with individuals involved in the experiments, and our own knowledge and experience. Nonetheless, for details on the design of the New Jersey experiment see Haveman and Watts (1976), Skidmore (1975), and Rossi and Lyall (1976), in addition to the New Jersey Final

Report. For RIME, consult Bawden (1970), Bawden and Harrar (1978), and Metcalf and Bawden (1976), in addition to Vol. I of the RIME Final Report. For SIME-DIME, see Kurz and Spiegelman (1971, 1972) and Conlisk and Kurz (1972). For G-X, see Kelly and Singer (1971) and Kehrer (1978). Our understanding of G-X was also helped by discussions with Andy Anderson, Co-Principal Investigator of G-X. For Mincome Manitoba, see Hum *et al.* (1979a,b), Mincome Manitoba Technical Reports 1 and 2. Consult also Table 1 in Ferber and Hirsch (1978).

2. Normal income is an economic concept connoting an income level from which transitory components have been removed. In most of the experiments, normal income was estimated on the basis of income information provided by families prior to enrollment in the experiment. The official U.S. poverty line in 1967 was $3300 per year for a family of four, hence a normal income in excess of $5000 rendered a family ineligible for the New Jersey experiment. An income cutoff was employed in every experiment and results in what is sometimes called a truncated sample.

3. Not all possible combinations were used. Originally, the 125% guarantee was not considered and the most generous and least generous combinations were not used. The plan consisting of the 125% guarantee and a .5 tax was implemented after New Jersey introduced its AFDC-UP program. Henceforth in the descriptions of the design space, we will only indicate the range or distinct values of guarantee levels and tax rates. Readers interested in specific plan combinations, time of introduction, etc., for the various experiments should consult the various design documents. Also, every one of the experiments had one or more control groups.

4. The central experiment focus on labor supply effects refers to the research orientation in determining the set of treatments or design space. Policy concerns also quite properly emphasized program costs. Since costs are related to labor supply effects, both viewpoints turn out to be merely a question of emphasis. Indeed, early on in the design discussions, the experimental objective was agreed to be "the estimation of the national transfer cost due to work response of a NIT" (Rossi and Lyall, 1976, p. 30).

5. See Kurz and Spiegelman (1971) for a justification of declining tax rates. See also the discussion by James Morgan in the same issue.

6. The original design called for an experiment in Seattle. The Denver site was subsequently added because of Seattle's highly irregular employment situation.

7. It might be helpful to compare the support levels of Mincome to other measures of low income levels often discussed in Canada. All comparisons are stated in terms of 1972 dollars and are for a family of size four. The low and high support levels for Mincome are $3301 and $5040, respectively. The Statistics Canada low-income line is $4922 as calculated by J. Podoluk (*Income of Canadians,* Queen's Printer, 1968). This figure of $4922 is the "unofficial" poverty line of the Economic Council of Canada and is also used as the low- income cutoff for the Consumer Finance Survey Reports. The Senate Committee on Poverty would place the poverty line for a family of four in 1972 dollars at $5556 (based on the 1969 poverty line adjusted by changes in the Consumer Price Index). Finally, to place all of this in perspective, the 1972 median income for a family of four was $11,234 [Income Distribution by Size in Canada: Preliminary Estimates (1972)].

8. The saturation site includes both the rural municipality and town of Dauphin, which is approximately 150 miles "as the crow flies" northwest of Winnipeg. The Town of Dauphin had a 1971 Census population of 8891; the Rural Municipality of Dauphin had a population of 3166. Slightly over 4000 households were eligible to be participants in the experiment.

9. The use of the earnings measure might also be justified as providing a straightforward way of weighting the relative importance of individual member responses (see Hollister, 1973, 1974). For a discussion of alternative aggregation rules in this context, see Sharir and Weiss (1975).

10. The experiments are in varying stages in terms of reported results. New Jersey, RIME, and G-X have released final reports, SIME-DIME has reported interim results on incomplete data, and Mincome has yet to undertake serious analysis on labor supply. The results of New Jersey, RIME, and G-X have also been subject to reanalysis and extensions by other researchers. In a sense, research concerning the experiments can be expected to continue for some time and it is not unlikely that initial findings will be subsequently challenged and corrected. Our purpose in this chapter is merely to describe the "first-round," "official report" results. In particular, the New Jersey results described here are from the experiment's final report, particularly the summary report. As well, we have relied on Hollister (1973, 1974), Rees and Watts (1975), and Haveman and Watts (1976).

11. A bias may exist in the use of earnings as a measure of response since experimental families learn more quickly than control families to report their income on a gross rather than net basis. There is some evidence to support this differential learning effect (Hollister, 1973, 1974).

12. The results described here are from the Summary Final Report of RIME. Assessment and criticism of the RIME findings may be found in J. Palmer and J. Pechman, editors (1979a,b).

13. The results described here are from Kehrer *et al.* (1979).

14. The results described here are from Keeley *et al.* (1977a,b,c).

15. Income effects were significant for wives (1% level) and female heads (5% level). Substitution effects were significant for husbands (5% level), wives (10% level), and female heads (10% level). Tests were performed using OLS although the estimated effects employed TOBIT analysis.

3 The Sample Design and Assignment Model of the Guaranteed Income Experiments

I. INTRODUCTION

The American income maintenance experiments were large-scale projects. The execution of the experiments included selecting participants from a number of sites and assigning them to alternative negative income tax programs for a number of years. Participants assigned to the treatment programs were given income-conditioned payments; a control group was also selected, but these participants were not entitled to a guaranteed income. Their role was to provide information for comparison purposes. This chapter is concerned with issues relating to the sample design and allocation model of the experiments.[1]

Both treatment and control group households provide valuable information for estimating the work response. Since the control group receives no payment, the cost of an observation for the control group is very low compared to an observation assigned to a treatment program. Additionally, the payments received by a household in the treatment program may be quite substantial. In the context of the sample design and assignment problem the issue is to determine simultaneously (1) the total sample size, (2) the allocation of the sample between control and treatment categories, and (3) the assignment of the treatment category households among the different treatment plans—all within a fixed budget constraint.

The detailed manner in which a sample frame is chosen and allocated among various treatments is a fundamental issue in experimental design. Given some decision on the number of experimental treatments to test, some analysis approach must be specified to allocate the sample. The common analysis of variance (ANOVA) procedure entails assigning to each treatment an equal number of observations, given equal cost for each sample point. Despite possible modifications to account for differing costs per treatment observation, unequal expected variances, different stratum populations, and unequal importance of experimental treatments, the ANOVA approach to sample allocation was not employed for a variety of reasons.

The sample selection and assignment process of the income maintenance experiments used a more complex model. The process required information from preexperimental interviews of the potentially eligible population to select participants. Having selected participants, a formal technique was used to allocate sample points among various experimental treatments in order to maximize the value of information generated by the experiment. The basis of this assignment model was a rigorous benefit–cost analysis of the alternative sample allocations that were feasible within a given budget constraint. In this application assumptions were made explicit and benefits measured in terms of reductions in the variances of certain predicted values. Costs were measured in monetary terms to reflect the financial budget constraint. The eventual sample allocation was therefore deemed "optimal."

The formal assignment model provides the experimenter with a structured means of making two types of complex tradeoff decisions. First, the experimental treatment was an income-conditioned negative income tax (NIT) program. Because several different NIT treatments are involved in the experiment, the costs of assigning an observation to a particular treatment plan varies with both the characteristics of the family (income, size, etc.) and the parameters of the NIT treatment. Thus the sample size itself is a variable that depends on the pattern of allocation of observations. The question is, "To what extent is the experimenter justified in trading expensive observations for more inexpensive observations in order to increase overall sample size, bearing in mind the extreme cost variations per observation that typify a multiyear income maintenance experiment?"[2]

Still another tradeoff arises from the fact that treatment plans vary in terms of their degree of importance, whether indicated by research reasons or policy relevance. If some treatments are more important than others, then the experimenter should allocate the sample in order to improve the ability to predict the response over the most relevant region of design points. But to what extent is it necessary to substitute sample points with relatively low policy importance in favor of sample points with relatively high policy importance?

The sample assignment algorithm used by the income maintenance experiments was developed by Conlisk and Watts and employed for the first time in the New Jersey experiment. The Conlisk – Watts algorithm (to be referred to as the Conlisk – Watts model) is a formal technique for optimizing experimental designs to estimate response surfaces. The analytic procedures of the model served as a guide in all the experiments; however, each experiment made minor adjustments or substantial modifications on the basis of external considerations or other information judged important. Nonetheless, the Conlisk – Watts model was the basis of the sample assignment process for all the experiments.

This chapter is divided into two parts. The Conlisk – Watts model is not standard in the literature on experimental design. Furthermore, original description of the model by Conlisk and Watts is both terse and compact, demanding an extremely high level of technical preparation simply to read it. Accordingly, the first part of this chapter is devoted to an unembellished description of the model in which we depict it in terms of more "basic" and readily recognized components. It is, of course, difficult to be merely descriptive, and our rendering of the formal Conlisk – Watts model in this section indicates the "estimation perspective" of the model's design.

Section III of this chapter is less descriptive. It examines the Conlisk – Watts model from the viewpoint of experimental design issues. It is fair to say that previous discussions of the Conlisk – Watts model tend to be confined to its alleged abilities to aid estimation precision. Not enough attention has been paid, in our judgment, to considering the model from the perspective of classical "experimental design," from which the Conlisk – Watts model represents a major departure. Section IV gives some final comments assessing the Conlisk – Watts model.

II. THE CONLISK – WATTS ASSIGNMENT MODEL: DESCRIPTION FROM AN ESTIMATION PERSPECTIVE

The income maintenance experiments were designed for certain research objectives. The primary objective was to investigate the impact of various guaranteed income programs on labor supply response. Given limited resources, a major problem was how to maximize precision in estimating these effects while observing additional constraints. The purpose of a formal assignment model was to optimize the allocation of sample points among experimental cells, given that observations placed in different cells yield different benefits with respect to some objective function and represent different levels of costs. The Conlisk–Watts assignment model employed by the experiments is composed of the following components: (1) a basic regression model, (2) a set of admissible regressor rows, (3) an objective function, and (4) a set of constraints on the choice set.[3] It thus represents a standard optimal experimental design well known in the statistical literature (see, for example Fedorov, 1972; Kiefer, 1959), implemented by means of a particular algorithm and program developed especially for income maintenance experiments.

The Response Function and Regression Model

Assume that the behavior under investigation can be adequately described by a quadratic response function and that the objective is to design an N-observation sample to estimate the response function:

$$Y_i = f(z_{1i}, z_{2i}, \ldots, z_{ki})\beta + \epsilon_i \qquad (3.1)$$

where Y_i is the dependent or response variable, the z_{ji} are design variables subject to experimental control, either directly or indirectly, β is a vector of coefficients, ϵ_i is a random error term, and $f(\cdot)$ is a known function so that Eq. (3.1) is linear in the unknown coefficients β. More specifically, (3.1) may be written, in matrix notation, as the conventional regression model:

$$Y = X\beta + \epsilon$$

$$E(\epsilon) = 0, \qquad \text{var}(\epsilon) = E(\epsilon\epsilon^T) = \sigma^2 I, \qquad \hat{\beta} = (X^T X)^{-1} X^T Y, \qquad (3.2)$$

$$V(\hat{\beta}) = \sigma^2 (X^T X)^{-1}$$

where Y is the dependent variable vector, X is the regressor matrix, ϵ is the error vector, β is the coefficient vector, $\hat{\beta}$ is the ordinary least squares estimate of β, and $V(\cdot)$ is the variance covariance matrix operator.

The Design Space and Admissible Regressor Rows

The independent variables z_{ji} are design variables, and a given choice of the matrix $Z = [z_{ji}]$ constitutes a particular design. The problem is then one of choosing some design Z, and therefore X, such that together with the response Y generated by the experiment, efficient inferences about β can be made.

The k design variables z_{ji} are subject to experimental control. They are selected, as in a normal regression context, on the basis of having a hypothesized effect on the response (dependent) variables. Consequently, the design variables are combinations of (a) socioeconomic (stratifying) variables (family type, income level, family size, number of earners, etc.), and (b) treatment variables, which are varied directly (guarantee level, offset tax rate).

Specifying a value for each of the k design variables yields a design point. Each observation on the design variables (each row of Z) will be constrained to lie at one of the m prechosen (and distinct) design points in the design space. Let the m design points be designated by the m k-element row vectors $Z_1^T, \ldots, Z_m^T$, and n_i be the number of observations taken at the ith treatment. The design matrix will then comprise n_1 rows like Z_1^T, n_2 rows like Z_2^T, and so on.

The regressor matrix X depends, row for row, on the design matrix Z, so that corresponding to each distinct row of Z (admissible row) is an admissible regressor row for X. The mapping from a row of Z to a row of X depends on the hypothesized functional relationship of the design variables on the response. The X and Z matrices are identical (except for an intercept term) only for the case in which the relationship is linear with no interaction terms. Usually, however, the design variables will contain terms of degree higher than 1 as well as interaction terms.[4] In sum, each row of Z represents an observation at a particular design point for which there is a corresponding admissible regressor row and each of these m distinct rows of Z (and also X) may be represented a number of times. Consequently, if X_i^T is the ith admissible regressor row corresponding to the ith row of the design vector Z, the regressor matrix X will be composed of n_1 rows of X_i^T, n_2 rows of X_2^T, and so on.

The admissible rows of the design matrix Z represent design points for which there are corresponding admissible rows of X. The m design points may be viewed alternatively as strata; the response is expected to be heterogeneous across strata and homogeneous within strata. Generally, the experimenter must choose the location of the design points so as to give the region of interest in the design space adequate coverage. By limiting the coverage of this region to m distinct design point locations, the choice of an N-observation sample reduces from choosing the Nk elements of Z to the much simpler one of choosing m nonnegative numbers $n_1, \ldots, n_m$. Conveniently, note that the total sample size N and the regressor cross-product matrix are given in terms of n_i and X_i,

$$N = \sum_{i=1}^{m} n_i, \qquad X^T X = \sum_{i=1}^{m} n_i X_i X_i^T \qquad (3.3)$$

The Objective Function

Criteria to rank alternative designs are embodied by specifying an objective function. If we adopt an estimation viewpoint, the goal of the experiment may be stated as accurately estimating a vector $P^T\beta$ of linear combinations of the elements of β, where P is a known matrix, the rows of which specify the linear combinations of regressor variable values for which a prediction is desired.[5] Therefore the objective is to minimize some measure of the prediction error of linear combinations of the estimated regression equation, which can be different for each design point.

The best linear unbiased estimator of $P^T\beta$ is $P^T\hat{\beta} = P(X^TX)^{-1}X^TY$, so it is natural to specify the objective function in terms of some scalar function of the matrix estimation error[6] $V(P^T\hat{\beta})$. In particular, assume the experimenter wishes to minimize a weighted sum of the variances of the elements of $P^T\hat{\beta}$. The objective function may be written as $\mathrm{tr}[W \, \mathrm{var}(P^T\hat{\beta})]$, where $\mathrm{tr}(\cdot)$ is the trace operator and W is a positive definite diagonal weight matrix whose diagonal elements measure the relative importance (policy relevance) to the experimenter of the elements of $P^T\beta$. Accordingly, substituting from (3.2) and (3.3) and multiplying by σ^{-2}, the objective function can be stated as[7]

$$
\begin{aligned}
\phi(n_1, n_2, \ldots, n_m) &= \sigma^{-2} \, \mathrm{tr}[WV(P^T\hat{\beta})] \\
&= \sigma^{-2} \, \mathrm{tr}[P^T WPV(\hat{\beta})] \\
&= \sigma^{-2} \, \mathrm{tr}[P^T WP\sigma^2(X^TX)^{-1}] \\
&= \mathrm{tr}\left[D\left(\sum_{i=1}^{m} n_i X_i X_i^T \right)^{-1} \right]
\end{aligned}
\tag{3.4}
$$

where $D = P^T WP$.

Constraints on the Choice Set

The choice set will generally be constrained to a proper subset of all nonnegative integer m-tuples $(n_1, \ldots, n_m)$. The design point sample sizes n_i must satisfy the budget constraint $c_i n_i \leq C$, where c_i is the cost of one observation at the ith design point, n_i is the number of observations at the ith design point, and C is the total available budget. In addition, there may be further linear constraints delimiting the choice set, written $L(n_1, \ldots, n_m) = 0$. These additional constraints may involve minimum lower bound values, absolute maximum limits, specific budget shares allocated to various design points, and so on.

Formal Statement of the Design Model

The experimental design problem for regression analysis consists of four basic components: (1) a response function and regression model, (2) a set of design points and the corresponding admissible regressor rows X_i^T, (3) the objective function matrices P and W, and (4) budgetary and other constraints on the choice set. Formally, the problem can be stated:

$$\text{Minimize } \phi(n_i, n_2, \ldots, n_m) = \text{tr}\left[P^T W P \left(\sum_{i=1}^{m} n_i X_i X_i^T \right)^{-1} \right]$$

subject to:

$$\sum_i c_i n_i \leq C, \quad L(n_1, n_2, \ldots, n_m) = 0, \quad n_i \geq 0, \quad i = 1, 2, \ldots, m$$

$$(3.5)$$

This is a well-behaved programming problem involving minimization of a convex objective function over a set of linear constraints.[8] In sum, the experimental design and sample allocation model can be defined in terms of a flexible and tractable mathematical programming model.

Choice of Response Function in Design: Relative Efficiency

The true response form is usually not known in advance. This problem is also aggravated by the fact that the sample assignment is extremely sensitive to the response form incorporated in the objective function. Furthermore, quantitative techniques for assessing benefits and losses associated with different forms of the response function are often lacking.[9] We briefly discuss the choice of the response function and the problem of comparing alternative design assignments.

The sensitivity of the optimal design to the choice of response function can be attributed to the paramount concern with efficiency, although differential costs of observations are also important. For example, if the shape of the response function is linear, the optimal design under equal costs per observation would assign all observations at boundary design points. On the other hand, if the response function is nonlinear, the optimal design must also assign observations to interior treatment points in order to estimate curvature. In general, the higher the degree of the assumed polynomial describing the response surface and the greater the assumed irregularities, the more interior design points must be covered. In the extreme case where the response function consists solely of a set of dummy variables indicating whether or not the observation lies at a particular treatment point, the model is identical to a one-way analysis of variance design and all treatments receive substantial allocations.[10]

Given the sensitivity to alternative specifications of the response function, some measure to compare efficiency of different designs is useful. The relative efficiency of any design allocation $(n'_1, \ldots, n'_m)$ to a reference design $(n_1, \ldots, n_m)$ may be measured by the ratio of objective function values: $\phi(n'_1, \ldots, n'_m)/\phi(n_1, \ldots, n_m)$. The objective function $\phi(n_1, \ldots, n_m)$ is seen upon inspection to be homogeneous of degree -1 in its arguments. This permits the derivation of certain scale properties, most notably that for a given percentage allocation $(n_i/N, \ldots, n_m/N)$, any change in the total budget C will result in an equiproportional change in the value of ϕ. For example, a doubling of the budget will double the sample size of all treatments and halve the value of the objective function. Since the objective function is a measure of variance, the relative efficiency measure can be given the following interpretation. If the ratio of objective function values associated with two designs is, for example, $\frac{1}{2}$, so that one assignment has .5 efficiency relative to another, a doubling of the budget is required to bring the one design up to the accuracy level of the other. Accordingly, the relative efficiency measure can be used to make pairwise comparisons of alternative design allocations in the Conlisk – Watts model.

Divergence between Initial Allocation and Final Treatment Sample Size

The Conlisk – Watts assignment model specifies the optimal allocation of sample points on the basis of the best prior specification of the response and pattern of sample development over time. In other words, the sample available for analysis at the end of the experiment could differ substantially from the starting sample sizes recommended by the formal assignment model. This can occur because of attrition of treatment units, splitting and recombination of units, creation of new treatment units, and misclassification of units. The problem of attrition can cause immense difficulties for the eventual estimation of work responses.

The formal assignment model can in theory be adapted to take account of these problems. One possibility is to specify or estimate how the pattern of attrition, splitting, recombinations, and so on, will vary across treatment cells and over time and incorporate this information in the model. Given some specification of these retention probabilities, the formal assignment model can then generate optimal starting sample sizes based on desired final treatment sample sizes. This approach requires for its success accuracy in predicting retention rate patterns over time. However, it may not be possible to provide acceptably accurate estimates of retention rates prior to the start of the experiment. Moreover, it may be necessary on occasion to modify prior estimates or incorporate design changes to the experiment. In such situations the formal assignment model may be applied as a sequential sampling strategy.

III. THE CONLISK – WATTS MODEL: A CRITIQUE FROM AN EXPERIMENTAL DESIGN PERSPECTIVE

Given a sample of measurements and a statistical estimator in closed (analytic) form, it is always possible to determine whether the estimator possesses optimal properties, that is, whether it is unbiased (consistent), efficient, and sufficient. For example, it is well known that the Gauss – Markov estimator under given conditions is unbiased and has a smaller variance than any other estimator. Consequently, least squares estimators are routinely used in analysis of variance (covariance) and regression models, for both experimental and nonexperimental data. When considering an experimental design it is possible to ask a second, closely related question: Given an *estimator* with optimal properties, how should a regression experiment be designed (how should we choose the values of the design matrix X) so as to yield optimal estimates? That is, is it possible to design an experiment that results in the smallest possible *value* of the variance? If the answer is yes, then not only is the estimator optimal but it also has the smallest possible measured sample variance. This situation results in maximum precision for some fixed sample size n (or conversely, the smallest possible sample size, given a fixed variance – covariance matrix of the estimator). When both the estimator and its value in a given experiment possess minimal variance, the corresponding experiment is said to be of optimal design, or simply optimal.

Historically, optimal experimental designs were employed exclusively in the classical laboratory (or agricultural) environment, where one has an infinite population and (presumably) no measurement error on the treatment variables. Classical optimal experimental design typically addressed the problem of minimizing the sample variance of an unbiased, efficient estimator, and thereby minimizing the sample size taken. This was achieved by a judicious choice of observations and design. To fix ideas, consider the familiar OLS estimator $\hat{\beta} = (X^T X)^{-1} X^T Y$. This estimator is unbiased and has minimal variance (given by the diagonal elements of

$\sigma^2(X^{\mathsf{T}}X)^{-1}$) under normal experimental conditions (the Gauss–Markov assumptions). We can prove (see, for example, Tocher 1952) that elements of X that minimize the variance of any regression coefficient $\hat{\beta}_i$ yield a diagonal matrix $(X^{\mathsf{T}}X)$; that is, they are orthogonal. And since the purpose of a scientific experiment is to measure or uncover some lawlike behavior or property by drawing on an infinite hypothetical population of measurements, there is no question of sampling bias arising from the nonrepresentative nature of the data. Any experimental data from a properly designed experiment are representative, so long as the experiment meets the substantive requirements of the researcher. Further, as long as there are no errors of measurement in the treatment (independent) variables, there is also no possibility of statistical bias because of the measurement process.[11] The sole criterion of optimality is then sample variance.

The picture changes somewhat from the classical experimental setup when one considers the guaranteed income experiments. A sample of individuals is selected from a *finite* population, and these individuals are assigned to various treatment and control groups. Here the sample must be representative of the population, and assignment among treatments and controls carried out in such a manner (say, random assignment) as to obtain independence (orthogonality) between individuals and treatments. For example, care should be taken so the control group does not have higher preexperimental earnings. If not, then the experimental estimates will be biased. An optimal experimental design must therefore either adopt an alternative optimality criterion (such as mean squared error, which encompasses both bias and variance) or else adjust for bias during analysis by incorporating properly selected covariates or "control variables," a difficult thing to do. Thus notions and techniques from classical experimentation in the natural sciences cannot be used indiscriminately in socioeconomic experiments to uncover optimal designs.

There are also other difficulties that can wreak havoc in optimal experiments, particularly for large-scale, complex socioeconomic experiments with a finite population. For example, since cost was a direct constraint in the Conlisk–Watts assignment model, the sample allocation is no longer necessarily random. There was a tendency to allocate more individuals to the control or cheaper plans (higher tax rate and lower guarantee combinations) than would otherwise be the case. Furthermore, the optimality criterion was defined exclusively in terms of variance (see previous section) so that bias because of nonrandom selection and allocation is not necessarily minimized unless there is a proper weighting scheme. Weighting, however, has its practical limits, since, with the exception of a few economic and demographic variables, we do not know the correct population proportions. Additionally, the population is multivariate, whereas weights are usually known in their univariate form. Of course, bias can, in principle, be removed by introducing covariates or control variables to correct for nonrandom selection. But this procedure is not without its drawbacks. First, it is very tedious, since a large number of regression equations must be estimated in order to uncover the correct functional form and to eliminate statistically unimportant variables. Second, we can never know how much bias remains in spite of attempts to remove it by statistical modeling techniques. In the final analysis "optimal" experimental designs in the social sciences lose much, if not all, of their advantage. Bias is usually introduced. Furthermore, efficiency in estimating a particular model is not necessarily the same thing as detecting significance and magnitude of experimental effects.

In what follows we consider the main properties of the Conlisk – Watts model and the types of designs that it suggests and offer our assessment of its statistical validity and practical utility in social experiments.

The Issue of Weights

Recall that the regression model may be written in the matrix form: (3.2)

$$Y = X\beta + \epsilon$$

The vector of population coefficients, β, is to be estimated by the OLS estimator $\hat{\beta} = (X^\mathsf{T}X)^{-1}X^\mathsf{T}Y$, whose covariance matrix is given by $V(\hat{\beta}) = \sigma^2(X^\mathsf{T}X)^{-1}$. Since the estimates (and the estimator) are unbiased, the only criterion of optimal precision is efficiency, that is, minimal sample variance. Let $P^\mathsf{T}\hat{\beta}$ denote estimators of the linear combinations $P^\mathsf{T}\beta$, where P is a matrix of full column rank so that $P^\mathsf{T}P$ is positive definite. Also let $Q = P^\mathsf{T}P$ and $R = (X^\mathsf{T}X)$. Then the optimality criterion defined by Conlisk and Watts minimizes the trace of the covariance matrix $V(P^\mathsf{T}\hat{\beta})$; that is, the trace of

$$\begin{aligned}
V(P^\mathsf{T}\hat{\beta}) &= E[P^\mathsf{T}\hat{\beta} - P^\mathsf{T}\beta][P^\mathsf{T}\hat{\beta} - P^\mathsf{T}\beta]^\mathsf{T} \\
&= E[P^\mathsf{T}(\hat{\beta} - \beta)(\hat{\beta} - \beta)^\mathsf{T}P] \\
&= P^\mathsf{T}[E(\hat{\beta} - \beta)(\hat{\beta} - \beta)^\mathsf{T}]P \\
&= P^\mathsf{T}V(\hat{\beta})P \\
&= \sigma^2 P^\mathsf{T}(X^\mathsf{T}X)^{-1}P
\end{aligned} \tag{3.6}$$

For any two square matrices A, B we have $\mathrm{tr}(AB) = \mathrm{tr}(BA)$ (see, for example, Basilevsky, 1983). The trace of expression (3.6) can be written as

$$\begin{aligned}
\mathrm{tr}\, V(P^\mathsf{T}\hat{\beta}) &= \sigma^2\, \mathrm{tr}[P^\mathsf{T}(X^\mathsf{T}X)^{-1}P] \\
&= \sigma^2\, \mathrm{tr}[(X^\mathsf{T}X)^{-1}P^\mathsf{T}P] \\
&= \sigma^2\, \mathrm{tr}[(P^\mathsf{T}P)(X^\mathsf{T}X)^{-1}]
\end{aligned} \tag{3.7}$$

Q can also be decomposed into the canonical form $Q = RMR$, where M is a diagonal matrix (Conlisk 1974), so we can write (3.7) in the simpler form

$$\sigma^2 \operatorname{tr}[(P^{\mathrm{T}}P)(X^{\mathrm{T}}X)^{-1}] = \sigma^2 \operatorname{tr}(QR^{-1})$$
$$= \operatorname{tr}(RMRR^{-1})$$
$$= \operatorname{tr}(RM) \qquad (3.8)$$

where RM is diagonal.

An implication of minimizing (3.7) [or (3.8)] is that each element of the trace function is of equal importance. However, some variances of the linear combinations $P^{\mathrm{T}}\hat{\beta}$ may be of greater policy significance and consequently given greater weight in the criterion function. A set of additional coefficients or weights W can then be introduced, so the criterion becomes

$$\operatorname{tr}[WV(P^{\mathrm{T}}\hat{\beta})] = \sigma^2 P^{\mathrm{T}} WPV(\hat{\beta}) \qquad (3.9)$$

where W is a diagonal matrix.

As an example consider the linear model

$$Y = \beta_1 X_1 + \beta_2 X_2 + \beta_3 X_3 + \beta_4 X_4 + \beta_5(X_1 X_3) + \beta_6(X_1 X_4) + \epsilon \qquad (3.10)$$

Suppose we wish to estimate the weighted sum of β_1, β_2, $(\beta_1 + \beta_3 + \beta_5)$, $(\beta_2 + \beta_4)$, $(\beta_1 + \beta_4 + \beta_6)$, and $(\beta_2 + \beta_3)$ (see Keeley and Robins 1978, p. 11). The weighted objective function (3.9) then becomes

$$\operatorname{tr}\left\{ \begin{bmatrix} W_1 & & & & & \\ & W_2 & & & 0 & \\ & & W_3 & & & \\ & & & W_4 & & \\ & 0 & & & W_5 & \\ & & & & & W_6 \end{bmatrix} V \begin{bmatrix} 1 & 0 & 0 & 0 & 0 & 0 \\ 0 & 1 & 0 & 0 & 0 & 0 \\ 1 & 0 & 1 & 0 & 1 & 0 \\ 0 & 1 & 0 & 1 & 0 & 0 \\ 1 & 0 & 0 & 1 & 0 & 1 \\ 0 & 1 & 1 & 0 & 0 & 0 \end{bmatrix} \begin{bmatrix} \beta_1 \\ \beta_2 \\ \beta_3 \\ \beta_4 \\ \beta_5 \\ \beta_6 \end{bmatrix} \right\}$$

$$= W_1 \operatorname{var}(\hat{\beta}_1) + W_2 \operatorname{var}(\hat{\beta}_2) + W_3 \operatorname{var}(\hat{\beta}_1 + \hat{\beta}_2 + \hat{\beta}_5) + W_4 \operatorname{var}(\hat{\beta}_2 + \hat{\beta}_4)$$
$$+ W_5 \operatorname{var}(\hat{\beta}_1 + \hat{\beta}_4 + \hat{\beta}_6) + W_6 \operatorname{var}(\hat{\beta}_2 + \hat{\beta}_3) \qquad (3.10)$$

which illustrates expression (3.9).

We have seen that the Conlisk–Watts model is a well-defined programming algorithm that can incorporate various linear combinations of the OLS coefficients $\hat{\beta}_i$ by a specification of the matrix P. Linear combinations of the $\hat{\beta}_i$, and not merely the elements $\hat{\beta}_i$ themselves, must be allowed for since we have an experimental design in which the usual analysis of variance treatment effects are computed from dummy variable least squares coefficients $\hat{\beta}_i$, that is, from linear combinations of the $\hat{\beta}_i$. Efficient estimation of the β_i themselves, if desired, can be obtained by simply setting $P = I$, the identity matrix. Furthermore, a diagonal matrix W of policy weights can easily be incorporated in the objective function. The elements of W will reflect the importance of elements of $V(P^T\hat{\beta})$, that is, the relative importance of the prediction points and their variances. Policy weights W_i for each design points may reflect a number of concerns; for example, (1) income class weights to reflect the income distribution of the population, (2) treatment weights to reflect the relative policy importance of each (G,t) combination, and (3) so-called pyramidal weights to reflect special interest in a given subgroup. For instance, interest may center heavily on the working poor rather than those with no income at all or those with incomes above the poverty level. Introducing differential weights W_i to the objective function can result in a greater number of the working poor being selected.

The Optimization Criterion

To minimize the sampling variance of the weighted linear combinations $WP^T\hat{\beta}$ Conlisk and Watts select the trace of the covariance matrix $V(WP^T\hat{\beta})$ as the objective function. Two choices for a scalar function of a covariance matrix are available to summarize multidimensional variance — the determinant and the trace. The determinant is the multivariate extension of the variance of a random variable; therefore it is known as the generalized variance. It is proportional to the square of the area contained by the column vectors of X; that is, $(\text{area})^2 = |X^T X|$. Since the determinant is a function of all elements of a matrix the generalized variance depends on both variance and covariance terms of a set of k random variables.

A possible drawback of choosing the determinant as the objective function is that its minimization is not affected by a set of constant weights. This can be seen by considering the determinant of expression (3.9). We have, using (3.6),

$$
\begin{aligned}
|WV(P^T\hat{\beta})| &= |W|\,|V(P^T\hat{\beta})| \\
&= |W|\,|P^T V(\hat{\beta})P| \\
&= |W|\,|P|^2|V(\hat{\beta})| \qquad\qquad (3.11)
\end{aligned}
$$

so that minimizing the weighted expression $|WV(P^T\hat{\beta})|$ is equivalent to minimizing $V(\hat{\beta})$, because P and W are nonsingular, nonrandom matrices. We obtain the same point through minimizing the simpler expression $|V(\hat{\beta})|$ as by minimizing the left-hand side of (3.11). That is, it makes little sense to minimize the variances of linear combinations of $\hat{\beta}_1, \hat{\beta}_2, \ldots, \hat{\beta}_k$ as opposed to the variances of individual $\hat{\beta}_i$, $i = 1, 2, \ldots, k$. The optimum design therefore depends only on the structure of the design matrix X and the constraints. This perhaps unexpected result implies that we need not bother with matrices P and W and that optimality can be achieved in a more simple fashion.

However, the preceding property may be a drawback if one wishes to discriminate, for policy reasons, between the variances of different linear combinations of the $\hat{\beta}_i$. To incorporate weights P and W in the model Conlisk and Watts employ the trace of $WV(P^T\hat{\beta})$ as the objective function. The objective function now depends on the diagonal elements of the matrix. In other words, it depends only on the weighted variances of $P^T\hat{\beta}$; consequently, it is not affected by covariances between the linear combinations $P^T\hat{\beta}$. It does, however, depend on the covariance terms of the $\hat{\beta}_i$ for the case when $P \neq I$.

The Response Function

The Conlisk – Watts model assumes that a response function $Y = X\beta + \epsilon$ has been defined. Otherwise, linear combinations $P^T\beta$ cannot be estimated. Conlisk (1973) notes the important role played by the response function, since designs generated by the optimization procedure are very sensitive to the specified functional form of the regression equation. For example, if the regression equation is assumed linear in the variables but is in reality quadratic, the design generated can depart widely from optimality. This is a serious difficulty, since the functional form of the regression equation is rarely known in advance. Although Conlisk (1973, p. 646) writes that "the [form] specified for the design is not binding on the eventual analysis of data from the completed experiment," this is misleading, because it is only when the analysis is in accordance with the assumptions of the optimization model that we obtain optimal designs. Any departure from assumptions during analysis will destroy optimality, and thus the basic rationale for using the Conlisk – Watts optimization model.

As an example consider Conlisk's simulation exercise (Conlisk, 1973), in which a sample of young people of high school graduation age is given an educational trust fund. For a fixed period the money can be spent only for college or other approved post-high-school training activities, and any money left at the end of the period is turned over to the project. Let E be the response variable measuring the amount of education – training received; G be the amount, in dollar terms, of the trust grant; and S be the average schooling level of a subject's parents, where G and S are controlled experimentally — the first by direct (postsample) manipulation and the second by presample stratification. Further, assume randomization such that G and S are distributed independently of all other variables such as race, income, family type, and so on. The response function can then be denoted as

$$E = f(G,S) + \epsilon \tag{3.12}$$

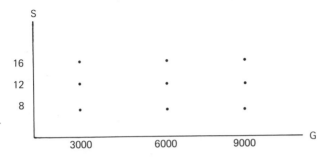

Fig. 3.1. *Trust experiment treatment points.*

Let the admissible values for a design variable pair (G,S) be the $m = 12$ treatment points shown on Figure 3.1. Let the total budget $C = 6{,}000{,}000$, and let the cost per observation c_i at the ith treatment point equal the trust amount G for that treatment plus a fixed administrative cost of 700 (with the c_i and C measured in dollars). The c_i vary from 700 to 9700; wide cost variation is characteristic of subsidy experiments and has strong influences on the nature of optimal designs. Finally, let the criterion matrix P be a matrix with ith row equal to $f(Z_i)$; that is, of interest are the heights of the response surface over the 12 treatment points. Assume further that each height is of equal importance so that no weighting of the rows of P is necessary. It only remains to specify the functional form of $f(\cdot)$.

Consider the following four increasingly complicated forms for the regressor row function $f(G,S)$, each labeled for later reference.

$(1,G,S)$,	linear form
$(1,G,S,G^2,S^2,GS)$,	quadratic form
$(1,DG_2\,DG_3,DG_4,DS_2,DS_3,GS)$,	7K form
$(D_1,D_2,\ \ldots\ ,D_{12})$,	AV form

Here DG_i is a dummy variable equal to 1 if the rth observation falls at the ith of the four G levels and zero otherwise. Similarly, DS_i is a dummy variable equal to 1 if the rth observation falls at the ith of the three S levels, and zero otherwise. Finally, D_i is a dummy equal to 1 if the rth observation falls at the ith of the 12 treatment points, and zero otherwise. The first two specifications yield linear and quadratic response functions in G and S. The 7K form handles each of the two design variables by a set of dummies, then adds an interaction term in continuous form. Without the last term, the 7K form would be a two-way analysis of variance form (AV) in main effects only. The AV form implies a one-way analysis of variance layout with a separate mean β_j for each treatment. Geometrically, the four forms allow varying amounts of response surface irregularity, or curvature, over the treatment points. At one extreme, the first form is a rigid plane, allowing no curvature. At the other extreme, the AV form allows maximal curvature by allowing the surface to have a different height β_j over each treatment point.

The optimal designs for the four specifications of $f(\cdot)$ are shown on the top half of Table 3.1, which also illustrates the dependence of n_i on functional form. In each case, the n_i for the lowest and highest S level are identical, and thus the correlation between G and S is zero. This is a result of the simple nature of the illustration; substantial correlations among design variables

Table 3.1

Designs for Educational Trust Illustration (Entries are the n_i)

Design	S-level	G-level			
		0	3000	6000	9000
Optimal for linear f	8	1208	0	0	222
	12	0	0	0	0
	16	1208	0	0	222
Optimal for quadratic f	8	530	169	0	145
	12	656	197	0	0
	16	530	169	0	145
Optimal for 7K f	8	447	107	95	106
	12	545	109	55	9
	16	447	107	95	106
Optimal for AV f	8	282	123	91	76
	12	282	123	91	76
	16	282	123	91	76
Treatment minima	8	958	61	46	134
	12	141	61	46	38
	16	958	61	46	134
Expected loss	8	600	165	55	87
	12	162	100	50	72
	16	600	165	55	87
Mixed estimation with $\sigma_d/\sigma = 5$	8	534	115	78	149
	12	298	48	10	1
	16	534	115	78	149
Mixed estimation with $\sigma_d/\sigma = 10$	8	410	127	75	105
	12	341	103	52	49
	16	410	127	75	105
Mixed estimation with $\sigma_d/\sigma = 20$	8	337	124	84	85
	12	318	117	78	68
	16	337	124	84	85

are common in optimal designs. Not surprisingly, the optimal design for the linear $f(\cdot)$ puts all observations at the corner treatments (for roughly the same reason that a table will be most stable if the legs are at the corners). The corners-only result is not inevitable, however; the cost at the corners could be high enough to rule them out. As the number of terms K in the successive regression forms increases, the model allocates stress more evenly over treatments. (Extra legs are needed to stretch the tabletop into a curved surface.) For the 12-coefficient AV form, all treatments receive a substantial allocation. (In a sense the table has no top; 12 legs support 12 separate points.)

The first four rows of Table 3.2 (above the line) show efficiencies for the designs under alternative assumptions about the true form of $f(\cdot)$, (with efficiency measured relative to the corresponding optimal design). Table 3.2 indicates the risk in designing for a given $f(\cdot)$ when one of the others is the true one. Therefore Table 3.2 is like a decision-theoretic loss table, in which columns correspond to states of nature, and rows to actions.

Table 3.2 also illustrates the experimenters' dilemma in specifying $f(\cdot)$. Prior beliefs about continuity of behavioral response, whatever its basis, often suggest that $f(\cdot)$ take a simple continuous linear form. However, a design based on this simple form leaves the experimenter very ill protected if response surface irregularities require a more complicated $f(\cdot)$. Table 3.2 shows this by the small entries to the upper right. At the other extreme, if the experimenter wants complete protection against irregularities and specifies the AV form, the resulting design is inefficient in the event the simple form is the true one; this is shown by the efficiencies to the left of the fourth row in Table 3.2. Clearly, there is no way to evade the dilemma; no design can be efficient with respect to all forms of $f(\cdot)$. This dilemma, if taken literally, can destroy much of the rationale for optimal designs.

Table 3.2
Design Efficiencies (Relative to Optimal Design for Column)

	True			
Design	Linear	Quadratic	7K	AV
Optimal for linear f	1.000	.000	.000	.000
Optimal for quadratic f	.749	1.000	.000	.000
Optimal for 7K f	.733	.936	1.000	.528
Optimal for AV f	.654	.859	.951	1.000

Conlisk (1973) proposes three possible strategies for overcoming this problem, each one offering some protection against mispecification of the functional form. But the fact remains that unless one knows the functional form in advance, there is a strong possibility of obtaining a design far from optimum. Of course, Conlisk's illustrative example is highly simplified; the functional form depends only on two (controlled) variables, G and S. Given the nonrandom nature of the allocation model, missing data, self-selection, and so forth, the response function will generally depend on a much larger set of variables, resulting in an analysis of covariance model. Again, however, it is usually not possible to predict which additional variables will be used; furthermore, since increasing the number of variables decreases degrees of freedom (and thus efficiency), the selected sample points n_i will typically not represent optimal values.

"Nonorthogonality" and the Cost Constraint

It was seen earlier that under certain assumptions orthogonality among the treatment variables leads to an optimal design. This condition is usually violated when a cost (budget) constraint is tacked onto an optimization model. In the negative tax experiments, orthogonality—or more generally, independence—would obtain if the support level assignment were independent of the tax rate assignment, that is, if the probability of assignment to a support level–tax rate combination were the product of the separate associated probabilities. This was not the case for the Conlisk–Watts model.

In a negative tax experiment the costs for different sample points vary greatly. Furthermore, the assumed response function depends on many variables in a nonlinear way. Thus quadratic (and cubic) functions, often involving many interaction effects, were routinely employed in the data analysis (see, for example, the New Jersey experiment). Given the high cost associated with certain tax rate and guarantee combinations, it was important for dollar economy not only to employ efficient estimators but also to choose the sample and design points such that the sample size was as small as possible.

Recall that the assignment model optimizes the allocation of sample points among the various experimental cells given that observations in different cells yield different benefits with respect to the objective function and represent different costs. It was therefore necessary to estimate these costs per cell in an accurate manner. Errors in estimating magnitude could result in either a smaller sample than possible (cost overestimated), with a resulting reduction in statistical precision, or a cost overrun (cost underestimated), with its attendant consequences. An error in estimating relative costs across cells implies a nonoptimal allocation of sample points and hence an inefficient use of scarce experimental funds. Consequently, all the experiments attempted to incorporate in the Conlisk – Watts model accurate cost estimates as well as allowances for attrition behavior and work responses. Although details varied from experiment to experiment, the Conlisk – Watts model virtually guaranteed by its logic a "nonorthogonal" result because of the priority of the cost constraint. Cost constraints are indeed a fact of life. But because the income maintenance experiments entailed such wide variation in costs among plans, the departure from orthogonality attributed to fixed resources was probably particularly significant.

IV. THE CONLISK – WATTS MODEL AND NEGATIVE TAX EXPERIMENTS: A FINAL COMMENT

The Conlisk – Watts model solves a well-behaved programming problem involving a convex objective function and linear constraints. Applied to a regression-type experiment, the Conlisk – Watts model determines the structure of a design matrix X. Alternatively, given X, the model determines the proportions of the sample to be allocated to experimental cells. Although the Conlisk – Watts model represents a powerful tool for designing optimal experiments, it has been criticized by many economic researchers[12] involved in the design (and analysis) of the income maintenance experiments (see, for example, Keeley and Robins). To understand this apparent paradox it is necessary to distinguish between the formal mathematical structure of the model itself and its application to a particular experiment. Thus although the Conlisk – Watts model leaves little to be desired from the computational viewpoint, we have two methodological reservations concerning its use in experiments where little (if any) a priori knowledge exists about the behavior of subjects. From the statistical point of view the objective function is usually mispecified when the model is used in an experiment with a sample drawn from a finite population. Further, the model requires stringent and narrow specifications of the response and objective functions together with constraints; this leaves little room for flexibility in the estimation stage of the experiment.

We remarked that an experiment conducted with an infinite population of measurements is always "respresentative" if care is taken to employ correct instruments and to avoid error in measuring independent variable(s) and if the experiment is properly isolated from outside influences (variables), either by randomization or by physical methods such as those used in laboratories to avoid "contamination" of the measurements. No bias can occur in the estimator(s) used and the sole criterion of precision in this context is, appropriately, sampling variance. Thus, all things being equal, an optimal experiment can guarantee sufficient accuracy and at the same time keep resources such as time, money, and general effort to a minimum.

The situation changes radically for an experiment conducted on a sample drawn from a finite population. This is so because experiments that draw on an infinite hypothetical population of measurements are established primarily to estimate (i.e., measure) lawlike functional behavior. On the other hand, surveys generally draw on a finite population of objects (individuals) in order to estimate characteristics of that population. Again assuming no measurement error, surveys on finite populations are subject to a source of potential bias that infinite-population experiments are not — namely, representativity of the sample. Because the Conlisk – Watts procedure employs an objective function that depends only on variance, and nonstatistical constraints of cost are imposed, the sample points chosen by the Conlisk – Watts assignment model are not necessarily representative of the target population. The measurements are thus not independent of the sample points and an estimator calculated over such a sample is biased. It cannot serve as the basis of an objective function.[13] To see why the sample points need not be representative of the population it is sufficient to consider the possible effects of the budget constraint. In a random allocation some individuals will face high guarantee levels and low tax rates. These observations cost more than those assigned low guarantee levels and high tax rates. Since this would result in a higher budget cost and lower sample size, the Conlisk – Watts model discourages expensive sample points and thus induces a nonrandom sampling scheme. Factors other than cost, such as the response and objective functions and the weights W, can also lead to high correlation between treatments and strata, tending to make the sample unrepresentative. Since any estimator applied to a nonrepresentative sample leads to biased estimates, elaborate means must be taken at the analysis stage to protect the integrity of the results. This explains the wide variety of adjustments performed by the subsequent researchers and the necessity of analysis of covariance methods. However, not all relevant covariates can always be found; their choice and availability can depend on a large number of factors. Consequently, the researcher is never certain how much bias (if any) still remains.

The second major difficulty with optimal experimental designs, and one that affects both finite and infinite populations, is the large amount of prior information required to design them correctly. This is a long-standing objection to optimal designs among statisticians and is exemplified by the heated discussion that followed Kiefer's 1959 paper on the subject. In what follows we enumerate some of the objections raised against optimal experimentation, knowing fully that controversy is likely to continue.

First, as indicated already, the behavioral response function must be known in advance, both its functional form and the variables that enter as arguments. We also know that designs generated by the Conlisk – Watts model are extremely sensitive to the specifications of functional form. For example, if the response function is assumed quadratic when in reality it is, say, cubic, then the allocation is no longer optimal (see Kendall and Stuart, 1968, Vol. 3, pp. 158 – 61). Nothing would then be gained from an optimal design; on the contrary, we now have a nonrepresentative sample. Although Conlisk (1973) proposed an approach to choosing a functional form by assigning a priori probabilities to various functional forms to minimize the expected loss (see Section III, under "The Response Function"), the difficulty with this approach is the usual lack of information concerning prior probabilities, and the relatively generous set of possible functional forms. As pointed out by Morris *et al.* (1980), it is not clear how one proceeds to assign zero probabilities to functional forms one is not willing to consider.

Second, the objective function must also be specified in advance. We noted that Conlisk and Watts use the trace rather than the generalized variance; that is, the determinant of the covariance (correlation) matrix of the linear combinations of the $\hat{\beta}_i$. Both the trace and determinant functions are covenient in the sense that both are continuous, differentiable, and convex. The Conlisk – Watts model employs the trace because it is a linear function of the elements of $V(\hat{\beta})$. This is not the case with the determinant. Furthermore, minimizing a weighted determinant is tantamount to minimizing its unweighted version, and this, it was felt, is an undesirable property of specifying the generalized variance as the objective function. However, a consequence of choosing the trace instead of the determinant is that the "optimal" design procedures ignore the covariances (correlation) between the linear combinations[14] $P^T\hat{\beta}$, thereby resulting once more in a nonoptimal design because of probable multicollinearity of the linear combinations of $\hat{\beta}_i$. In any case, it is not clear just how robust the "optimal" allocation is with respect to the variance measures. The objective function defined by Conlisk and Watts assumes that ordinary least squares estimators rather than the generalized least squares estimator will be used. This assumption turns out to be another important source of misspecification, and thus nonoptimality, since many analyses in fact used the generalized least squares estimator to take account of the panel nature of the data! Finally, and as an illustration of the sensitive nature of optimal designs, the

Conlisk – Watts objective function does not differentiate between the two objectives of point estimation and hypothesis testing, something on which an optimal design may depend (see Kiefer, 1959, p. 278).

The restrictive "optimal" design procedure of the Conlisk – Watts model can create many difficulties for analysis, particularly the estimation and evaluation of the effect(s) of the experiments. The first difficulty is again due to the budget constraint, the effect of which may be to reduce the sample size to such an extent as to preclude the detection of relatively small significant treatment effects. Spiegelman and West (1976) indicate that for the SIME – DIME assignment model[15] a sample six times as large as the one actually employed might be required to obtain statistically significant treatment effects. The introduction of monetary cost into the design has the effect of trading off sample information for dollars, a process that is statistically suspect. One should first determine whether the budget is large enough to finance a proposed experiment, and if it is not, then either the budget should be increased or the experiment should not be carried out at all. It may be possible to obtain statistically significant treatment effects with a small sample, but this approach usually requires regression-type modeling together with a priori "economic theory" of labor supply, a methodology that essentially ignores the experimental nature of the data. In fact, many of the studies took this approach. Thus paradoxically, although the purpose of the Conlisk – Watts model was to obtain an optimal allocation, the sample so obtained may require that the design model be abandoned when actually evaluating the experimental data (Keely and Robins, 1978).[16]

Another major problem associated with the highly restrictive nature of "optimal" designs is its lack of robustness. The design cannot usually yield information for a wide number of different questions. Given the high cost of the income maintenance experiments, the ability to address a fairly wide range of questions would appear to be particularly desirable. Versatility is probably more cost-effective in the long run than the unipurpose, uniobjective optimal design.

There may be problems even when the objective is confined to labor supply estimation. Since the Conlisk – Watts model depends on a *single* dependent labor supply variable as a function of treatments and sample strata, it is not necessarily flexible enough to provide answers to labor supply behavior when the dependent variable is altered during the estimation stage or when more than one dependent variable is to be used. As someone once said, when researching into the unknown it is better to have a design that allows one to be vaguely correct, rather than one that is precisely wrong. To conclude, the Conlisk – Watts model is formally correct and provides an efficient algorithm to an important experimental problem.[17] However, its application to complex, multipurpose socioeconomic experiments on a finite population most probably results in misspecification bias and non-representativity of the allocation, both of which are difficult to control for. Moreover, the Conlisk–Watts model represents a narrow channeling of potential research effort to answering limited, predefined labor supply questions.

NOTES

1. Other design issues include the length of the experiment and whether or not inferences about permanent effects could be drawn from temporary experiments; whether a nation-wide sample is preferable to the test-bore or cluster-sampling approach; whether dispersed sampling is adequate; and so on. We do not wish to imply these issues are not important. Our focus is on the work response findings and how the sample assignment model may have helped or hindered these research efforts. It would therefore serve little purpose to discuss alternative scenarios that were not implemented. In many instances, the costs and benefits were known and discussed at the beginning, and a variety of circumstances led to a judgment. Our purpose is not to second-guess these judgments.

2. It must be emphasized that, contrary to many experiments wherein the costs of sample points are usually roughly equal, costs of sample points in the negative income tax experiments differed greatly. For example, the ratio of cost between the most expensive design point and a control design point may be as high as 24 to 1, and not 1 to 1.

3. The model is from Conlisk and Watts (1969, pp. 150–6); Conlisk (1973, pp. 643–656); and an unpublished manuscript by Conlisk. The notation in this chapter corresponds to that of Conlisk and Watts.

4. In general, the number k of independent variables in a design row vector need not be equal to the number k of regression coefficients. For example, with $k = 2$ such that $f(z_{1i}, z_{2i}) = [1, z_{1j}, x_{1j}, \log(z_{2j})]$, this leads to the $k = 4$ regression form: $y_i = \beta_1 + \beta_2 z_{1j} + \beta_3 z_{1j} + \beta_4 [\log(z_{2j})] + \epsilon_i$.

5. The matrix P is chosen to reflect the region of prediction interest. For example, choosing $P = I$, the identity matrix, implies a primary interest in estimating the elements of β, that is, the individual terms of the coefficient vector. An alternative choice might be $P = (X_1, \ldots, X_m)^\mathsf{T}$, which implies a primary interest in estimating the height of the response surface above each of the m design points.

6. This assumes equal error variances in the regression model. If error variances are assumed to differ across the design points such that the error variance corresponding to the ith regressor row X_i is $\sigma^2 \cdot v_i$, the experimenter can specify the values for v_i and incorporate such information into the objective function. This is equivalent to a weighting process to remove heteroscedasticity from the regression equation by increasing the sample sizes of those cells with higher variances.

7. Minimizing the trace functions $\mathrm{tr}[\mathrm{var}(WP^\mathsf{T}\hat{\beta})]$ may be viewed as minimizing a weighted sum of variances of elements of $\hat{\beta}$. Note, however, that $\mathrm{tr}[\mathrm{var}(WP^\mathsf{T}\hat{\beta})]$ may also be written as $E[(\hat{\beta} - \beta)^\mathsf{T}(P^\mathsf{T}W^\mathsf{T}WP)(\hat{\beta} - \beta)]$ so that minimizing a weighted sum of variances of the regression coefficient estimates is equivalent to minimizing a weighted expectation of a quadratic loss function.

8. Although the problem is strictly one of integer programming, in practice the unknowns were treated as continuous.

9. For a discussion of three possible approaches, see Conlisk (1973).

10. Just as the linear form assumes no curvature is present, the analysis of variances response form can be viewed as allowing for maximum curvature, because it permits the response surface to have a different height over each design point. In addition, although the general design model does not usually have an explicit solution, the special case of a response function consisting exclusively of exhaustive binary variables can be shown to give the usual one-way analysis of variance allocation: that is, design point sample sizes n_i proportional to weight w_i and inversely proportional to the square root of the cost of the observation $C_i^{1/2}$.

11. There can be bias, of course, if the data are not analyzed by a correct model—for example, if interaction effects exist but are ignored in the subsequent analyses of variance.

12. Many researchers on the noneconomic aspects of the experiment were critical as well. In many instances their initial remarks were countered by the statement that the primary research objective was economic in nature.

13. Variance must be replaced by the more general concept of the mean squared error.

14. When $W = P = I$ the trace also ignores covariances between the $\hat{\beta}_i$.

15. Actually a somewhat simplified version of the SIME–DIME assignment model was used.

16. This point was also raised somewhat earlier by Henry in an unpublished memorandum, as well as in private conversation.

17. The originality of the Conlisk–Watts procedure lies in the efficiency and completeness of the algorithm rather than in the mathematical model itself, the components of which are more or less well known in the experimental literature. For a review of this literature see Fedorov (1972) or Kiefer (1959).

4 Methodological Issues and Experimental Data

I. INTRODUCTION

A truly distinctive feature of the income maintenance experiments conducted in the United States (and Canada) was their attempt to conform as closely as possible to the classic experimental design methodology. Thus selected sample families were allocated among several treatment groups and control groups. The treatment groups received monthly payments based on prespecified combinations of negative tax rates and guarantee levels. The control families were assigned to equivalent cells but received no payments. The major research objectives of the income maintenance experiments were (1) to determine whether a guaranteed income would reduce the labor supply of sampled families and (2) to predict such work change(s) for the entire eligible population in order to estimate the total transfer cost(s) of a national guaranteed income program.

The general superiority of well-designed experiments over ordinary survey methods is well known. It was hoped that the income maintenance experiments would provide data capable of yielding conclusions concerning the effectiveness of treatments (social intervention variables) that would be less ambiguous than earlier results based on surveys. It was believed that careful analyses of the New Jersey, Gary, Seattle/Denver, RIME, and Manitoba[1] data would yield clear answers to the preceding two policy mandates.

This initial anticipation has not been fully realized because social experimental data are, after all, still obtained by survey methods and in part suffer from the latter's deficiencies such as capture (measurement) error, nonresponse, and attrition. Thus despite the many optimal estimators based on experimental data, it has not been possible to take full advantage of their properties because of technical difficulties due to all social survey work and additional complicating factors. The methodological clarity and simplicity of the experimental design models developed to cope with problems encountered in agriculture and biology apparently are not able to compensate sufficiently for the simple fact that social experiments involve people, families, and other social units (and institutions), the substantive and sampling behavior of which is intrinsically more complex than that of a corn field treated with fertilizer. Also, and perhaps paradoxically, full advantage of the experimental nature of the data was not always taken into account or exploited to its full extent. Again this was probably due to the complex nature of the experiments as well as the fact that the constrained Conlisk – Watts procedure (see Chapter 3) did not yield a completely random sample. Furthermore, some researchers held that socioeconomic data could best be analyzed by econometric models (rather than by the more pragmatic statistical experimental techniques) because only these were well adapted to the requirements of economic theory and data. Still, the experimental nature of the research designs could not be totally dismissed. For example, although the New Jersey experiment attempted for the most part to adapt analysis of variance – covariance and spline regression models, SIME – DIME researchers virtually ignored the experimental nature of the data and concentrated on classic econometric techniques developed for time series and/or cross-sectional data. The result of such methodological laissez-faire was the emergence of research based on both the statistical traditions for evaluating experimental data and the econometric techniques evolved in the context of nonexperimental data. One consequence of this situation has been the difficulty, if not impossibility, of comparing or cross-validating the results of the various experiments.

This chapter describes several methodological issues confronting all researchers concerned with the four U.S. income maintenance experiments. We comment generally on the final models used, and highlight how the results concerning labor supply response might have been affected. Although all the experiments faced similar methodological difficulties concerning sampling strategy, choice and definition of variables, model specification, and the like, in each experiment the issues were resolved in somewhat different fashions. For a detailed account of each particular experiment the reader is referred to Chapters 5 through 8 and the original documents cited. The present chapter reviews issues common to all four experiments and is organized as follows. Section II describes the problem of choice and definition of variables; Section III is on the nonrandomness of the samples; Section IV is concerned with the issue of truncated and censored sampling; Section V is about modeling structural change; Section VI discusses functional form specification; and Section VII concludes with aspects relevant to panel data.

II. CHOICE AND DEFINITION OF VARIABLES

One of the first major research decisions concerns the variables of potential importance or interest, both dependent and independent. This section discusses the choice and definition of variables in the income maintenance experiments.

Choice of Variables

Generally speaking, four variables (indicators) or functions of these variables were employed as the dependent response for labor supply analysis:

1. labor force participation status,
2. employment – unemployment status,
3. hours worked per time period, usually one week, quarter year, or full year, and
4. earnings per time period.

The first two variables represent nominal scales (dichotomous categories) and the remaining two are continuous ratio scale variables.

The type of dependent variable(s) determines to a large extent the estimation methodology. Although the dependent response is "labor supply," there are several interrelated aspects of behavior that can be measured by the preceding variables. For example, an income maintenance program could reduce a respondent's number of work hours to zero either because the respondent has left the labor force altogether or else is in the process of changing jobs. Even though such observed behavior is measured as a "dummy" 0–1 variable, the underlying probability of response may not depend on the same set of independent variables. On the other hand, given that a respondent is working, his/her labor supply may be measured by the number of hours worked per time period (usually per week, assuming that it is possible to vary this variable continuously[2]), or earnings (net, gross, or both depending on the sample composition) per time period. Actual earnings capture a dimension that number of hours worked does not, namely, the earning capacity of an individual (independently of the number of hours worked), which may change due to reclassification, job change, and so on. Of course, the four dependent variables are usually intercorrelated and should be analyzed jointly by least squares models, which allow for more than a single dependent variable. None of the experiments took this approach, preferring to consider each dependent variable separately within a single equation. Thus an important source of sample information was omitted, resulting in less efficient estimators. We will return to the topic of dependent variable(s) when we discuss the statistical models actually used in the analyses. In passing we note that although econometric practice often analyzes a single dependent variable at a time (except in a simultaneous equations situation), the statistical and experimental tradition is to consider several intercorrelated dependent variables through methods of MANOVA or least squares regression (see, for example, Seal, 1964).

The choice of independent variables is obviously wide. It is guided by both statistical and experimental design requirements as well as substantive considerations of theory about behavior. For example, the appropriate set of independent variables will differ according to whether the sample is concerned with male youths, female heads of households, or farm operators. The influence of statistical requirements on the choice of independent variables requires a further comment, however. Let Y represent a dependent variable. Then, generally, we can write

$$Y = f(X, Z) + \epsilon \tag{4.1}$$

where Eq. (4.1) represents a class of models containing both continuous (ratio scale) variables X and dichotomous variables Z representing categories or classifications. $f(\cdot)$ is some specified functional form and ϵ is a residual term. This model is well known in both econometric work and statistical analysis of experiments (analysis of covariance). However, some of the income maintenance experiments used the two sets of variables X and Z in a manner opposite to that common in statistical work, reflecting perhaps the differing substantive perspectives of the econometric and experimental disciplines. In most cases the continuous economic variables X have a natural interpretation or a theoretical counterpart of particular interest to economists and econometricians; the dummy variables Z merely act as control variables. In contrast, an analysis of covariance of experimental data would focus principally on the dichotomous treatment variables Z, because only these measure the experimental parameters. Here the X are considered as "covariates" whose role is to account for systematic influence(s) beyond the control of the experimenter but that influence control and experimental differentials. Both views seem to have been held in the income maintenance experiments at one time or another. For example, the New Jersey experiment adopted an analysis of covariance methodology in order to detect significant experimental effects. On the other hand, the SIME – DIME and Gary experiments focused on continuous variables defined in terms of wage rates and total income, using the experimental dummy variables as control variables. This led to different estimation methodologies and models; and the reported results of these income maintenance experiments cannot, strictly speaking, be directly compared.[3]

Another major difference between the analysis of covariance approach and econometric modeling lies in the functional form of Eq. (4.1). In analysis of experimental data Eq. (4.1) is typically specified as a second-order polynominal, linear in the parameters, and usually estimated by a suitable analysis of covariance method based on the general linear model.[4] The nonlinear product terms then reflect the interaction effects between the design variables and/or the design variables and the covariates, if such interactions exist. In econometric work, however, more general estimation procedures and functional forms are frequently used. This difference is considered further in the sections that follow.

Definition of Variables: Use of Normal Wage Rates and Incomes

More than one response indicator can be selected as the dependent variable, and this indeed has been the case in the income maintenance experiments. Experimental design methods would probably construe any particular choice as arbitrary, that is, as being determined by the particular application at hand. Econometricians have much stronger views on the subject. Their procedure is to base the choice of dependent variable on economic "theory," by which is meant an a priori model conformable to intuition whereby some utility function is maximized subject to constraints. In spite of its formal framework, this procedure is ultimately not less arbitrary than others that might be used. The variables that influence utility are also assumed from economic theory; the major underlying premise is that the standard assumptions (and results) of microeconomic demand theory is the best way to model labor supply behavior under experimental conditions. In fact, economic theory provides little aid for specifying the complete set of independent variables to use or for choosing the functional form for labor supply equations. These two factors are, of course, vitally important in empirical work, with either experimental or survey data.

A major disadvantage of the econometric approach is that it can result in biased estimators. Suppose for any ith individual,

H_i is the number of hours of paid work, per time period (say one week),
Y_i is the total (annual) income,
W_i is the wage rate,

and let X and Z be defined as in (4.1). The standard utility maximization exercise results typically in the specification of a labor supply function

$$H = f(W, Y, X, Z) + \epsilon \qquad (4.2)$$

where W and Y are variables of prime economic interest and variables X and Z are included as control variables. The regression coefficients associated with Y and W, when transformed to percentage rates of change[5] (in order to remove the effects of units of measurement), are known respectively as the income elasticity (income effect) and the substitution elasticity (wage effect, substitution effect) of the labor supply function (4.2).

There are several statistical problems with formulation (4.2). By the usual least squares assumption the residual error ϵ is only associated with the dependent variable H. Since the wage rate W is often constructed as total earnings per number of hours worked, the variable W is also observed with error. This will bias most least squares estimators. The problem disappears, of course, if W is captured independently of the number of hours worked, say, by means of workers' pay stubs or other records. This was attempted by the experiments.

Another difficulty is that the relevant sample often consists of both employed and unemployed members of the labor force. By definition, unemployed workers cannot have an observed nonzero wage rate, even though their *potential* wage rates are generally nonzero. To avoid both of the preceding difficulties the observed wage rate W is replaced, in Eq. (4.2), by the so-called normal wage rate $\hat{W}$. This variable is commonly computed from an OLS regression equation (see, for example, Keeley *et al.*, 1978; Horner, 1973) of the form

$$\hat{W} = \hat{\alpha}_0 + \hat{\alpha}_1 V_1 + \hat{\alpha}_2 V_2 + \cdots + \hat{\alpha}_r V_r \qquad (4.3)$$

estimated from the employed workers only. The V_i ($i = 1, 2, \ldots, r$) denote either r lagged, observed wages W_{t-r}, or alternatively, variables that "explain" the wage rate structure of the labor force, or both. These variables must be collected internally by the experiment—from either respondents, employers, or both. Generally speaking, this procedure can purge W of error terms and also provide estimated wage rates for the unemployed by assigning them hypothetical wages they *would* have earned had they been employed, that is, their "normal" wage rate. The procedure is not without its difficulties, however. Several major assumptions are re-

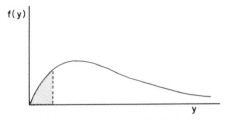

Fig. 4.1. *A truncated distribution.*

quired for this approach. These assumptions include (1) the labor force characteristics (regression slopes) of the employed and unemployed are identical; (2) Eq. (4.3) is properly specified; that is, the appropriate functional form has been selected and no independent variables have been omitted; and (3) variables V_i possess no error terms. When the preceding assumptions are not satisfied, the normal wage rates $\hat{W}$ will be biased, and consequently the labor supply estimates of Eq. (4.2) will also be biased. This appears to have been the case for most of the income maintenance experiments that used this approach. Other problems exist when estimating W, and these will be discussed in the context of the particular experiments.

Equivalent considerations apply when "normal" incomes are used to draw the initial sample. Annual income was one of the experimental variables measured. Unlike other parameters, however, income cannot be controlled by the experiment. Now, the observed income Y is composed of the "normal" or long-term ("equilibrium") income $\hat{Y}$ as well as a short-term ("transitory") component T, such that $Y = \hat{Y} + T$. Therefore all the experiments based their sample design on $\hat{Y}$ rather than Y to ensure that families' incomes would not, in the long run, systematically exceed certain prespecified income levels. Inaccurate estimates of $\hat{Y}$ could therefore result in a poorly selected sample, or possibly high attrition rates. Finally, because individuals with "high" incomes were systematically omitted, the result is a truncated sample as indicated by Figure 4.1. The problem of truncation and censorship of samples is considered in detail in the next section.

III. SAMPLE-POPULATION INFERENCE: NONRANDOMNESS OF EXPERIMENTAL SAMPLES

Social experiments have a high likelihood of a nonrandom sample. In the income maintenance experiments nonrandomness can be attributed to two principal reasons: one is the sample design, and the other is missing data due to attrition, "self-selection" of individuals (families), truncation, and/or censorship. Before considering more detailed aspects of the income maintenance experiments we make several observations of a more general nature relating to sampling and experimentation.

There is often insufficient appreciation of the difference between an *experiment* and an *evaluation program*. Generally speaking, an experiment (say, in the agricultural sciences) is conducted to estimate hypothesized lawlike behavior for same hypothetical infinite population of measurements. On the other hand, a social program (such as the income maintenance experiments) is established to estimate behavior of a finite human target population. Since the target population consists of those individuals about whom the researcher (or policymaker) wishes to make inferences, many "traditional" difficulties associated with experiments need not arise. For example, nonrandomly missing data associated with sample censorship and/or attrition, far from causing bias (inconsistency) in estimates, may in fact be an essential ingredient in preventing bias (inconsistency). This would happen if the target population is defined as that which would remain in a social program if it became universally implemented. Furthermore, if estimating the cost of a national income maintenance program were the main mandate of an economic "experiment," then clearly sample attrition, over time, would be a necessary ingredient.

Another important difference between an experiment and an evaluation program is that the latter often consists of periodic cross-sectional samples taken from nonstationary populations. As a result, at the estimation stage the researcher ends up modeling what is, essentially, a nonstationary stochastic process rather than a fixed response surface. It may be essential to regard attrition of the longitudinal sample as essential rather than as a statistical inconvenience. Of course, if the purpose is to make inference about a wider stationary population (such as a national adult population), then representativity of the sample implies that it must be replenished periodically during the experimental period. Inference, however, may be extremely difficult to make over time for a nonstationary population if the duration of the "experiment" is short.

Sample Design

As already noted, the Conlisk – Watts model was not fully random in the sense of assigning experimental units to treatment or control status with equal probability. This in itself does not pose intractable problems for sample-population inference, since such nonrandomness can, in principle, be taken into account by means of control variables (covariates). Moreover, the fact that normal income $\hat{Y}$ rather than observed income Y was used for drawing a sample[6] does not necessarily destroy its representative nature. This is so even when the normal income estimates are inaccurate, since $\hat{Y}$ can be expected to be distributed in a manner similar to Y. When estimates of normal income are low, however, a relatively larger proportion of the experimental units will earn incomes higher than the break-even levels over the duration of the experiment. This will result in a reduced sample size for analysis if one is mainly interested in families that received payments.

Two criticisms have been advanced against the Conlisk – Watts Model. It can be argued that monetary cost should have no bearing on establishing the truth or otherwise of a scientific hypothesis, however desirable this may be from an administrative point of view. Although budget constraints are employed in statistical survey sampling, there the main objective is to estimate an expected value of some random variable as efficiently as possible. The objective function of the Conlisk – Watts procedure is, it can be argued, statistically much too complex. And, it is difficult to evaluate directly the effect(s) of the budget constraints on the labor supply Eq. (4.2). A second criticism of the Conlisk – Watts model is that it imposes severe limits on alternative statistical models. For example, the Conlisk – Watts objective function entails minimizing the trace of the covariance matrix of regression slopes, thereby neglecting the covariances between the weighted coefficients of the independent variables. This latter comment was often voiced by the noneconomists associated with the experiments but largely fell on unsympathetic ears. Other criticisms of the Conlisk – Watts approach were discussed in Chapter 3 and need not be repeated. Our purpose here is to mention the nonrandomness problem associated with the Conlisk – Watts model.

Missing Data

A further difficulty that biases and/or renders estimators inefficient is missing data due to self-selection, censorship, or truncation. Since participation in a social experiment is voluntary, any individual may decide (at the outset or eventually) not to participate. If nonparticipants are significantly different from participants, clearly any estimates computed from a sample that did not take self-selection into account will be biased. Furthermore self-selection may reduce the sample size so that estimates exhibit higher variance; it then becomes more difficult to detect relatively small experimental effects. Sample selection bias may also arise as a direct consequence of the researcher—for example, when analyzing labor supply responses of married men (women), the sample is often confined to families that remained intact during the life of the experiment.

Because socioeconomic experimental data are obtained by more or less standard sampling survey instruments, many difficulties inherent in survey data gathering are also present in social experiments. However, missing data need not have a decisive influence on the experimental results if their effects are counteracted. One such procedure is to exploit both the cross-sectional and time series nature of the data to increase degress of freedom and reduce unexplained (error) sums of squares. Since experimental data from the income maintenance experiments consist of periodic observations recorded for experimental and control units over a number of years, and since sequential socioeconomic time series are usually serially correlated, a classic experimental approach comparing treatments and controls at each recorded time point (interval) would ignore this dependence. Two interdependent approaches have been used to sharpen the experimental analysis. The first is to consider only the treatment sample and utilize each individual as his/her own control over time. Thus change in behavior (if any) for each individual upon receipt of payments becomes the basis for determining the presence or absence of treatment effects. Since socioeconomic samples are highly interdependent over time, a great deal of the variance may be accounted for in this way. Hausman and Wise (1976), for example, find that about 85% of the total labor supply response variance in the New Jersey experiment is due to the time behavior of individual participants. The second, and more general, method is to consider both treatment–control and time variation by means of a components of variance model (described later). By drawing on as many sources of variance (information) as the sample permits, it is possible to greatly reduce the effects of missing data.

Although a nonrandom self-selection process will generally bias the statistical estimators, the presence or absence of "bias" may also depend on how the target population has been defined. For example, if the relevant population is considered to be all eligible members of the labor force ("the working poor"), then attrition and nonresponse will bias the usual estimators of labor supply for this group. However if, owing to policy considerations (such as determining the total cost of a national guaranteed income program), the target population is defined as those eligible adults who *in fact* will participate in such a program, then the self-selection process may become an essential ingredient of the experiment. The focus is then on cost estimation, and nonparticipants have no bearing here. Therefore "nonrandomness" resulting from self-selection becomes an important issue only if the experiment is to reflect the labor supply population for both participants and nonparticipants.

Although the missing data problem can frequently be defined out of existence, or minimized by combining all data panels into a single analysis, missing data will often still occur. This introduces biases and inefficiency into estimators, the magnitudes of which cannot usually be determined beforehand. Specialized estimators are needed to determine how much bias (if any) has been caused by missing data. Several methods have been proposed to deal with missing data in the context of estimating labor supply equations. A statistical model to deal with biases arising from self-selection and censoring has been proposed by Heckman (1977; 1979) and modified by Greene (1981); Hausman and Wise (1976, 1977a) have considered the problem of truncation and its effect on experimental estimates. Although both situations may appear similar in practice, they differ theoretically. It was already noted that not all members of the labor force are of equal interest. Experimental samples are "truncated" with respect to certain *variables* such as income or location. Thus sample points (individuals or families) with values for stratifying variables, such as normal income, that exceed a specific predetermined level are systematically excluded and are therefore unobserved. The resulting random variable is then said to be truncated (see Figure 4.1). A similar situation applies to certain dependent variables in the labor supply Eq. (4.1) when it is not possible to observe values smaller than some limit point. For example, the number of hours worked per week (H) is necessarily nonnegative. Although reasons for not observing certain values are different for both variables (values for income are excluded by the researcher while the number of hours worked is "logically" a nonnegative number), they are both usually referred to as truncated random variables.

When a sample contains missing (unobserved) values it is also said to be truncated, or else censored. A sample is truncated when it is not possible to use sample evidence to estimate the probability that a hypothetical observation will be observed; a sample is censored when it is possible to estimate this probability from the observed data. It is possible then to have truncated variables in either a truncated or a censored sample. We now consider three models that are used with censored and truncated samples, either with or without a truncated dependent variable.

The Tobit Model: Censored Samples with a Truncated
Dependent Variable

A regression model containing a "limited" dependent variable was developed by Tobin (1958). We illustrate the model using the bivariate regression equation, although the estimation procedure applies to any number of independent (exogenous) variables. Let

$$Y_i = \beta_0 + \beta_1 X_i + \epsilon_i \qquad (4.4)$$

where the dependent variable Y_i is observed only for individuals for whom

$$Y_i > L, \qquad i = 1, 2, \ldots, n \tag{4.5}$$

For example, let L equal 0, Y_i be hourly wage rate of individual i, X_i be number of years of schooling completed by individual i. Clearly, we only observe a wage rate for those individuals employed, so that a random sample of all employable adults will consist of the following observed values of Y,

$$Y_i = \begin{cases} Y_i^*, & \text{if } i \text{ employed} \\ 0, & \text{if } i \text{ unemployed} \end{cases}$$

The variable Y_i is therefore truncated.[7] The model can be written (assuming a lower bound L) as

$$Y_i = \begin{cases} \beta_0 + \beta_1 X_i + \epsilon_i, & \text{if } Y_i = \beta_0 + \beta_1 X_i + \epsilon_i > L, \quad Y_i \text{ observed} \\ L, & \text{if } Y_i = \beta_0 + \beta_1 X_i + \epsilon_i \le L, \quad Y_i \text{ unobserved} \end{cases} \tag{4.6}$$

To estimate model (4.6) we might use ordinary (or generalized) least squares on all the observed values of Y_i, including the values $Y_i = L$. In this example we would be attempting to compute the influence of education (schooling) on the wage rate, using $L = 0$ wages for the unemployed. This approach yields biased estimators because, clearly, unemployed workers will receive a nonzero wage rate on being employed. Using least squares on all data points would yield erroneous (biased) predicted wage rates for *all* elements in the vector Y.

A second approach might be to use only that part of the sample for which $Y > L$; that is, compute least squares estimates for (4.6) only for employed workers. This procedure may also result in biased estimators. First, the residuals do not satisfy the condition $E(\epsilon) = 0$ (in the population); so the least squares estimator of β_0 is necessarily biased.[8] Second, β_1 may also be biased since individuals with an observed wage rate need not represent a random sample of the population. If the original sample (including both employed and unemployed) were taken randomly, excluding unemployed workers may result in a nonrandom sample since unemployed workers may not represent a random subset of all workers—they may, for example, possess less formal education than the employed.

Another general estimation method that can be used is maximum likelihood. Assuming (as Tobin did) that ϵ is distributed normally with mean zero and constant variance σ^2, the joint distribution of the (independent) ϵ_i is

$$\prod_{i \in n_1} \frac{1}{\sigma\sqrt{2\pi}} \exp\left[-\frac{1}{2\sigma^2}(Y_i - \beta_0 - \beta_1 X_i)^2 \right]$$

$$\times \prod_{i \in n_2} \frac{1}{\sigma\sqrt{2\pi}} \int_{-\infty}^{L} \exp\left[-\frac{1}{2\sigma^2}(Y_i - \beta_0 - \beta_1 X_i)^2 \right] dY_i \tag{4.7}$$

where n_1 observations are observed (above point L) and n_2 are not observed. The likelihood function (4.7) is usually written in the abbreviated form

$$L = \prod_{i \in n_1} \frac{1}{\sigma} f\left(\frac{Y_i - \beta_0 - \beta_1 X_i}{\sigma}\right) \prod_{i \in n_2} F\left(\frac{-\beta_0 - \beta_1 X_i}{\sigma}\right) \tag{4.8}$$

where $f(\cdot)$ is the standard normal density and $F(\cdot)$ is the cumulative normal density and depends on the parameters β_0, β_1, and σ^2. The nonlinear function (4.8) is maximized with respect to β_0, β_1, and σ^2. The problem does not allow the estimators of β_0, β_1, and σ^2 to be expressed in explicit (closed-form) notation. The approach can be expanded to include more than a single independent variable. Also other functional forms may be used (such as a quadratic), and densities other than the normal could also be utilized for the likelihood (4.8), such as the standardized Sech-squared distribution whose cumulative density is the logistic (see Maddala, 1977). The logit model is often more appropriate since survey data often contain a slightly higher frequency of outliers than would be expected under the normal curve.

The following properties of the Tobit model can be noted.

1. The treatment parameters (regression coefficients) are not interpreted in the same way as least squares regression. Whereas least squares coefficients measure the response rate(s) of the entire sample, Tobit coefficients yield response rates for that sample portion with nonzero values for the dependent variable. Sample points for which $Y = L = 0$ are included in the regression largely to increase efficiency.

2. The predicted values Y (or H) are constrained by the Tobit method to assume nonnegative values and, in this sense, agree more closely with the observed values. Least squares predicted values can be negative and are therefore more difficult to interpret.

3. The variance–covariance matrix of the parameter estimates can be obtained and hypotheses on the regression slopes tested by the χ^2 statistic.

Amemiya (1973b) has proved the Tobit model consistent and asymptotically normal. He also provides an alternative estimator that is simpler to compute than the Tobit estimator.

The Hausman and Wise Model: Truncated Samples

Values below L are assumed "unobserved" in the Tobit model. In one sense the point L is a logical bound since we can never observe a negative number of hours worked. It would be more exact to characterize values lying below (or above)[9] the point L as unobservable rather than unobserved; that is, the Tobit case corresponds to a censored sample. Hausman and Wise (1977a) define a different model in which the dependent variable Y_i is not observed below (or above) a certain value L_i; that is, Y is sampled in a truncated sample. Consider the model (4.4) in the general form

$$Y_i = X_i\beta + \epsilon_i \qquad (4.9)$$

where Y denotes a $(n \times 1)$ vector of observations on some indicator of labor supply (such as earnings) and X is a $(n \times k)$ matrix of k explanatory variables. The error term ϵ is again assumed normal with mean 0 and (constant) variance σ^2, although this again is not logically necessary. For a randomly drawn experimental sample, least squares will provide unbiased estimators of β under the usual condition that X is uncorrelated with ϵ. Assume, however, that the cutoff level varies from sample point to sample point; that is,

$$Y_i < L_i \qquad (4.10)$$

For example, assume families are selected from an eligible population, and those whose incomes are subsequently higher than a given percentage of the poverty level (say, 150%) are eliminated from the study. Since the poverty level is dependent on family size, the cutoff point for Y is generally different for each family; therefore the truncation takes the form (4.10), where L_i depends on family size, and we have

$$Y_i = \begin{cases} X_i\beta + \epsilon_i \le L_i, & \text{included} \\ X_i\beta + \epsilon_i > L_i, & \text{excluded} \end{cases} \qquad (4.11)$$

that is, although values of $Y_i > L_i$ exist in the population they are excluded from the sample. What we have in this case is a "measuring device" that "misses" all observations above L rather than assigning them the value L as in the Tobit situation.

As with the Tobit model, estimating (4.9) by least squares using only the included portion of the sample ($Y_i \le L_i$) may introduce bias to all coefficient estimates. It is instructive to consider Hausman and Wise's original example (Figure 4.1). Suppose the "working poor" are characterized in terms of some long-run average income Y, and that this income is related to education by means of model (4.9):

$$\begin{aligned} Y &= Y^* + \epsilon \\ &= \beta_0 + \beta_1 X + \epsilon \end{aligned} \qquad (4.12)$$

where $Y^* = \beta_0 + \beta_1 X$ is average long-run income and X denotes the level of education. The (population) error term ϵ represents unexplained, random transitory income variations peculiar to an individual year. If one chooses a sample over a single year period, some individuals will have a temporarily high transitory income (resulting in a positive ϵ_i) and some will have a temporarily low transitory income (negative ϵ_i). By the truncation rule (4.10) one ends up, on balance, with more negative ϵ_i because the levels L_i act as "trapping barriers" for individuals possessing low transitory incomes. The result is again similar to the Tobit situation; that is, $E(\epsilon) \neq 0$ and the intercept term β_0 cannot be estimated without bias by least squares.[10] To see that the slope coefficient β_1 may also be biased, further argument is necessary. It can be assumed (with some justification) that the condition $E(\epsilon) \neq 0$, produced by using least squares only on the observed portion of the sample, can destroy the representative nature (randomness) of the sample. However, statistically the condition $E(\epsilon) \neq 0$ need not lead to bias in $\hat{\beta}_1$. Furthermore, since long-run earnings are determined by other (exogenous) variables that presumably do not influence transitory income, it is uncertain whether the truncation rule results in an unrepresentative sample of the working poor, particularly if L is set well above the poverty line. A labor supply function estimated from a truncated sample of low-income workers therefore need not yield biased estimates for the entire coefficient vector.[11]

Should bias also exist in the slope coefficients a maximum-likelihood estimation procedure developed by Hausman and Wise (1977a) can be used. Let F be the cumulative distribution function of those values of Y less than or equal to L_i (see Figure 4.1). Then

$$F(Y_i) = P(Y_i \leq y_i | Y_i \leq L_i)$$
$$= \begin{cases} 1, & \text{if } y_i > L_i \\ P(Y_i < y_i)/P(Y_i < L_i), & \text{if } y_i \leq L_i \end{cases} \tag{4.13}$$

in standard notation. The density function of Y given X_i is then

$$f(Y_i) = F'(Y_i) = \begin{cases} 0, & \text{if } Y_i > L_i \\ \hat{\phi}(Y_i) / \int_{-\infty}^{L_i} \hat{\phi}(Y_i)\, dY_i, & \text{if } Y_i \leq L_i \end{cases} \tag{4.14}$$

where $\hat{\phi} = N(X_i\beta, \sigma^2)$ is the normal density function and

$$\Phi[(L_i - X_i\beta)/\sigma] = \int_{-\infty}^{L_i} \hat{\phi}(y_i)\, dy_i \tag{4.15}$$

The likelihood function for n observed individuals is then given by

$$L = \prod_{i=1}^{n} f(Y_i) = \prod_{i=1}^{n} \hat{\phi}(Y_i) \Big/ \Phi[(L_i - X_i\beta)/\sigma] \tag{4.16}$$

and maximizing $\log_e L$ with respect to β and σ yields the required regression line. Equation (4.16) is not globally concave and a numerical procedure with good convergence properties is discussed by Hausman and Wise (1977a). The procedure is also compared to ordinary least squares using New Jersey data; the ML coefficients tend to be larger than OLS values by two to three times, with some being five to six times larger. Hausman and Wise therefore conclude that OLS underestimates experimental effects when the dependent variable is truncated. This comparison, of course, need have nothing to do with bias since it may reflect differences in efficiency of the two estimators (or the computed variance in a particular sample). The SEE of the OLS equations is approximately .39, whereas for the ML equations it is roughly .62, indicating that the ML procedure results in a poorer fit. Consequently, most of the standard errors of the ML coefficients are higher than the OLS values. When t statistics are compared for the two specifications, the difference becomes smaller.[12]

The Heckman Model: Censored Samples

We have seen for the Tobit model that censored samples arise in practice and that unless specialized models are used the estimated equations are biased. A more general method to correct for missing data is the Heckman (1976, 1979) model, which corrects for bias of nonrandom samples due to censorship (see also Maddala and Lee, 1976). Heckman essentially shows that the problem is equivalent to that of an omitted explanatory variable (correlated with included explanatory variables) and can be corrected by including in the equation an appropriate estimate of the excluded variable. The source of bias is also known as "selectivity bias" in program evaluation research and can be defined as "bias (which) arises in program evaluations when the treatment (or control) status of the subjects is related to unmeasured characteristics that themselves are related to the program outcome under the study" (Barnow *et al.* 1980; p. 43). The outcome is a biased estimate of the effect of treatment on outcome, such as labor supply.

Following Heckman (1977), consider a random sample of $I = I_1 + I_2$ individuals where I_1 are observed and I_2 are unobserved, and consider the following equations for any ith individual:

$$Y_{1i} = X_{1i}\beta_1 + \epsilon_{1i} \tag{4.17a}$$

$$Y_{2i} = X_{2i}\beta_2 + \epsilon_{2i} \tag{4.17b}$$

where X_{1i} is a $(1 \times k)$ vector of measurements for individual i and the usual OLS assumptions hold. In general, for the population we have

$$E(Y_{1i}|X_{1i}) = X_{1i}\beta_1 \tag{4.18}$$

but when data are missing on Y_{1i} the regression corresponding to the I_1 individuals is

$E(Y_{1i}|X_{1i}|\text{sample selection rule}) = X_{1i}\beta_1 + E(\epsilon_{1i}|\text{sample selection rule})$

Now assume that

data on Y_{1i} are available if $Y_{2i} \geq 0$,
data on Y_{1i} are not available if $Y_{2i} < 0$

in which case the available subsample regression for I_1 individuals is

$$E(Y_{1i}|X_{1i}, Y_{2i} \geq 0) = X_1\beta_1 + E(\epsilon_{1i}|Y_{2i} > 0) \cdot$$
$$= X_1\beta_1 + E(\epsilon_{1i}|\epsilon_{2i} \geq -X_{2i}\beta_2) \quad (4.19)$$

in view of the sample selection rule. When the second term is zero, the missing data create no bias, and the only consequence is lower efficiency resulting from decrease in the degrees of freedom. When the term is not zero, however, Eqs. (4.18) and (4.19) differ, and to correct for bias it is necessary to include the second term (or its estimate) in Eq. (4.17a). Therefore the bias can be viewed as resulting from an omitted "variable" $E(\epsilon_{1i}|\epsilon_{2i} \geq -X_{2i}\beta_2)$ that is correlated with the error term ϵ_{1i} of Eq. (4.17a), since generally ϵ_i, ϵ_2 are not independent.

The bias may affect either the constant term of (4.17a) or the entire set of coefficients. Assume the only term in the vector X_{2i} that determines sample selection of individual i is the constant vector $X_{2i} = (1,1, \ldots ,1)$. The probability of sample inclusion is the same for all individuals; the conditional mean $E(\epsilon_{1i}|\epsilon_{2i} \geq -X_{2i}\beta_2)$ is a constant, and the only term in (4.17a) that is biased is the intercept. However, when X_{2i} contains other nontrivial terms, all coefficients of (4.17a) are generally biased.

Using the theory of truncated bivariate normal distributions, where ϵ is truncated (see Johnson and Kotz, 1972, pp. 112–13) it can be shown that

$$E(\epsilon_{1i}|\epsilon_{2i} \geq -X_{2i}\beta_2) = \sigma_{12}/(\sigma_{22})^{1/2}\lambda_i \quad (4.20)$$

where σ_{12} and σ_{22}^2 are covariance and variance terms, respectively (involving ϵ_{1i}, ϵ_{2i}) and λ_i is the inverse of the so-called Mill's ratio; that is,

$$\lambda_i = \phi(Z_i)/[1 - \Phi(Z_i)] \quad (4.21)$$

where ϕ and Φ are the density and cumulative density of a standardized normal variable, respectively, and

$$Z_i = -X_{2i}\beta_2/[(\sigma_{22})^{1/2}] \quad (4.22)$$

Heckman's method is to estimate Z_i (and hence λ_i) and to use λ_i as a regressor variable in order to eliminate the bias; that is, Eq. (4.19) becomes

$$E(Y_{1i}|X_{1i}, Y_{2i} \geq 0) = X_{1i}\beta_1 + [\sigma_{12}/(\sigma_{22})^{1/2}]\lambda(Z_i) \quad (4.23)$$

with an equivalent regression holding for Y_{2i}. Heckman's is therefore a two-step estimation procedure whereby the function (Z_i) is computed first and then used in a second step OLS estimation as a supplementary variable. Although Heckman proves the resultant estimator consistent, his proposed algorithm (estimation procedure) appears in error; the interested reader is referred to Greene (1981) for a corrected (and more simplified) estimation procedure (see also Heckman, 1980, addendum, pp. 70–74).

An alternative restatement of the theory is provided by Barnow *et al.* (1980) in the context of selectivity bias rather than censored samples per se. It was seen earlier that difficulties associated with nonrandomly missing data can be solved by using a model that reduces the missing data problem to that of a missing variable problem, so as to avoid inconsistent regression estimates, or the so-called selectivity bias. Let the observed variables be

$Y =$ labor supply outcome

$$Z = \begin{cases} 1, & \text{treatment group} \\ 0, & \text{control group} \end{cases}$$

$X =$ matrix of covariates/control variables (including the constant)

and denote the unobserved variables by w and t where w is an unobservable latent trait, say "taste for work" and t is selection.

We assume that

$$Y = \beta w + \alpha Z + \epsilon_0 \qquad (4.24)$$

where the error term ϵ is assumed well behaved and normally distributed. Also, because the unobserved variables w and t can be expected to be highly correlated with the socioeconomic and demographic covariates X we have

$$w = \theta_1 X + \epsilon_1 \qquad (4.25)$$

$$t = \theta_2 X + \epsilon_2 \qquad (4.26)$$

Clearly, when X correlates perfectly with w and t, no bias (inconsistency) is introduced as a result of self-selection — however, the lower the correlation, the greater is the expected bias. It is further assumed that the disturbances ϵ_1 and ϵ_2 are bivariate normal, that each satisfies the usual ordinary least squares assumptions, and that both ϵ_1 and ϵ_2 are independent of ϵ_0. Substituting (4.25) into (4.24) we obtain

$$\begin{aligned} Y &= \beta \theta_1 X + \alpha Z + (\beta \epsilon_1 + \epsilon_0) \\ &= \gamma X + \alpha Z + \epsilon_3 \end{aligned} \qquad (4.27)$$

As before [see Eq. (4.19)] the selection rule implies that for treatments $(Z = 1)$ we obtain $t = \theta_2 X + \epsilon_2 > 0 \Rightarrow \epsilon_2 > -\theta_2 X \Rightarrow \epsilon_2/\sigma_2 > -\theta X$ where

$\sigma_2 = \text{var}(\epsilon_2)$ so that $-\theta X$ is a standardized normal variate.[13] Likewise for the controls $(Z = 0)$ we have $\epsilon_2/\sigma_2 \le \theta X$, so that

$$E(Z|X) = \text{Prob}(Z = 1|X) = \Phi(\theta X) \qquad (4.28)$$

where θ can be estimated by maximum-likelihood probit analysis of the dummy binary variable Z on X. Following Heckman's argument it follows that

$$E[(\epsilon_2/\sigma_2)|X_1, Z = 1] = \phi(\theta X)/\Phi(\theta X) \qquad (4.29)$$

and

$$E[(\epsilon_2/\sigma_2)|X, Z = 0] = -\phi(\theta X)/\Phi(\theta X) \qquad (4.30)$$

Combining (4.29) and (4.30) then yields the conditional expectation of ϵ_2/σ_2 given X, Z,

$$E[(\epsilon_2/\sigma_2)|X, Z] = Z\phi(\theta X)/\Phi(\theta X) - (1 - Z)\phi(\theta X)/[1 - \Phi(\theta X)]$$
$$= h(X, Z; \theta) \qquad (4.31)$$

say, so that $E(\epsilon_2|X, Z) = \sigma_2 h(X, Z; \theta)$. Thus the conditional expectation of ϵ_3 in Eq. (4.27) is given by

$$E(\epsilon_3|X, Z) = (\sigma_{12}/\sigma_{22})E(\epsilon_2|X, Z)$$
$$= \mu h(X, Z; \theta) \qquad (4.32)$$

Thus the regression of Y on X and Z in (4.27) is given by the conditional expectation

$$E(Y|X, Z) = \gamma X + \alpha Z + \mu h(X, Z; \theta) \qquad (4.33)$$

The parameters γ, α, and μ can be estimated consistently by nonlinear least squares, given the probit maximum-likelihood estimate of θ.

The Heckman–Maddala–Lee model provides a *theoretical* solution to selectivity bias. Little evidence is yet available, however, as to its practical feasability in evaluating response to large-scale social experiments. First, the model is conditional on normality of the disturbance terms in Eqs. (4.25) and (4.26), and some evidence exists that indicates lack of robustness to normality (Crawford, 1979). Second, the model provides a qualitative solution to least squares regression bias (nonconsistency) rather than a quantitative one in the sense that it is not usually known just how much bias is removed from the estimated treatment effects. Given the usually high degree of multicollinearity of unobserved variables with the socioeconomic and demographic covariates the selection bias incurred by using ordinary (generalized) least squares may be very small in practice—smaller perhaps than the decrease in precision of Heckman's model that often results owing to high multicollinearity between $h(X,Z;\theta)$ and X,Z in the second stage of the estimation.

Truncation and censorship are particular instances of a wider problem commonly encountered in virtually all sample surveys, namely, missing data due to nonresponse and attrition. Much has been written on the topic recently and a complete review of missing data problems is not possible within the present context. For a review of the literature and missing data estimates the reader is referred to Anderson, Basilevsky, and Hum (1983), as well as Little (1982) and Greenless *et al.* (1982) for new approaches to the problem.

IV. MODELING STRUCTURAL CHANGE: POLYNOMIAL SPLINE FUNCTIONS

A novel feature of experimental analysis to emerge from the New Jersey experiment is the use of spline functions to model structural (nonlinear) change or behavioral difference(s) in a response variable. Spline functions originated in mathematical approximation theory and it is only in relatively recent times that they have found application in econometrics or statistics.

Many relationships in the social sciences seem inherently discontinuous. For example, when causal (explanatory) variables consist of nominal scales such as ethnicity, religious and political affiliation, or sex of a given individual, the underlying causal models used to analyze such variables should also be discrete. Frequently, points of discontinuity are identified in terms of "structural" or purely qualitative changes in the behavior of a dependent variable. Much of contingency table analysis, for example, falls into this category as well as certain hierarchical clustering models used to search for structural change (see, for example, Sonquist *et al.* (1973)). In terms of the general linear (regression) model we encounter the familiar situation in which dummy variables, properly interacted with other independent variables, are used to model structural change in both intercept and slope(s) of a regression surface. Here both discrete and continuous independent variables can be used when discontinuity (change in structure) does not occur in all dimensions.

The dummy variable approach assumes that the function shifts permanently (and instantaneously) as a result of structural change. In many instances this is too crude an approximation to the real situation. Structural change may occur in a continuous fashion except at certain fixed points. This is viewed as a smooth response along a continuous curve except at points marked by a break in derivatives, depending on whether a linear, quadratic, or cubic response form is used for modeling purposes. For example, experimental treatments may in reality be continuous, although by design they are observed only at a small number of discrete points, often designated simply as "low," "medium," and "high" treatment levels. In the income maintenance experiments the various payment plans were not independent of each other but contained similarities in terms of either common tax rate(s) or guarantee level(s). In this situation it can be argued that one should employ models that are essentially continuous, yet capable of reflecting change(s) in structure of response at particular points. A class of such models is represented by spline functions, which, conveniently, can be estimated by usual least squares regression. We briefly outline the salient points of spline function analysis as it concerns statistical curve fitting. Our discussion is largely based on Poirier (1973, 1976) and Buse and Lim (1977).

Linear Splines

A polynomial spline function of degree n can be defined as a piecewise polynomial function, which, in turn, is composed of polynomial sections, each of degree n or less, such that the polynomial spline as well as its derivatives of degree $n - 1$ or less are continuous (the derivative of degree n is discontinuous) (Poirier, 1976). For the special case $n = 1$ we obtain the linear spline, which is illustrated in Figure 4.2. The linear spline can therefore be viewed as a linear relationship between X and Y that undergoes structural change at a finite number of points, known as "knots." Figure 4.2 portrays five linear segments, each joined together at the knot points $\bar{X}_1 < \bar{X}_2 < \bar{X}_3 < \bar{X}_4$ where structural change has occurred. Although the segments are continuous, the linear spline has discontinuous first derivatives at the knots.

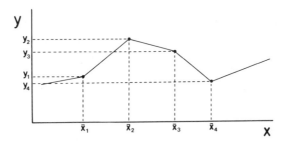

Fig. 4.2. *A linear spline function with four knots at* $\bar{x}_1, \bar{x}_2, \bar{x}_3, \bar{x}_4$.

The linear spline function can be represented (parametrized) in several ways. The most convenient for estimation purposes follows closely the dummy variable format so that a linear spline can be specified (and estimated) as a linear equation in $k + 1$ variables, where k denotes the number of knots. Let $W_1 = X$ be the explanatory variable. Then define

$$W_2 = \begin{cases} X - \overline{X}_1, & X > X_1 \\ 0 & \text{otherwise} \end{cases}$$

$$W_3 = \begin{cases} X - \overline{X}_2, & X > X_2 \\ 0, & \text{otherwise} \end{cases}$$

$$\vdots$$

$$W_k = \begin{cases} X - \overline{X}_k, & X > X_k \\ 0, & \text{otherwise} \end{cases}$$

(4.34)

The linear spline can be written as

$$S_\Delta(X) = \beta_0 + \beta_1 W_1 + \cdots + \beta_{k+1} W_{k+1}$$

(4.35)

and estimated by the usual methods of multiple regression analysis. The coefficients β_i of Eq. (4.35) are related to changes in slopes of the linear segment. Thus for the example in Figure 4.2, β_1 denotes the slope of the spline $S_\Delta(X)$ over the first interval, β_2 the change in slope from the first interval to the second interval, β_3 the change in slope from second to third interval, and so on. To obtain the actual slopes over the various segments it is necessary to add the slopes. Thus the slope over the first segment is β_1 (as before), the slope over the second segment is $\beta_1 + \beta_2$, and the slope over the ith segments is $\beta_1 + \beta_2 + \cdots + \beta_i$. In an actual statistical regression the variables W_i will usually be insufficient to explain behavior and other variables (both continuous and discrete) are added as "controls" or covariates. For an illustration of the use and interpretation of linear spline regression see Poirier (1976, pp. 12–20).

Quadratic and Cubic Splines

The linear spline equation (4.35) assumes that segments that join at the knots are straight lines, hence the term linear spline. More generally a spline of degree n will comprise segments that are polynomials of degree n (or less). In practice, polynomials of degree greater than $n = 3$ are rarely used and the most immediate generalization of Eq. (4.35) is the cubic spline, in which segments joining the knots consist of cubic (quadratic, linear) functions. The reason for this parsimony is that the choice of spline function can be viewed as an attempt to provide the greatest smoothness of fit in the sense of minimizing curvature. Commonly, this can usually be achieved by specifying the cubic (or quadratic, as the case may be) spline function. Halladay's theorem (see Ahlberg *et al.,* 1967, p. 376) states that for a set of knots $X_0 < X_2 < \cdots < X_k$ having abscissa values $y_0, y_1, \ldots, y_k$ $(k > 2)$ the cubic spline is the solution to

$$\min_{f(X)} \int_{x_0}^{x_i} |f''(X)|^2 \, dx \qquad (4.36)$$

where $f(X_i) = Y_i$ $(i = 0,1, \ldots, k)$, $f''(X)$ denotes the second derivative, and the minimization is over function $f(X)$.

When analyzing experimental data the position of the knots x_i depend on the treatments and are therefore known. For nonexperimental data this is frequently not the case and there is an additional problem of estimating the locations of the knots (see Gallant and Fuller, 1973). Although cubic spline functions were first developed for purposes of numerical approximation (Ahlberg *et al.,* 1967), Poirier (1973) has employed them to develop a new piecewise regression model. More recently, Buse and Lim (1977) have shown that regression based on cubic splines can be formulated as restricted least squares regression, a well-known model in the econometric literature. Both the Poirier and the Buse–Lim formulations yield identical results. However, the restricted least squares formulation seems more flexible for testing statistical significance of a priori restrictions.

V. ELASTICITY ESTIMATION AND FIRST DIFFERENCES

All the experiments allocated a portion of the sample for control purposes. The initial intention in having control groups was to use standard experimental design techniques (analyses of variance, covariance) to test for labor supply response. This approach was not adopted by all research groups. Instead, since data were available longitudinally (at regular time intervals and sometimes continuously) for the same set of individuals, the treatment units were used as their own controls and labor supply response was measured by considering paired differences at two different time points. Under this research strategy the principal variables are measured as first differences $\Delta X = X_{after} - X_{before}$ and then substituted in a regression equation. We consider briefly the statistical–econometric implications of expressing variables as first differences, and particularly the interpretation of regression parameters in this context.

Let

$$\Delta Y = \alpha_0 + \alpha_1 \Delta X_1 + \alpha_2 \Delta X_2 + \cdots + \alpha_k \Delta X_k \qquad (4.37)$$

denote a linear equation in terms of first differences ΔY and ΔX_i ($i = 1$, $2, \ldots, k$) in the dependent and independent variables respectively, where

$$\Delta Y = Y_t - Y_{t-1}, \qquad \Delta X_i = X_{it} - X_{i,t-1} \qquad i = 1, 2, \ldots, k \quad (4.38)$$

are measured at two time points t and $t - 1$. If the first differences (4.38) are good approximations to the total differentials dY and dX_i; that is

$$\Delta Y \simeq dY, \qquad \Delta X_i \simeq dX_i \qquad (4.39)$$

then Eq. (4.37) can be approximated by

$$\begin{aligned} dY &= \alpha_0 + \alpha_1 \, dX_1 + \alpha_2 \, dX_2 + \cdots + \alpha_k \, dX_k \\ &= \alpha_0 + \alpha_1 (YX_1/YX_1) \, dX_1 + \cdots + \alpha_k (YX_k/YX_k) \, dX_k \quad (4.40) \end{aligned}$$

for each sample point. Because Eq. (4.40) gives the total differential dY of a dependent variable in terms of total differentials dX_i of independent variables, we have

$$\alpha_i = \partial Y/\partial X_i \qquad i = 1, 2, \ldots, k \qquad (4.41)$$

Dividing (4.40) by Y and substituting for α_i we have

$$\begin{aligned} \frac{dY}{Y} &= \frac{\alpha_0}{Y} + \left(\frac{\partial Y}{\partial X_1} \frac{X_1}{Y} \right) \frac{dX_1}{X_1} + \cdots + \left(\frac{\partial Y}{\partial X_k} \frac{X_k}{Y} \right) \frac{dX_k}{X_k} \\ &= \beta_0 + \beta_1 \frac{dX_1}{X_1} + \cdots + \beta_k \frac{dX_k}{X_k} \qquad (4.42) \end{aligned}$$

where $\beta_0 = \alpha_0/Y$ and $\beta_i = (\partial Y/\partial X_i)(X_i/Y)$ represent continuous percentage rates of change, or elasticities. For an actual sample the discrete analogs of the β_i are

$$\beta_i^* = \frac{\Delta Y}{\Delta X_i} \frac{X_i}{Y} = \frac{\Delta Y/Y}{\Delta X_i/X_i} \qquad (4.43)$$

whose average values for the whole sample can be obtained directly from the regression equation

$$\frac{\Delta Y}{Y} = \beta_0^* + \beta_1^* \frac{\Delta X_1}{X_1} + \cdots + \beta_k^* \frac{\Delta X_k}{X_k} + \epsilon \qquad (4.44)$$

Because the β_i^* are average elasticities they can be interpreted as logarithmic (exponential) rates of change. Note, however, that the average elasticities β_i^* cannot be obtained from a regression based on Eq. (4.37) because

$$(Y/X_i)\beta_i^* = \alpha_i \qquad (4.45)$$

so that the X_i generally vary for each sample point; that is, for each different value of Y and of X_i. Consequently, when elasticities are estimated from Eq. (4.37), they are usually expressed at the mean point as

$$(\overline{Y}/\overline{X}_i)\beta_i^* = \overline{\alpha}_i \qquad (4.46)$$

It is preferable, however, to compute the elasticities β_i^* directly from Eq. (4.44) because the X_i lose precision for sample points further away from the means $\overline{Y}, \overline{X}_1, \overline{X}_2, \ldots, \overline{X}_k$.

Another way to view model (4.44) is in terms of a linear approximation to some (labor supply) equation whose exact functional form is not specified. This interpretation is particularly useful because economic theory cannot provide sufficient a priori specification of the labor supply functional form. Let

$$Y = f(X_1, X_2, \ldots, X_k) \qquad (4.47)$$

be a labor supply function. Expanding Y into a k-variable Taylor series yields the linear approximation (omitting the cross-product terms) as

$$Y \simeq X_1 \frac{\partial Y}{\partial X_1} + X_2 \frac{\partial Y}{\partial X_2} + \cdots + X_k \frac{\partial Y}{\partial X_k} \qquad (4.48)$$

Taking the total differential we have

$$dY \simeq \frac{\partial Y}{\partial X_1} dX_1 + \frac{\partial Y}{\partial X_2} dX_2 + \cdots + \frac{\partial Y}{\partial X_k} dX_k \qquad (4.49)$$

which is the same as Eq. (4.40).

VI. COMPONENTS OF VARIANCE AND COVARIANCE

Social experiments typically provide both cross-sectional and time-series measurements, that is, so-called panel data whereby observations on each variable vary by individual (family) in addition to time intervals (usually quarterly in the income maintenance experiments). Data of this form are relatively rare, and research possibilities abound. Not only can treatment individuals be compared to control individuals (as in analysis of variance–covariance) but treatment individuals may also be compared to themselves across time.[14] Thus, loosely speaking, each treatment unit can also act as its own control. One complication is that each cross-sectional "panel" at time t is no longer independent from a panel at time $t - j$, and therefore cannot be analyzed by the usual analysis of variance–covariance methods. In other words, treatment effects cannot be assumed constant over time. Indeed, under the components of variance–covariance model, they form a set of random variables. For this reason the variance–covariance components model is known in the statistical experimental design literature as the random effects model. For a thorough review of the literature the reader is referred to Searle (1971), Kendall and Stuart (1968, Vol. 3, pp. 57–84), Scheffe (1959), and Graybill (1961). Recently, the model has been introduced in econometrics as well (see Swamy, 1971). First consider the experimental design model

$$Y_{ij\ldots k} = \mu + \alpha_i + \beta_i + \cdots + \epsilon_{ij\ldots k} \tag{4.50}$$

where the treatments α_i, β_j are considered fixed (nonrandom). It is well known that the model can also be written (and estimated) as the OLS equation

$$Y = X\beta + \epsilon \tag{4.51}$$

where each X_i is a vector with, say, elements equal to either 0 or 1. The components of variance model is written as

$$Y = 1\mu + X\beta + \epsilon \tag{4.52}$$

where μ is the overall mean and the coefficients β are unobservable random variables with variance σ^2. There are thus $k + 1$ random components in Y (the k treatment effects and ϵ) such that

$$
\begin{aligned}
E(\epsilon) &= 0, & \sigma_\epsilon^2 I &= E(\epsilon\epsilon^T), & \text{cov}(\beta_i,\epsilon) &= 0 \\
E(\beta_i) &= \mu_i, & \text{var}(\beta_i) &= \sigma_{\beta_i}^2, & \text{cov}(\beta_i,\beta_i) &= 0
\end{aligned} \tag{4.53}
$$

This implies that the variance in Y can be written as

$$
\begin{aligned}
\sigma_Y^2 &= \sigma_{\beta_i}^2 + \sigma_{\beta_2}^2 + \cdots + \sigma_{\beta_k}^2 + \sigma_\epsilon^2 \\
&= \sigma_\beta^2 I + \sigma_\epsilon^2 I
\end{aligned} \tag{4.54}
$$

and the purpose of the components of variance approach (random coefficients model) is to estimate the σ_β^2 and σ_ϵ^2 so that the usual hypotheses concerning the treatments can be tested. Equation (4.51) implies K groups, each containing n_i observations, that is,

$$
\begin{bmatrix} y_{11} \\ y_{12} \\ \vdots \\ y_{n_1} \\ \vdots \\ y_{k1} \\ y_{k2} \\ \vdots \\ y_{kn_k} \end{bmatrix}
=
\begin{bmatrix}
1 & 0 & \cdots & 0 \\
1 & 0 & \cdots & 0 \\
\vdots & \vdots & & \vdots \\
1 & 0 & \cdots & 0 \\
\vdots & \vdots & & \vdots \\
0 & 0 & \cdots & 1 \\
0 & 0 & & 1 \\
\vdots & \vdots & & \vdots \\
0 & 0 & \cdots & 1
\end{bmatrix}
\begin{bmatrix} \beta_1 \\ \beta_2 \\ \vdots \\ \beta_k \end{bmatrix}
+
\begin{bmatrix} \epsilon_{11} \\ \epsilon_{12} \\ \vdots \\ \epsilon_{1n_1} \\ \vdots \\ \epsilon_{k1} \\ \epsilon_{k2} \\ \vdots \\ \epsilon_{kn_k} \end{bmatrix} \tag{4.55}
$$

For panel data the K groups represent K time periods.

When the same number of observations are available for each individual the data are said to be "balanced." When data are balanced the usual (analysis of variance) estimator has minimum variance. For unbalanced data (when some data are missing), great caution is necessary when selecting an estimator since uniqueness, optimality, and unbiasedness are not guaranteed.

The concept of components of variance can also be applied to the residual term of an analysis of covariance regression equation. Let

$$Y_{it} = \beta_0 + \beta X_i + d Z_{it} + u_{it}, \qquad i = 1, 2, \ldots, n, \quad t = 1, 2, \ldots, T \tag{4.56}$$

for n individuals and T time periods, where X_i represents the experimental effects (variables) and Z_{it} denotes the control covariates.[15] As with the random coefficient model the observations are not independent owing to time. To take time dependence into account we can decompose u_{it} as

$$u_{it} = \mu_i + \tau_t + v_{it} \tag{4.57}$$

where μ_i is the time-persistent individual residual attribute variation, constant through time for each individual, τ is the individual pervasive time effects, constant for all individuals at time t. This component can occasionally be omitted if time is explicitly taken into account, and v_{it} is the usual properly behaved error term (homoscedastic, uncorrelated). The following is assumed for the disturbance terms.

$$E(\mu_i) = E(v_{it}) = 0$$

$$\text{cov}(\mu_i, \mu_i') = \begin{cases} 0, & \text{different individuals} \\ \text{var}(\mu) = \sigma_\mu^2, & \text{same individuals} \end{cases}$$

$$\text{var}(v_{it}) = \sigma_v^2, \qquad \text{var}(\mu_i) = \sigma_\mu^2$$

where

$$\sigma_u^2 = \sigma_\mu^2 + \sigma_v^2 \tag{4.58}$$

Since u_{it} is no longer homoscedastic or uncorrelated, the appropriate estimation procedure is generalized least squares (GLS). The following procedure can be used to estimate the equation (see also the New Jersey report, see D.IV, p. 5). First compute the usual analysis of variance components by means of OLS regression to obtain the total sum of squares of the u_{it}, the between (individual) and within sum of squares. This permits the construction of a heteroscedastic error covariance matrix. Second, use GLS to reestimate the regression coefficients. As mentioned, considerable care must be taken with unbalanced data. Note this procedure assumes the slopes to be constant across individuals and time, but the intercept random since it is now equal to $(\beta_0 + \mu_i)$ and therefore varies across individuals (but not time).

VII. CONCLUSION

This chapter has described several methodological developments and research issues common to all the income maintenance experiments. It has also outlined a number of different analysis approaches and attempted to consider them from both a statistical and econometric perspective. With this as background, we can now consider the models and results of each of the four income maintenance experiments.

NOTES

1. Unlike its American counterparts, no labor supply analysis has yet emerged from the Manitoba income maintenance experiment.

2. Respondents may have part-time work either as a sole job or in addition to regular employment which normally cannot be varied for a given individual in a continuous manner. On the average, however, the discontinuities can be expected to be small in number for a given sample.

3. As will be seen from Chapters 7 and 8, even the "econometric" models used in SIME-DIME and Gary differ substantially.

4. Although analysis of covariance does not explicitly use least squares regression, it can always be reformulated (and solved) as a least squares problem.

5. Coefficients are transformed to percentage rates of change when the dependent and independent variables are measured in such disparate physical units that interpretation becomes difficult or impossible. The aim of such an exercise is not unlike standardizing a variable to unit variance. Where this is not the case, there is no advantage in the transformation.

6. The sample is therefore not random for a second reason namely, that individuals who earn over a certain income have a zero probability of being sampled. The sample is therefore truncated with respect to income.

7. In a sense the wage rate is observed for the unemployed, namely, $y = 0$. However, this is a consequence of being unemployed and is not due to the potential wage rate being zero. Thus a (potential) wage rate exists even for the unemployed but cannot be observed.

8. Note, however, that β_1, need not be biased simply because $E(\epsilon) \neq 0$.

9. The point L can also serve as an upper bound value.

10. Note again that least squares does not necessarily result in bias for the slope coefficient(s) simply because $E(\epsilon) \neq 0$. The intercept and slope coefficients are distributed independently.

11. Hausman and Wise (1977a) prove that $E(Y_i/X_i)$ is biased (Appendix A), but do not show that bias must necessarily exist in the slope coefficients (rather than in the intercept).

12. In the case of age 35–45 the ML coefficient is reported to be 6.7 times larger than the OLS value, although neither are significant at the .90 level.

13. That is, $\theta = \theta_{2/\sigma_2}$. The original notation in Barnow *et al.* is confusing since it is not clear whether primes or the transpose of θ are used.

14. A mistaken notion that has made its way into the econometric literature is that components of variance obviate the use of controls. Naturally, control individuals can also be used.

15. The X_i and Z_{it} may interact.

5 The New Jersey Graduated Work Incentive Experiment

I. INTRODUCTION

The New Jersey experiment was a milestone in empirical research and sparked much of the methodological debate concerning "controlled" economic experimentation. A large portion of the discussion centered on the choice of statistical technique to analyze socioeconomic experimental data; in particular, data containing dichotomous and nonnegative dependent variables, high attrition rates, missing data, and truncated dependent variables. Analysis of data from the New Jersey experiment can be conveniently divided into two main categories.

The first category consists of studies carried out by researchers officially affiliated with the experiment; these results were initially released in four volumes and received limited circulation as the *New Jersey Final Report*. The labor supply findings were subsequently edited and published by Academic Press (Watts and Rees, eds., 1977); abridged versions of these studies appeared in a special issue of the *Journal of Human Resources* (Vol. 9, No. 2, 1974), and in Rees and Watts (1975). A summary report written for a nontechnical audience was released by the U.S. Department of Health, Education, and Welfare (1973). These publications constitute the "official" published results of the New Jersey analysis.

The "official" New Jersey results were immediately greeted with acclaim, partly due to the unique nature of the experimental data and partly due to

84

sincere admiration for the dedication and ability of the New Jersey researchers. But there was also critical scepticism of the results and interpretations, ranging all the way to questioning the policy relevance of the findings (Barth *et al.*, 1975; Mahoney and Mahoney, 1975) to doubting the appropriateness of the sampling procedure, experimental design, and statistical analysis of the data (Aaron, 1975; Cogan, 1978; Hall, 1975; Heckman, 1977; Hausman and Wise, 1976; Rossi and Lyall, 1976). The statistical analyses contained in the massive *New Jersey Final Report* were based mainly on econometric and statistical models and the use of spline regression techniques to model nonlinear treatment effects (Poirier, 1973a,b,c). No attention was given to the fact that some dependent variables were either dichotomous, nonnegative, or truncated. Consequently, this formed the basis of much criticism of the "official" findings; and that, in particular, the New Jersey research team had possibly introduced a downward bias in their estimates of the expected labor supply response. Subsequent reworking of the New Jersey data taking account of these difficulties constitute a second category of results — the "postofficial" interpretation.

The next section describes the models and results of the *New Jersey Final Report* in general terms. This is followed by a discussion of the specific findings of the Final Report, that is, the "official" results. The final section considers the "postofficial" interpretations.

II. MODELS AND RESULTS OF THE NEW JERSEY FINAL REPORT

This section presents a general description of the labor supply results from the Final Report. It is important to bear in mind that the New Jersey data constitute a nonrandom sample owing to income truncation and attrition; the target population is the urban working poor rather than the entire labor force, and the allocation of the sample is affected by the special nature of the Conlisk – Watts model.[1] There were also changes introduced in the welfare programs by the U.S. government both during and after the experiment.

The main stress in this chapter is on methodological rather than policy issues since these constitute a novel feature in the design and analyses of experiments. We focus especially on the extent to which methods actually met experimental requirements.

The New Jersey experiment found no widespread abandonment of work by intact husband – wife experimental (payment) families, either for husbands, wives, or families taken as a whole. Four response (dependent) variables[2] were used to measure labor supply — total earnings, total (weekly) number of hours worked, employment status, and labor force participation. It is clear from Tables 5.1 – 5.4 that significant control – experimental differences, if they exist, are not large. Although estimates of the labor supply response vary from one response variable to another, from one group of participants to another, and from one model to another for most experimental groups, the various measures show reductions (relative to the control group) of less than 10%. Many of these differentials are in fact smaller and

Table 5.1

Mean Total Family Income ($ per week) of Intact Husband – Wife Families (n = 693)

Family	Pre	1st year	2nd year	3rd year
Experimental	102.30	117.32	129.45	140.28
Control	104.34	117.30	132.71	148.93
Total	103.09	117.31	130.71	143.63

Source: Watts and Rees (1977).

Table 5.2

Mean Total Family Earnings ($ per week) of Intact Husband – Wife Families (n = 693)

Family	Pre	1st year	2nd year	3rd year
Experimental	95.18	108.16	113.63	123.93
Control	94.54	105.31	113.41	127.80
Total	94.93	107.06	113.55	125.43

Source: Watts and Rees (1977).

Table 5.3

Mean Total Family Hours Worked per Week, Intact Husband – Wife Families (n = 693)

Family	Pre	1st year	2nd year	3rd year
Experimental	40.6	39.9	39.2	50.8
Control	40.7	42.6	42.4	44.9
Total	40.6	40.9	40.4	42.4

Source: Watts and Rees (1977).

Table 5.4
*Number of Employed Persons per Family,
Husband–Wife Families (n = 693)*

Family	Pre	1st year	2nd year	3rd year
Experimental	1.071	1.066	1.035	1.067
Control	1.041	1.159	1.153	1.190
Total	1.059	1.102	1.080	1.115

Source: Watts and Rees (1977).

not significantly different from zero (at the .05 level). Indeed, for blacks there is no significant reduction in labor supply and, in a number of cases, a statistically significant *increase* in work effort was observed. Only for wives (especially whites) were large and significant percentage reductions observed, but these do not constitute large absolute reductions since truncating family incomes during sample selection resulted in extensive deletions of families with wives in full-time employment. Consequently, females in the experimental sample worked, on the average, a very small number of hours. In fact, the 15–20% reduction in work effort on the part of wives may actually represent an upwardly biased figure. Another interesting finding was the insignificance of the various treatment plans when taken separately; this is probably due to the small differences in actual cash payments represented by these plans. Labor supply differentials based on regression estimates are given in Tables 5.5–5.7.

The summary statistics presented in Tables 5.1–5.4 provide a very rough indication of experimental effects because complete randomness of samples cannot be assumed, and the effect(s) of the treatments (payment plans) cannot be determined. To compare more than two mean responses requires an analysis of variance model; but since other factors (covariates) typically affect experimental–control differentials, the analysis of variance model becomes, in effect, an analysis of covariance with covariates representing control variables. The unique feature of the New Jersey analysis is that the treatment parameters, as well as other variables such as age, are modeled by continuous spline functions rather than discontinuous (and orthogonal) dummy variables. The spline function specification appears more appropriate for two reasons. First, the treatments (payment plans) are not independent of one another since they contain either a common tax rate or guarantee level. Second, the response surfaces in the treatments (payment plans) are, in reality, continuous.

In order to partition response variance along a set of dimensions, a surface of the form

$$Y = f(Z) + R(X,XZ) + u \qquad (5.1)$$

is estimated, where Y is a dependent labor supply response variable, $f(Z)$ represents control variables (covariates) such as age, education, and other individual characteristics, and $R(X,XZ)$ measures the response to payment treatments X as well as interactions XZ. The term u is a residual normal error variate that can be further decomposed into components since cross sections and time series are both available. The response surface $R(X,XZ)$ contains, as a subset, linear spline functions of the form

$$S(k) = \sum_{i=1}^{n} a_i S_i(x,g,t), \qquad k = 1, 2, \ldots, 8 \qquad (5.2)$$

The a_i are parameters, and spline functions S_i (which depend on the tax rate t and guarantee level g) are defined as

$$S_1 = x = \begin{cases} 1, & \text{treatment} \\ 0, & \text{control} \end{cases}$$

$$S_2 = S_1(g - .75)$$

$$S_3 = S_1(t - .50)$$

$$S_4 = \max(S_2,0) = \begin{cases} S_2, & S_2 \geq 0 \\ 0 & \text{otherwise} \end{cases} \qquad (5.3)$$

$$S_5 = \max(S_3,0) = \begin{cases} S_3, & S_3 \geq 0 \\ 0, & \text{otherwise} \end{cases}$$

$$S_6 = \max(g - 1.00,0) = \begin{cases} g - 1.00, & g \geq 1.00 \\ 0, & \text{otherwise} \end{cases}$$

$$S_7 = S_2 S_3 - S_4 S_5$$

$$S_8 = S_4 S_5$$

Thus S_1 is the usual experimental–control dummy whose coefficient a_1 measures the differential mean response in labor supply between the payment and control groups, that is, the experimental differential evaluated at $g = .75$ and $t = .50$. Coefficients a_2 and a_3 are associated with splines S_2 and S_3 and represent the "slopes" (rates of change) of the linear portions of the response curve with respect to $g' = g - .75$ and $t' = t - .50$; thus the estimated response to the (1.00,.70) plan, all else kept constant, is $a_1 + 25a_2 + .20a_3$. Coefficients a_4, a_5, and a_6 measure the response to nonlinear (but additive) effects of g and/or t on labor supply, while a_7 and a_8 represent nonlinear and nonadditive interaction effects associated with S_7

and S_8. The coordinate $(g,t) = (.75,.50)$ is arbitrarily selected as the origin in the guarantee – tax rate (or treatment) space from which interplan variation is measured. Equations of the form (5.2) are used to estimate normal incomes $\hat{Y}$ and normal wage rates $\hat{W}$, which, in turn, are used in labor supply regressions estimated separately for male heads, female heads, and the entire family.

Unfortunately the chapters dealing with labor supply in the New Jersey experiment have not been coordinated; the individual authors were "free to follow their own choices . . . in specifying analytical and statistical models for explaining the phenomenon of labor supply response" (Watts *et al.* 1973, p. BI-1). As a result the studies from the New Jersey experiment are uneven in style and methodology, and this effectively removes any possibility of comparing labor supply response among different groups. Consequently, we must review the results by considering in turn each major subgroup, and the issues raised by that group.

III. SPECIFIC FINDINGS AND MODELS OF THE NEW JERSEY FINAL REPORT

Male Family Heads (Husbands)

The New Jersey report found no significantly large withdrawal of labor supply for husbands in intact families who remained with the experiment from beginning to end (Watts *et al.*, 1973; Rees, 1974; Watts *et al.*, 1974; Horner, 1973). Watts (1973a) and Horner (1973) carried out independent analyses employing different methods; in what follows both approaches are considered, but first, it is necessary to consider the estimation of normal wage rates and normal income.

Estimation of Normal Wage Rates and Normal Incomes

The variables required to compute "normal" wage rates and "normal" incomes should be independent of experimental parameters; that is, normal wage rates must be independent of experimental effects. However, an experimental – control difference was detectable in hourly earnings (i.e., observed wage rates), particularly during the first half of the experiment (Watts *et al.*, 1973, pp. BI-25, BI-26). Wage rates for experimental and control husbands are depicted in Fig. 5.1. The average rate is 7% higher for experimentals than controls at preenrollment, and remain higher throughout the experiment.

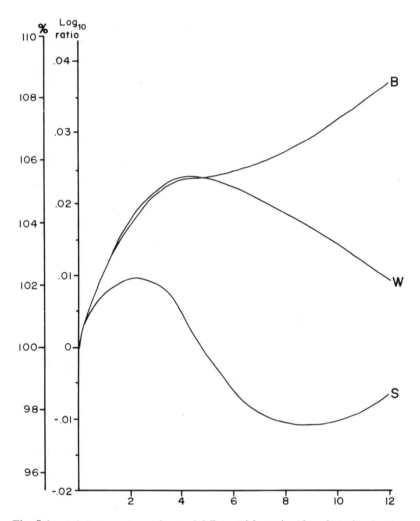

Fig. 5.1. *Relative experimental-control differential for males (the cubic spline* $f \rightarrow (x_{10})$).

Watts and Mallar (1973) investigated whether the experimental–control differential was due to measurement error (i.e., experimentals tending to report gross wages and controls tending to report net wages). A set of four cubic spline variables denoting experimental time is used to measure the relationship of experimental wages to the overall time trend in wages. The time (experimental) variable has three "knots" at quarters 2, 6, and 12, and by evaluating the coefficients of these knots for a given quarter, the difference between experimental wages and control wages[3] can be estimated.

After considering various hypotheses Watts and Mallar (1973) conclude that only for black husbands is it reasonable to suggest an endogenous wage change by the experiment; the experimental–control differences for whites and Spanish-speaking males are probably due to systematic reporting error so that wages are independent of experimental effects. The evidence notwithstanding, it is difficult to believe that wage differentials were mainly produced by differential misreporting by the experimental and control groups.

Nonetheless, because of the possibility that observed wages (and incomes) may respond to some extent to experimental effects, the New Jersey experiment employed normal wage rates $\hat{W}$ rather than observed wages W (see Chapter 4). The common logarithm of the wage rate of husband i at time t, W_{it}, is decomposed as the linear form[4]

$$W_{it} = \hat{W}_{it} + \tilde{W}_{it} + \epsilon_{it} \tag{5.4}$$

where the "normal" component depends on the husband's personal traits as well as the job characteristics; that is,

$$\hat{W}_{it} = f_1(x_1, x_2) + f_2(x_3, x_4) + f_3(x_5) + f_4(x_6) + f_5(x_7) \tag{5.5}$$

where x_1 is the current age, x_2 the years of completed education, x_3 the industrial code of job, x_4 the occupational code of job, x_5 the site code, x_6 the employment status of spouse, x_7 the current calendar time, and $f_i(\cdot)$, $i = 1$, 2, . . . , 5, represent spline and dummy variable functions (see Watts *et al.*, 1973, pp. BI-29, BI-30 for greater detail). The term $\tilde{W}_{it}$ captures the impact of the experimental plan assignment;[5] that is,

$$\tilde{W} = f_6(x_8, x_9) + f_7(x_{10}) \tag{5.6}$$

where x_8 is the tax rate, x_9 the guarantee level, x_{10} the experimental time, and $f_6(\cdot)$ and $f_7(\cdot)$ are spline functions. Finally, the term ϵ_{it} is a random residual term with two components.

The sample is restricted to continuous husband–wife families present at the eighth and twelfth quarters; and the data comprise 9009 observations on 693 families from which 4361 observations are deleted either because the husband was not working full time[6] or because of miscoding (errors in variables). A further 308 observations are discarded on the basis of education attainment and age; husbands completing more than 12 years of schooling, or over 55 years old, are excluded.

Normal incomes $\hat{Y}_{it}$ are estimated in similar fashion although the details are different. Here the complete panel data consisting of 13 observations on 693 families are used. The basic equation is specified as

$$Y_{it} = \hat{Y}_{it}(Z) + \tilde{Y}_{it}(\hat{Y}, X) + u_{it} \tag{5.7}$$

Normal incomes $\hat{Y}_{it}(Z)$ are assumed to depend on a set Z of family characteristic variables; that is, x_1 is the husband's age (years), x_2 the husband's education (years), x_3 the wife's age (years), x_4 the wife's education (years), x_5 the experimental site, x_6 the calendar time in months (from August 1968), x_7 the month of year (January $= 1$), x_8 the family composition variable, and x_9 the health of husband at quarters 2 and 6. The term $\hat{Y}_{it}(\hat{Y}, X)$ represents the effect of the experiment on family income at time t. Note that $\hat{Y}_{it}$ is specified to depend on normal income $\hat{Y}$ as well as experimental variables X that consist of x_{10} the experimental status variable (dummy), x_{11} the guarantee level, x_{12} the tax rate, x_{13} the experimental time (quarters), x_{14} the "normal welfare ratio."[7] Unlike the normal wage specification it is assumed that the vectors $\hat{Y}$ and X interact. The terms $\hat{Y}_{it}(Z)$ and $\hat{Y}_{it}(\hat{Y}, X)$ therefore depend on spline dummy variable subfunctions.

Labor Supply Response of Husbands

We first consider the analysis by Watts (1973a). The labor supply equation (for white, black, and Spanish-speaking husbands) is defined as

$$S = \beta_1 \left(\frac{\hat{Y}}{PL(n)} \right) + \beta_2 \hat{W} + \beta_3 \left(\frac{1}{\hat{W}} \right) + \beta_4 \left(\frac{\hat{Y}}{\hat{W}} \right) + \beta_5 H_p$$
$$+ \beta_6 E_b + f(\text{treatment variables}) + \epsilon \qquad (5.8)$$

where S is one of four labor supply response measures, $\hat{Y}$ the normal family income, $\hat{W}$ the normal wage rate, $PL(n)$ the poverty level used to define guaranteed income, H_p the preenrollment hours worked per week, E_b the number of weeks employed in base year, and f the function containing treatment variables formulated in terms of dummy variables.

Treatment status (payment) is indicated by the usual $0-1$ dummy variable codes, and the variables $\hat{Y}$, $PL(n)$, $\hat{W}$, H_p, and E_b are employed as covariates or "control" variables. Regressions of the form (5.8) are estimated, and then used to compute differential treatment effects according to the usual covariance analysis. Thus $\hat{Y}$ and $\hat{W}$ are used primarily as control covariates for the treatments rather than to obtain income or substitution effects (as in SIME–DIME; see Chapter 7).

Watts's results are presented in Table 5.5A, which is drawn from the *New Jersey Final Report* (reprinted in Watts and Rees (1977)) and Table 5.5B, which is reproduced from a subsequent journal article. A major shortcoming of the chapter in the Final Report is the lack of specimen regression information or example calculations to determine the four methods used to compute Table 5.5. It is also difficult to verify which of the standard statistical models or assumptions are being employed and to what degree the data conform to the assumptions made. For example, evaluating statistical

Table 5.5A

Experimental Response According to Plan "Generosity" for Four Indicators of Labor Supply by Ethnicity and Time Span

			Plan					
	Quarter	Base	Low	Medium	High	F_3	F_2	R_2
Participation								
White	1–4	95.8	−1.3	1.5	4.5[a]	1.64	1.63	.40
	5–8	97.7	−3.8	−2.6	2.3	1.59	2.36[a]	.33
	9–12	94.4	−4.1	− .7	3.9	1.59	2.31	.28
	3–10	96.9	−2.8	−1.2	2.9	1.39	2.04	.37
Black	1–4	98.3	1.8	.7	−1.0	0.23	.34	.25
	5–8	97.8	−3.3	2.0	2.7	1.03	1.43	.26
	9–12	99.3	−5.8	5.7	− .8	2.05	3.08[b]	.26
	3–10	97.5	−2.0	2.6	1.5	.65	.87	.28
Spanish-speaking	1–4	99.0	3.0	.4	− .1	.19	.27	.22
	5–8	100.6	1.9	− .2	.3	.09	.12	.30
	9–12	99.3	1.9	2.2	− .8	.42	.59	.22
	3–10	99.6	2.4	.0	.1	.13	.18	.29
Employment								
White	1–4	92.5	−1.7	.2	2.6	.52	.67	.45
	5–8	92.5	−6.7[a]	−4.3	.1	1.52	1.66	.47
	9–12	87.6	−9.6[b]	−4.7	−3.0	1.52	.86	.37
	3–10	91.6	−6.3[a]	−4.2	− .1	1.55	1.60	.50
Black	1–4	94.0	3.1	3.1	3.5	.50	.01	.41
	5–8	93.9	.1	− .9	2.1	.22	.30	.37
	9–12	92.9	1.1	2.2	2.7	.15	.04	.42
	3–10	92.6	1.7	1.6	2.7	.26	.06	.44
Spanish-speaking	1–4	96.6	.1	−3.8	−2.5	.40	.23	.31
	5–8	95.7	3.2	−3.6	− .6	.35	.47	.33
	9–12	97.0	8.1	2.3	−1.8	.74	1.08	.42
	3–10	95.7	4.9	−2.9	−0.5	.58	.83	.42
Hours per week								
White	1–4	37.2	1.4	−1.0	−1.0	.73	.99	.56
	5–8	35.8	−3.9[a]	−1.5	−0.9	1.33	1.05	.49
	9–12	35.2	−2.5	−4.4[b]	−3.2[b]	2.48[a]	.34	.47
	3–10	36.2	−2.7	−2.1	−1.3	1.29	.37	.58
Black	1–4	36.4	3.0	2.5	1.9	1.05	.15	.43
	5–8	35.7	1.5	.8	1.1	.26	.06	.51
	9–12	36.5	1.3	.7	1.8	.34	.13	.47
	3–10	35.7	2.1	1.2	1.3	.60	.12	.56
Spanish-speaking	1–4	37.5	−2.7	− .8	−1.9	.53	.26	.38
	5–8	37.8	2.3	− .6	−0.3	.30	.44	.44
	9–12	37.7	5.6[a]	1.9	0.9	1.19	1.15	.47
	3–10	37.4	3.1	−0.2	0.1	.65	.95	.54

(continues)

Table 5.5A
(Continued)

			Plan				
Quarter	Base	Low	Medium	High	F_3	F_2	R_2
Earnings per week								
White 1–4	93.0	10.4[b]	1.1	2.2	1.72	1.81	.63
5–8	93.8	−6.0	−3.1	− .5	.63	.61	.68
9–12	88.4	−4.5	−13.4[c]	−5.8	2.51[a]	1.32	.61
3–10	92.9	−3.4	−4.3	− .6	.67	.58	.75
Black 1–4	95.5	8.7	11.2[b]	8.6[a]	2.24[a]	.15	.52
5–8	92.3	16.8[c]	10.1[b]	9.6[b]	3.54[b]	.82	.60
9–12	95.8	14.7[b]	8.2	9.3[a]	1.80	.39	.54
3–10	92.5	16.3[c]	9.8[b]	9.6[c]	5.02[c]	1.09	.68
Spanish-speaking 1–4	96.3	−9.6	2.4	2.5	1.28	1.87	.63
5–8	94.7	1.3	−2.9	.5	.18	.26	.59
9–12	94.4	9.6	1.2	4.9	.76	.63	.64
3–10	93.9	3.4	−1.3	3.5	.62	.77	.73

Note: From regressions controlling on $S_c[\hat{Y}, \hat{W}, \text{PL}(n)]$, and *preexperiment values* for hours per week and weeks per year. The base is for head with $\hat{Y} = \$100$, $\hat{W} = \$2.50$, $\text{PL}(n) = \$80$, who worked 40 hours at preenrollment and for 50 weeks the previous year.

F_3 is the F-statistic for the null hypothesis that all three experimental coefficients are zero, that is, all experimental group means are the same as the base. F_2 is the F-statistic for the null hypothesis that all three experimental coefficients are the *same* (i.e., no variation by generosity).

[a] Statistically significant at the .10 level.
[b] Statistically significant at the .05 level.
[c] Statistically significant at the .01 level.
Source: Watts and Rees (1977), Chapter 3.

significance by the F tests requires that the residual term be normal, yet no mention is made, even in passing, of whether this is the case.

The main results obtained by Watts may be summarized as follows: (1) Only 19 of the 144 response coefficients of Table 5.5 are "significant" at the .10 level (or better). This is apparently slightly more than implied by random draws. Watts concludes that the payment plans do not have very much overall effect on the four measures of labor supply. Such reasoning, however, is incorrect—the 19 "significant" coefficients cannot be used as independent indicators of treatment effects because the 144 coefficients given in Table 5.5 are not all independent. Hence the theory of simple random draws does not apply. (2) In Table 5.5, 12 of the 19 significant coefficients are found in the "earnings per week" equations, particularly for the black subsample. Not only are more coefficients significant for the measure "earnings per week" but also the R^2 values are higher, indicating

Table 5.5B

Husband Totals: Regression Estimates of Differentials in Labor Force Participation, Employment, Hours, and Earnings for Quarters 3–10[a]

Group	Labor force participation rate	Employment rate	Hours worked per week	Earnings per week
White				
Control group mean	94.3	87.8	34.8	100.4
Absolute differential	− .3	−2.3	−1.9	1
Absolute group mean	94.0	85.5	32.9	100.5
Percent differential	− .3	−2.6	−5.6	1
Black				
Control group mean	95.6	85.6	31.9	93.4
Absolute differential	0	.8	.7	8.7
Treatment group mean	95.6	86.4	32.6	102.1
Percent differential	0	.9	2.3	9.3
Spanish-speaking				
Control group mean	95.2	89.5	34.3	92.2
Absolute differential	1.6	−2.4	− .2	5.9
Treatment group mean	96.8	87.1	34.1	98.1
Percent differential	1.6	−2.7	− .7	6.4

Note: These figures differ from Final Report figures (p. B11a-87), Table 2.

[a] The data for these tables consist of 693 husband–wife families who reported for at least eight of the 13 quarters when interviews were obtained. The reported differentials in each measure of labor supply are the experimental treatment group mean minus the control group mean, as measured in a regression equation in which the following variables were controlled: age of husband, education of husband, number of adults, number of children, sites, preexperiment labor supply variables of the husband. These means and the associated control–treatment differentials may therefore be interpreted as applicable to control and treatment groups with identical composition in terms of these variables. Percent differentials are computed using the mean of the control as base.

Official government labor force concepts, used in the experiment, define someone in the labor force if he or she is employed or unemployed. Someone is unemployed if he or she is actively seeking employment, waiting recall from layoff, or waiting to report to a new wage or salary job.

Source: This and the following two tables appear as Tables 1, 2, and 3 in U.S. Department of Health, Education, and Welfare (1973).

better explanatory power. The significant coefficients also tend to be larger in magnitude, thereby indicating that significance is due not only to small variance (higher R^2) but also to a stronger response.

The treatment effects are considered in terms of a "base" male family head rather than in terms of the controls. This appears to be due to a particular requirement of the New Jersey experiment, whereby payment families filled out income reports every four weeks while controls did not. As a result, a suspected differential bias in reporting earnings may have crept in between the two subsamples. The payment families realized more quickly that gross rather than net incomes were required. Since the response of earnings to treatments did not appear to match the number of hours worked, the earnings variable was deleted from any further analysis.

Treatment – Income Interaction

Labor supply response is postulated to depend on the magnitude of the payment; therefore individuals receiving low payments or whose incomes are above the breakeven point should contribute very little to the general response effect. The size of the treatment effect (or payment) is therefore expected to decrease gradually and to eventually vanish at the breakeven point. To handle this situation Watts (1973a) defines a parameter θ where

$$\theta = \begin{cases} 0, & \text{for controls and payment husbands who} \\ & \text{are more than 20 hours-worth of income} \\ & \text{above breakeven} \\ \dfrac{M + 20\hat{W} - \hat{Y}}{10\hat{W}}, & \text{otherwise} \end{cases} \qquad (5.9)$$

where M is the breakeven (dollar) level for a household, given its assigned guarantee G, tax rate t, and poverty level $\mathrm{PL}(n)$; $\hat{W}$ the normal wage rate, and $\hat{Y}$ the normal income. The parameter θ measures the distance from breakeven. For example, θ assumes the value 2 for an observation whose normal income $\hat{Y}$ is exactly at the breakeven point, and so on. For greater comparability among respondents, the index θ is further rescaled in terms of hours of work.

A quadratic labor supply response function in θ is defined to take account of nonlinearities. We have

$$X = (\alpha_{11} + \alpha_{12}S_2 + \alpha_{13}S_3)\theta + (\alpha_{21} + \alpha_{22}S_2 + \alpha_{23}S_3)\theta^2 \qquad (5.10)$$

where $S_2 = G - .75$ and $S_3 = t - .50$ are linear splines. The α_{ij} are coefficients to be estimated iteratively. Labor supply response to the experimental parameters G and t is measured by the derivatives

$$\frac{dX}{dG} = X'_G + X'_t \frac{dt}{d\theta} + X'_\theta \frac{d\theta}{dG} \qquad (5.11)$$

$$\frac{dX}{dt} = X_t' + X_G' \frac{dG}{dt} + X_\theta' \frac{d\theta}{dt} \tag{5.12}$$

where X_G', X_t', and X_θ' are the partial derivatives

$$X_G' = \alpha_{12}\theta + \alpha_{22}\theta^2 \tag{5.13}$$

$$X_t' = \alpha_{13}\theta + \alpha_{23}\theta^2 \tag{5.14}$$

$$X_\theta' = (\alpha_{11} + \alpha_{12}S_2 + \alpha_{13}S_3) + 2(\alpha_{21} + \alpha_{22}S_2 + \alpha_{23}S_3)\theta \tag{5.15}$$

The preceding expressions are then used to estimate the income effect

$$\left. \frac{dX}{dG} \right]_{dt=0} = X_G' + X_\theta' \frac{d\theta}{dG} = X_G' + X_\theta' \frac{PL(n)}{10t\hat{W}} \tag{5.16}$$

the (uncompensated) price effect

$$\left. \frac{dX}{dt} \right]_{dG=0} = X_t' + X_\theta' \frac{d\theta}{dt} = X_t' - X_\theta' \frac{PL(n)M}{10t\hat{W}} \tag{5.17}$$

and the coefficient

$$\left. \frac{dX}{dG} \right]_{dM=0} = X_G' + \frac{t}{G} X_t' \tag{5.18}$$

which measures effects induced by the experimental guarantee G and tax rate t. Here $M = G/t$ is the breakeven level so that coefficient (5.18) embodies compensating movements in t and G so as to maintain constancy in the breakeven level M. The compensated price change ("substitution effect") is obtained as

$$\left. \frac{dX}{dt} \right]_{dB=0} = X_t' + X_G' \frac{\hat{Y}}{PL(n)} - X_\theta' \left(\frac{PL(n) - t\hat{Y}}{10t^2\hat{W}} \right) \tag{5.19}$$

where the net benefit B is kept constant. Numerical estimates of these derivatives are obtained for an average plan and an average male head for $G = 100$, $t = .50$ (so that $S_2 = .25$ and $S_3 = 0$), $PL(n) = \$80.00$, $\hat{Y} = \$100.00$, $\hat{W} = \$2.50$. The family size is slightly larger than six to produce a poverty line of $80.00 per week. Hence the breakeven point is $160.00 per week and consequently $\theta = 4.4$. The derivatives can then be calculated directly at $\theta = 4.4$, $S_2 = .25$, and $S_3 = 0$ to obtain

$$\left. \frac{dX}{dG} \right]_{t=.5} = S_G' + 6.4X_\theta' \tag{5.20}$$

$$\left. \frac{dX}{dG} \right]_{M=2} = X_G' + .5X_t' \tag{5.21}$$

$$\left.\frac{dX}{dt}\right]_{G=1} = X'_t - 12.8X'_\theta \tag{5.22}$$

$$\left.\frac{dX}{dt}\right]_{B=30} = X'_t + 1.25X'_G - 4.8X'_\theta \tag{5.23}$$

using the partial derivatives (5.13) to (5.15), which, in turn, depend on the estimated values of the α_{ij}.

The values of the derivatives are summarized in Table 5.6 where x is the response in employment. Watts *et al.* (1974) report that the negative coefficients predicted by "economic theory" are significant only for the Spanish-speaking husbands, and even here the magnitude of response is not very large (Table 5.7). For whites only the hours regression indicates significance, whereas for the black sample all responses are insignificant.

A sample of parameters that measure the labor supply response to treatment plans is given in Table 5.6. Watts *et al.* present only a limited sample of derivatives and associated elasticities. The elasticities are evaluated at the mean (see above) owing to the complex interaction of the guarantee and tax rates as defined by θ. The first column contains the "gap" effect ($dx/d\theta$), which decreases with increasing values of θ, indicating a mild disincentive effect. The second column corresponds to the income effect (keeping tax rate constant); the third corresponds to a simultaneous

Table 5.6

Selected Derivatives and Elasticities for Prototype Cases from Regressions Using Middle Two-Year Averages of Husband's Hours[a]

Group	θ	$\left.\dfrac{dx}{d\theta}\right\|$ "Gap" effect	$\left.\dfrac{dx}{dG}\right\|^{dt=0}$ Income effect	$\left.\dfrac{dx}{dG}\right\|^{dM=0}$ "Pivot" effect	$\left.\dfrac{dx}{dt}\right\|^{dG=0}$ Price effect	$\left.\dfrac{dx}{dt}\right\|^{dB=0}$ Substitution effect
White	4.4	$-$ .8($-$.09)[b]	.7(.02)	2.9(.08)	4.5(.06)	5.3(.07)
	6	$-$1.2($-$.30)	2.4(.10)	3.9(.16)	3.0(.06)	5.4(.11)
Black	4.4	.2(.02)	$-$1.0($-$.03)	1.5(.04)	5.3(.07)	3.9(.05)
	6	$-$ .2($-$.06)	$-$1.1($-$.05)	$-$ .3($-$.01)	1.6(.03)	0.5(.01)
Spanish-	4.4	$-$1.9($-$.22)	$-$3.4($-$.09)	$-$4.0($-$.11)	$-$ 1.1($-$.01)	$-$ 5.4($-$.07)
speaking	6	$-$3.0($-$.74)	$-$1.9($-$.04)	$-$7.6($-$.31)	$-$13.3($-$.28)	$-$14.3($-$.30)

[a] The prototype plan refers to a guarantee G of 1.00 times the poverty level and a tax rate t equal to .50. The poverty level is approximately $80 per week.

[b] Numbers in parentheses are elasticities assuming 38 hours as base for $\theta = 4.4$ and 24 hours as base for the $\theta = 6$ prototype.

Source: Watts *et al.* (1974).

Table 5.7

F-*Ratio Tests of Hypotheses on Experimental Response Regressions on Averages of Middle Two Years*

Group	All experimental (8)	Terms using θ^2 (3)	Tax rate terms (2)	Guarantee terms (2)	Tax and guarantee terms (4)	R^2
White husbands (275)						
Participation	.43	.09	.11	.44	.46	.417
Employment	1.03	1.15	.50	1.02	1.33	.492
Hours	2.40[b]	.86	.95	2.57[b]	2.58[a]	.637
Black husbands (201)						
Participation	.84	.45	.63	.36	.35	.442
Employment	.87	.35	.24	.45	.36	.540
Hours	1.28	1.41	2.07	1.16	1.07	.658
Spanish-speaking husbands (137)						
Participation	3.81[c]	6.53[c]	13.06[c]	9.85[c]	6.99[c]	.521
Employment	5.79[c]	7.20[c]	19.72[c]	15.79[c]	9.86[c]	.638
Hours	3.10[c]	3.28[b]	10.33[c]	8.87[c]	5.29[c]	.687

[a] Significant at the .10 level.
[b] Significant at the .05 level.
[c] Significant at the .01 level.
Source: Watts *et al.* (1973).

increase in the guarantee level and tax rate so as to keep the breakeven point $M = G/t$ the same. In other words, it indicates the consequence of increasing the guarantee level without changing the level of income at which benefits begin. Finally, the fourth and fifth columns yield the price and income-compensated substitution effects respectively, where the latter is derived under the constraint that benefits B remain constant under a change in the tax rate. As pointed out, the results conform to "economic theory" only in the case of the Spanish-speaking husbands, and white husbands show mildly significant (but low-magnitude) response only for hours worked.

The preceding supply responses are limited to healthy husbands, that is, those with at most one chronic illness and who missed fewer than seven days of work in the year preceding the experiment.[8] The New Jersey results indicate that husbands with impaired health have lower hourly earnings, with a larger response to illness being concentrated among husbands with low earning rates. Health status produces weak interactive effects with the guarantee level and tax rate, but only in the first year of the experiment. Differentials because of health status tend to increase at low guarantees and high tax rates. Attitudinal scales are also constructed for the following psychological variables: work involvement, "anomie," occupational flexibility, self-esteem, personal efficiency, job satisfaction, present–future time orientation, and perception of financial need. Regression results fail to indicate any significant influence of psychological attitudes on labor supply. Rather, the opposite process seems to occur. The poor indicate a strong motivation to work; but when external factors interfere adversely with their labor effort, this results in negative attitudes toward work.

Experimental Response and the Cobb–Douglas Function: Dependent Variables as First Differences

Horner (1973) adopts a different approach to analyzing the sample of husbands. His orientation is more along econometric lines in that the empirical equations are constrained a priori to conform to "economic theory." Horner begins by assuming a utility function of the form:

$$U = A + a \ln(Y) + b \ln(L_m) - c \ln(L_f) + d \ln(L_o) \qquad (5.24)$$

where Y is the income, representing inputs in the "production" of family activity, and L_m, L_f, L_o are the leisure time of the male head, the female head, and other adults (if any) in the household. Horner then derives an estimation equation

$$\Delta H_i = \beta_0 Q_i + \beta_1 D_i Q_i + \beta_2 P_i Q_i + \beta_3 F_i Q_i + \beta_4 M_i Q_i \qquad (5.25)$$

where ΔH is the first difference in the number of hours worked per week (thereby measuring the change in work effort), Q the vector of demographic characteristics as well as "human capital" variables such as the amount of job training, education, and so on, possessed by the individual, P the vector containing work history and labor status, F the vector of family structure variables, and M the welfare history.

Only a single experimental variable is defined:

$$Q = Y_s / W_{m2}(1 - t) \qquad (5.26)$$

where Y_s is the level of nontaxable income subsidy, t is the tax rate, and W_{m2} represents the husband's wage rate at the end of the experimental period.[9] Equation (5.25) consequently consists of two sets of explanatory variables, say X and Q, and may be rewritten in the form

$$\Delta H = B_0 X + BXQ + e \qquad (5.27)$$

where ΔH and Q are defined as before and X denotes a matrix of variables characterizing the head and his family.

Horner's sample consists of 799 husbands; it is not limited to husbands in the continuous husband–wife sample. Further, observations from the preenrollment survey in addition to the 12 quarterly interviews during the experiment are employed; the final sample contains all husbands for whom data exists in the preenrollment period, the fourth quarter, and at least three other quarters.[10]

The dependent variable is then defined as

$$\Delta H = (H_7 + H_8 + H_9 + H_{10}/4) - H_0 = \overline{H} - H_0 \qquad (5.28)$$

where H_i denotes the number of hours worked in quarter i. The difference-averaging process implied by (5.28) is used for two reasons: first, to smooth an (uneven) seasonal pattern, and second, to account for any adjustment in work effort due to the terminations of payments by the experiment.[11] This was termed the "wind-down effect."

Horner estimates three separate regression equations of the form (5.27), and these are given in Table 5.8. Given the definition of ΔH in (5.28) the elasticities of labor supply response are computed from regressions I and II only. For regression I we have

$$e_{1G} = \frac{G}{\overline{H}} \frac{\partial \overline{H}}{\partial G} = \frac{G}{\overline{H}} \frac{\partial \overline{H}}{\partial Q} \frac{dQ}{dG}$$

$$\qquad (5.29)$$

$$e_{1t} = \frac{t}{\overline{H}} \frac{\partial H}{\partial t} = \frac{t}{\overline{H}} \frac{\partial \overline{H}}{\partial Q} \frac{dQ}{dt}$$

with similar expressions holding for regression II.

Horner's development at this point (see Horner, 1973, pp. BII b-17 to BII b-20) becomes obscure owing to typographical error as well as poor presentation. Although discussion of the preliminary economic–econometric aspects are well covered, and the final results summarized in tables, it is impossible for the reader to go from the one to the other. Therefore any technically qualified reader wishing to consider the methodology (and results) of Watts (1973a) or Horner (1973), or to enhance their understanding of the computational procedures used to obtain experimental responses, will encounter continual frustration. In any case Horner's main results are given in Table 5.9, where we learn that for individuals near the minimum wage who receive subsidies equal to the poverty level, and who face a 50% tax rate on their earnings, a 1% increase in either the guarantee or the tax rate will decrease labor supply by 0.66% or 0.137%, depending on whether regression I or II is applicable[12] (Horner, 1973, BII b-19). However, it is virtually impossible to relate the notation and certain entries in the tables with the verbal explanation of the text. For instance, e_{1G}, e_{1t} and e_{2t}, e_{2G} are used to denote elasticities with respect to guarantee and tax rate in regression

Table 5.8
*Coefficients for the Three Primary Models of the
Labor Supply Response of Male Family Heads to
Negative Income Taxation*

Independent variable	Regressions		
	I	II	III
Q	-1.11942^a		-13.2258
	$(.62166)$		(8.2207)
Q^2		$-.55964^a$	
		$(.29506)$	
EQ			-1.7173
			(1.5610)
AQ			$.64380$
			$(.43629)$
A^2Q			$.007843$
			$(.005543)$
H_0	$-.80394^a$	$-.80359^a$	$-.80087^a$
	$(.03064)$	$(.03064)$	$(.03072)$
$1/\overline{W}$	3.1835	4.9963	3.4827
	(6.4735)	(6.6456)	(6.4821)
A	$.95020^a$	$.95133^a$	$.39839$
	$(.37424)$	$(.37414)$	$(.54497)$
A^2	$-.011792^a$	$-.011817^a$	$-.004902$
	$(.004851)$	$(.004849)$	$(.007133)$
L	-5.7097^b	-5.6604^b	-5.5571^b
	(1.3413)	1.3410	(1.3427)
E	1.8514	-1.8631	3.0967^a
	(1.1523)	(1.1520)	(1.529)
P	$.28171^a$	$-.28122^a$	$.27857^a$
	$(.04064)$	$(.04063)$	$(.04071)$
C_1	$.4983$	$.4960$	$.4394$
	(1.4653)	(1.4643)	(1.4693)
C_2	2.0367	2.0561	1.9913
	(1.3654)	(1.3653)	(1.3672)
C_3	1.2470	1.2782	1.1843
	(1.4396)	(1.4396)	(1.4424)
Constant	-5.8725	-6.7946	4.2714
	(7.8711)	(7.8696)	(10.6391)
R^2	$.4800$	$.4803$	$.4829$

Note: Standard errors are in parentheses. Sample size is 799.
[a] Statistically significant at the .05 level, one-tailed test.
[b] Statistically significant at the .05 level, two-tailed test.
Source: Horner (1973), reprinted in Watts and Rees (1977, p. 68).

Table 5.9

*Elasticities of the Labor Supply Response for
Alternative Levels of* G, T, *and* W

G	t	W	e_{1g}	e_{2g}	e_{1g}	e_{2t}
50	50	1.60	.033	.033	.034	.034
50	50	2.67	.020	.020	.012	.012
50	50	3.50	.015	.015	.007	.007
100	30	1.60	.059	.012	.070	.030
100	30	2.67	.036	.007	.025	.011
100	30	3.50	.027	.006	.015	.006
100	50	1.60	.066[a]	.066[a]	.137	.137
100	50	2.67	.040	.040	.049	.049
100	50	3.50	.030	.030	.029	.029
100	70	1.60	.138[a]	.157[a]	.381[a]	.888[a]
100	70	2.67	.083	.094	.137	.319
100	70	3.50	.063	.072	.080	.186
125	50	1.60	.083	.083	.214	.214
125	50	2.67	.049	.049	.077	.077
125	50	3.50	.038	.038	.045	.045

Note: All elasticities are negative.
[a] Inconsistent with Horner's text.
Source: Horner (1973).

I and II, respectively. The column headings of Table 5.9, on the other hand, employ a different notation, which confuses the issue again, and typographic error adds even further to the confusion.

Horner offers little justification for the three equations except that the "theory" of "human capital" indicates that certain variables be present.[13] Since the experimental effects are picked up by the least squares coefficient of Q (or Q^2), all three regressions in Table 5.8 indicate a significant decrease in work effort. But here the similarity between the three regressions ends. Although all three equations appear to have insignificantly different R^2 values, the magnitude of the coefficients of Q and Q^2 (the experimental effects) differ enormously. The coefficient of Q in regression III is more than 11 times larger (in magnitude) than the coefficient of Q in regression I, and more than 23 times the magnitude of the coefficient of Q^2 in regression II, evidently owing to high multicollinearity in regression III. This problem, as with all other statistical difficulties, is not addressed. Again, using the seventh line of Table 5.9 ($G = 100$, $t = 50\%$, and wage rate $W = \$1.60$) Horner's estimates[14] of work disincentive can be increased by a large margin. This is due to the sensitivity of the coefficients of Q and Q^2 to the specification of the regression equations given in Table 5.8, particularly for respondents on minimum wages and assigned to generous payment plans.

Conclusions

An examination of Table 5.6 indicates that when the sample of husbands is partitioned by race (ethnicity), response to experimental parameters is very uneven in terms of labor force participation, employment, hours worked per week, and weekly earnings. Indeed, only 19 of 144 regression coefficients are significantly different from zero; all negative responses fall in the interval 0–7% response rate, with blacks (for reasons not yet understood) showing no significant withdrawal of labor supply. Here the response differentials are computed with respect to the preexperimental levels of the treatment (payment) husbands and controlling for demographic variables. When treatment husbands are compared to controls (Table 5.6), no large significant differences emerge. Therefore the New Jersey researchers conclude that no evidence was found for a large reduction of labor supply among the working poor under a negative income tax scheme. Further refinements such as incorporating treatment–income interactions, or the use of Cobb–Douglas type labor supply functions, also failed to reveal significant labor force withdrawal in excess of 6–7%, although higher but statistically insignificant figures were sometimes obtained. These higher figures may be the basis for the recent view that "major differences were observed by ethnic groups . . ." (Ferber & Hirsch, 1978, p. 61), but it is clear from the report that most of these differences were not statistically significant.

Female Family Heads (Wives, Husbands Present)

The New Jersey experiment failed to uncover large-scale reductions in the labor supply of husbands. This is intuitively acceptable, since husbands in intact families probably have a firm attachment to the labor force, their jobs, or their careers. But secondary earners, such as wives, might be more prone to reduce their work effort once family income is guaranteed not to fall below a certain level. In terms of whether or not to work, and the hours of work once the decision to work has been made, women generally face less social and economic pressures than husbands. Consequently, married women (with husbands present) are expected to withdraw more readily from the labor force or to reduce the number of hours worked under a guaranteed income.

Cain *et al.* (1973; 1974) analyze a sample containing 450 payments status and 292 control status wives.[15] The husband is present in all cases, presumably in the labor force, so that the wife's labor supply is in fact conditional on the husband's labor supply. The basic equation analyzed is of the form:

$$L_{ij} = f(X_{ij}, Z_{ij}, L_{i,j-1}, T_{ij}, T_{ij}Z_{ij}) + \epsilon_{ij} \qquad (5.30)$$

where L_{ij} is the labor supply (dependent) response measure for individual i at time period j, X_{ij} the control variables that do not interact with experimental treatments T_{ij}, Z_{ij} the control variables that do interact with treatments T_{ij}, $L_{i,j-1}$ the preexperimental values of the dependent variable, and ϵ_{ij} the vector of residual (unexplained) terms.

Unfortunately, the treatment variables T are parametrized slightly differently for the wives than for the husbands. Consequently, direct comparison of results between husbands and wives is not possible from the strictly statistical point of view. Also, three dependent variables are used in the analysis of wives' labor supply; the percentage of quarters in which the wife reported being in the labor force for the survey week,[16] the average hours worked by the wife as reported in the survey week, and average earnings of the wife as reported in the survey week. Experimental treatments are parametrized by the following variables: general treatment effect;

$$T = \begin{cases} 1, & \text{treatment} \\ 0, & \text{control} \end{cases}$$

guarantee level G; treatment guarantee (as a fraction of the poverty level) minus .75;[17] the tax rate t; and the treatment tax rate[18] minus .50. Separate regression equations are estimated for each dependent variable. Experimental–control differentials are then computed from the estimated regression coefficients associated with the treatment variables T, G, and t, after controlling for the effects of site, ethnicity, and other variables. (See Cain *et al.*, 1973.) Cain *et al.* present a large number of tables giving various "coefficients" of labor supply response; one table is reproduced here for illustration and discussion (see Table 5.10). Although significance levels for the coefficients are reported, it is not clear what the magnitudes actually measure, nor how the mean differential labor supply responses quoted in the text are related to the coefficients given in the tables. An actual example of how (rather than why) the differential mean responses are computed would have been particularly useful, particularly since the method of coding used seems to differ from the usual regression-type analysis of variance–covariance. The coefficients are further confusing in that apparently equivalent tables in Cain *et al.* (1973) and Cain *et al.* (1974) contain coefficients whose magnitudes differ (at times) by a factor of 100.

Cain *et al.* (1973) reach the following conclusions with respect to working wives (husband present);

Table 5.10

Wife Totals: Regression Estimates of Differentials in Labor Force Participation, Employment, Hours, and Earnings for Quarters 3–10[a]

Group	Labor force participation rate	Employment rate	Hours worked per week	Earnings per week
White				
Control group mean	20.1	17.1	4.5	9.3
Absolute differential	6.7[b]	−5.9[b]	−1.4	−3.1
Absolute group mean	13.4	11.2	3.1	6.2
Percent differential	−33.2	−34.7	−30.6	−33.2
Black				
Control group mean	21.1	16.8	5.0	10.6
Absolute differential	−.8	−.3	−.1	.8
Treatment group mean	20.3	16.5	4.9	11.4
Percent differential	−3.6	−1.5	−2.2	7.8
Spanish-speaking				
Control group mean	11.8	10.7	3.4	7.4
Absolute differential	−3.8	−5.2	−1.9	−4.1
Treatment group mean	8.0	5.5	1.5	3.3
Percent differential	−31.8	−48.3	−55.4	−54.7

[a] The data for these tables consist of 693 husband–wife families who reported for at least 8 of the 13 quarters when interviews were obtained. The reported differentials in each measure of labor supply are the experimental group mean minus the control group mean, as measured in a regression equation in which the following variables were controlled: age of wife, number of adults, number and ages of children, sites, preexperiment family earnings (other than wife's), and preexperiment labor supply variables of the wife. These means and the associated control–treatment differentials may therefore be interpreted as applicable to control and treatment groups with identical composition in terms of these variables. Percent differentials are computed using the mean of the controls as base.

[b] Significant at the .95 level (two-tailed test).

Source: Cain *et al.* (1973).

1. Wives in the treatment group generally work less hours than wives in the control group. This reduction is apparently due almost entirely to white wives.[19]

2. The measurement of treatment effects is not sensitive to the "welfare effect"; that is, it makes little difference whether or not welfare families are included in the analysis.

3. There is a decrease of 50 hours of labor time per year for *all* treatment

wives. Whenever labor supply decreases significantly (for white wives only) the decrease was proportionately large, in the order of a 30–40% reduction. However, since wives work little to begin with (see Table 5.10), the large percentage reduction translates to a small number of hours.

Cain *et al.* (1973, p. B.III.a-79) note that these results (particularly their unevenness) are at odds with findings for wives in the survey-type, nonexperimental literature. Experimental data are perhaps not strictly comparable to the usual survey-type data. But it should also be remembered that the normal family income criterion most certainly biased the results.[20] A disincentive effect might result even where none exists since a disproportionately large number of part-time working wives was enrolled. And part-time workers, if anything, would *probably* have less attachment to the labor force than full-time workers.

Papers reporting the findings for wives (Cain *et al.*, 1973, 1974) are fairly weak in terms of explicating the "how" of the statistical methodology employed. And since different models were used for the sample of husbands, the results for husbands and wives cannot be directly compared, nor is a more detailed appraisal of the findings for wives possible. Given the complex structure of the sample and the highly complicated computing algorithms used for analysis, computing error could be responsible for some seemingly "puzzling" results that appear inconsistent with "economic theory."

Young Adults (School Enrollment and Labor Force Participation)

Young adults are another source of secondary family earners. On a priori grounds, their attachment to the labor force might be even weaker than wives' since a guaranteed income might encourage them to attend educational or vocational training schools instead of working.[21] In short, would guaranteed incomes cause a substitution of school attendance for labor market participation? Or would it tend to create "dropouts," that is, young adults who participate neither in the labor force nor educational training?

A sample[22] of young adults between 16 and 18 years of age and living in continuous husband–wife families was analyzed by Mallar (1973) using regression-type models of the form

$$Y_i = Z_i\beta + X_i\gamma + \epsilon_i \qquad (5.31)$$

where Z is a matrix of demographic (personal, family, and location) variables, X are variables describing experimental status, and ϵ is the usual residual vector. The dependent variables Y_i, $i = 1, 2, 3$, are dichotomous and are defined as follows:

$$Y_1 = \begin{cases} 1, & \text{if enrolled in school and/or in the labor force} \\ 0, & \text{otherwise} \end{cases}$$

$$Y_2 = \begin{cases} 1, & \text{if enrolled in school} \\ 0, & \text{otherwise} \end{cases}$$

$$Y_3 = \begin{cases} 1, & \text{if in labor force} \\ 0, & \text{otherwise} \end{cases}$$

Three separate regression equations are estimated by ordinary least squares[23] and a nonlinear probit model for each of nine quarters. The parametrization of experimental statuses entails simply inserting a dichotomous ("dummy") variable in the regression and interacting this dummy with other explanatory variables such as age, ethnicity, and sex. Given this model, detection of experimental effects should proceed through examining the significance of corresponding regression coefficients. However, the coefficients are not interpreted and the analysis is, in fact, only qualitative; we are not told magnitudes for any significant experimental effects. Additionally, ordinary least squares is not appropriate for this type of dependent variable if efficient estimates of the individual coefficients are desired.[24] A multivariate probit (or logit) model would be more appropriate owing to correlation of the dependent variables. The final results reported are rather mixed and are summarized in Table 5.11. Mallar (1973) concludes that experimental effects, if present, "tend" to increase activity. The tendency is for school enrollment to increase for 18-year-olds and labor force participation to increase for ethnic minority youths. Again, no quantitative measures of the experimental effects are given (even in terms of summary statistics), and it is difficult to see how the coefficients of a probit regression curve can yield differential experimental–control probabilities for school attendance or labor force participation when many of the estimated regressions do not appear to include the experimental variable X (see, for example, Mallar's Table A-17; 1973, p. BIV-48).

The Family

It is important to determine whether experimental effects influence the labor supply behavior of the family as a whole. Hollister (1973; 1974) reports results for three ethnic–race groups using two dependent variables: hours worked and earnings. Hollister estimates regressions using the aggregate income of the family rather than adopting a simultaneous equations approach. The latter is often advocated when cross-sectional microdata are

Table 5.11
*Significance of Experimental Effect in
Young Adults*

Quarter	School enrollment	Labor force
1	Yes[a]	Yes[b]
2	—	—
3	—	—
4	—	—
5	Yes[c]	Yes[d]
6	—	—
7	—	—
8	—	—
9	—	Yes[e]

[a] Positive effect for 17-year-olds and negative for blacks.
[b] Positive effect for 16-year-olds.
[c] "Large" and positive for 18-year-olds; negative Spanish-speaking experimental interaction.
[d] Positive, Spanish-speaking experimental interaction.
[e] Positive black experimental interaction and Spanish-speaking experimental interaction.
Source: Mallar (1973).

available to estimate income and substitution effects (Ashenfelter and Heckman, 1974). Hollister correctly points out that although estimates of income and substitution effects could be computed from experimental data to compare these with the nonexperimental literature, this was not the central objective of the New Jersey experiment—namely, to calculate the direction and magnitude of responses to an income support plan, and the cost implications of these responses. Hollister remarks that simultaneous equations estimation (structural or reduced form) would place too great a burden on a priori specification, particularly since the economic literature involving structural models of family labor supply is neither well developed nor extensive. The Hollister approach, therefore, is to estimate the family labor supply response directly via a single equation using *total* family earnings and hours worked as dependent variables. The experimental plan parameters are entered as an (independent) linear or nonlinear combination of terms, with another set of terms interacting the experimental variables with family demographic characteristics (or functions of such characteristics). The single equation specification also allows Hollister to implement the spline function regressions in conjunction with the components-of-variance models described in Chapter 4. Given the experiment and its objectives, we tend to agree with Hollister's basic strategy although it would have been interesting to estimate a simultaneous equations model as well, if only for comparative purposes especially since the two dependent variables are correlated.

Hollister's tactics are to begin with relatively simple specifications and test certain necessary assumptions, then proceed to more complex (and more realistic) estimates of family labor supply. We follow Hollister's development in describing his work.

Simple Models of Family Response

Hollister employs the same sample used to analyze the responses of husbands, wives, and young adults — continuous husband – wives families for the duration of the experiment. However, two major modifications are introduced. First, experimental families whose budget constraints are dominated by welfare amounts are deleted.[25] Second, the "averaged[26] results" sample is further reduced since fewer inputations are made for missing data.

The initial experimental – control differentials for the two response variables, hours worked and earnings, are based on an analysis of variance approach, and presented in Tables 5.12 – 5.14 for the three ethnic – racial groups. In Table 5.12 the entry -8.13 represents the central experimental differential in terms of hours worked; that is, it is an estimate of the difference between *average* hours worked per week by families in the central experimental plan (where $G = 100$ and $t = .50$) and *average* hours worked per week by control families. The slope coefficients for $G = 1.00$ and $t = .50$ are the linear effects on response of differences in experimental plans, measured from that central plan. For example, the estimate of response for families facing a $G = .75$, $t = .50$ plan is obtained by multiplying the $(G - 1.0)$ slope by .25, and subtracting that product from the central experimental differential. For whites (Table 5.12) we have, for example, a response given by $-8.13 - (5.23)(.25) = -9.44$ hours per week, and so on. Similarly, estimates for the plan with $G = 1.0$ but $t = .70$ are obtained by multiplying the slope of $(t - .50)$ by .20 and *adding* it to the central experimental differential. Tables 5.12 – 5.14 reveal that the effects of particular plans are not significant for all three subsamples. Significant effects emerge only for the central experimental differentials,[27] so that the difference in average hours worked per week between experimentals and controls is significant only when the experimental group is taken as a whole; *within* the experimental plans (treatment) the experimental–control differences are not significant. Note that for the black subsample, experimental families worked, on average, 3.91 hours per week more than control families.

The estimates in Tables 5.12–5.14 of the "pooled" data are obtained by using a rather different model, one which exploits the fact that the sample consists of time-series and cross-sectional data. Consequently, in addition

Table 5.12
Experimental-Control Differentials: Whites

				Quarters		
Parameter	Slope	R^2	n	4	8	12
Hours						
Averaged						
Central experimental differential ($G = 1.0$, $t = .5$)[a]					− 8.13	
$G - 1.0$					5.23	
$t - .5$	.0408		228		− 7.87	
Pooled						
Controls				39.35	40.80	48.74
Experimentals				33.85	34.94	38.21
Central experimental differential ($G = 1.0$, $t = .5$)[a]				− 5.50	− 5.86	−10.53
$G - 1.0$					− 2.09	
$t - .5$	.0236		3575		− .17	
Earnings						
Averaged						
Central experimental differential ($G = 1.0$, $t = .5$)[a]					−14.53	
$G - 1.0$					.75	
$t - .5$	.0295		228		− 7.93	
Pooled						
Controls				82.18	90.69	111.07
Experimentals				78.04	80.63	89.98
Central experimental differential ($G = 1.0$, $t = .5$)[a]				− 4.12	− 10.06	−21.09
$G - 1.0$					− 13.51	
$t - .5$	.0413		3575		10.55	

[a] Statistically significant at the .01 level.
Source: Hollister (1973).

Table 5.13

Experimental-Control Differentials: Blacks

Parameter	Slope	R^2	n	Quarters 4	8	12
Hours						
Averaged						
Central experimental differential ($G = 1.0$, $t = .5$)[b]					3.91	
$G - 1.0$					− 8.78	
$t - .5$	.0743		175		18.35	
Pooled						
Controls				46.18	41.13	41.60
Experimentals				45.81	43.93	44.98
Central experimental differential ($G = 1.0$, $t = .5$)[a]				− .37	2.81	3.38
$G - 1.0$					− 6.28	
$t - .5$	.0130		2613		15.65	
Earnings						
Averaged						
Central experimental differential ($G = 1.0$, $t = .5$)[c]					22.07	
$G - 1.0$					−13.61	
$t - .5$	.0505		275		50.21	
Pooled						
Controls				104.81	92.86	100.04
Experimentals				115.36	108.72	115.81
Central experimental differential ($G = 1.0$, $t = .5$)[a]				10.55	15.82	15.77
$G - 1.0$					−11.99	
$t - .5$	.0133		2613		43.84	

[a] Statistically significant at the .10 level.
[b] Statistically significant at the .05 level.
[c] Statistically significant at the .01 level.
Source: Hollister (1973).

to using the control portion for comparison purposes, the experimental families are used also as their own controls (over time). The output for the "pooled" data in Tables 5.12–5.14 is reported for three time periods. Although the pooled sample is "richer," it does not yield higher R^2 values,

Table 5.14

Experimental-Control Differentials: Spanish-Speaking

Parameter	Slope	R^2	n	Quarters 4	Quarters 8	Quarters 12
Hours						
Averaged						
Central experimental						
differential ($G = 1.0$,						
$t = .5$)[a]					-6.01	
$G - 1.0$					.90	
$t - .5$	.0114		127		.77	
Pooled						
Controls				43.26	42.16	45.88
Experimentals				38.71	38.60	40.79
Central experimental						
differential ($G = 1.0$,						
$t = .5$)				- 4.55	- 3.56	- 5.09
$G - 1.0$					3.22	
$t - .5$	.0182		1781		2.01	
Earnings						
Averaged						
Central experimental						
differential ($G = 1.0$,						
$t = .5$)					- 8.99	
$G - 1.0$					- 6.71	
$t - .5$	.0339		127		-18.14	
Pooled						
Controls				100.51	99.30	112.40
Experimentals				97.91	95.84	101.11
Central experimental						
differential ($G = 1.0$,						
$t = .5$)				- 2.60	- 3.46	-11.29
$G - 1.0$					5.61	
$t - .5$	.0174		1781		- 2.24	

[a] Statistically significant at the .05 level.
Source: Hollister (1973).

which are all very low. Note also that the pooled results are generally lower in magnitude than those from the averaged data.[28] This difference may be due to differences in the samples, differences in the models, or both.

To summarize, there is a highly significant *negative* experimental differential between experimental families (as a whole)[29] and control families, in terms of both the earnings and hours, and for both the white and Spanish-speaking subsamples. However, there is a significant *positive* experimental differential for blacks, also in both earnings and hours. This implies that black experimental families took advantage of the guaranteed income to improve their earnings by working more hours!

Family Response, Controlling for Normal
Earnings Capacity

The preceding analysis is valid only if experimental and control families were assigned in a completely random fashion, in which case labor supply response is independent of other factors. Since nonrandomness of assignment is suspected, Hollister uses an analysis of covariance. Hollister's basic strategy here is to construct a single variable—an estimate of the normal earnings capacity for each family—and to use this measure to control for possible nonrandom effects. Again two different estimates of normal earnings are developed: one for the *averaged* estimates and one for *pooled* estimates.[30] The underlying method is that employed to estimate normal wage rates. Total family earnings Y are regressed on a set of independent values, $\hat{Y}$ is obtained, and each entry $\hat{Y}_i$ of Y is divided by the poverty line for that family size. This procedure yields a measure of earnings capacity relative to family size. The resulting variable, known also as the welfare ratio, is denoted by $\hat{Y}/\text{pov}$.

The results are presented in Tables 5.15–5.20, where entries are interpreted in the same way as those in Tables 5.12–5.14. Thus in Table 5.15, for example, the first row of the averaged estimates indicates the central experimental differential at the average plan values *and* at the average value of $\hat{Y}/\text{pov}$ for all racial–ethnic groups combined.[31] The next row gives the linear slope for adjusting the control–experimental differential for values of $\hat{Y}/\text{pov}$ that differ from 1.32; that is, for ($\hat{Y}/\text{pov} - 1.32$); and the next two rows yield the linear slopes for adjusting the control–experimental differential for values of $\hat{Y}/\text{pov}$ that differ from their mean of 1.32 (see preceding section of this chapter). The last two rows give the nonlinear interaction effects, that is, coefficients for making adjustments when varying both $\hat{Y}/\text{pov}$ and G, or $\hat{Y}/\text{pov}$ and t from their central values. The pooled results have a similar interpretation except coefficients are available for three quarters. For example, consider Table 5.15 for the pooled regressions. Examine the results in quarter 8, and assume one wants the estimates of the experimental–control earnings differentials for those families who are facing a guarantee of $G = .75$ and a tax rate $t = .30$, and for whom the welfare ratio is

Table 5.15
Experimental Response Conditioned by $\hat{Y}/pov$ Earnings of White Families

	Quarters		
	4	8	12
Pooled			
Central experimental differential ($G = 1.0$, $t = .5$, $\hat{Y}/pov = 1.12$)	−6.48	−11.00	−25.91
Slopes:			
$\hat{Y}/pov − 1.12$	3.88	− 2.89	12.85
$G − 1.0$		− 8.45	
$t − .5$		15.63	
Interactions:			
$(\hat{Y}/pov − 1.12)(G − 1.0)$		− 1.60	
$(\hat{Y}/pov − 1.12)(t − .5)$		20.11	
$R^2 = .3016$			
$n = 3575$			
Mean $\hat{Y}/pov − 1.22^a$			
Overall experimental response significant at .01 level			
$\hat{Y}/pov$ effect on response not significant			
Averaged			
Central experimental differential ($G = 1.0$, $t = .5$, $\hat{Y}/pov = 1.32$)		− 1.66	
Slopes at central point:			
$\hat{Y}/pov − 1.32$		−34.82	
$G − 1.0$		5.91	
$t − .5$		−19.72	
Interactions:			
$(\hat{Y}/pov − 1.32)(G − 1.0)$		− 15.04	
$(\hat{Y}/pov − 1.32)(t − .5)$		34.07	
$R^2 = .2773$			
$n = 228$			
Mean $\hat{Y}/pov = 1.44$			
Overall experimental response significant at .10 level			
$\hat{Y}/pov$ effect on response significant at .05 level.			

[a] Mean $\hat{Y}/pov$ gives the mean value for this ethnic group. The value $\hat{Y}/pov = 1.12$ is the mean $\hat{Y}/pov$ for all ethnic groups combined.
Source: Hollister (1973).

Table 5.16

Experimental Response Conditioned by $\hat{Y}/pov$ Hours of White Families

	Quarters		
	4	8	12
Pooled			
Central experimental differential ($G = 1.0$, $t = .5$,			
$\quad \hat{Y}/pov = 1.12$)	-3.15	-3.40	-7.01
Slopes:			
$\quad \hat{Y}/pov - 1.12$	-5.75	-3.31	-8.80
$\quad G - 1.0$		0.62	
$\quad t - .5$		-2.36	
Interactions:			
$\quad (\hat{Y}/pov - 1.12)(G - 1.0)$		-6.74	
$\quad (\hat{Y}/pov - 1.12)(t - .5)$		21.88	
$R^2 = .1342$			
$n = 3575$			
Mean $\hat{Y}/pov = 1.22$			
Overall experimental response significant at .01 level			
$\hat{Y}/pov$ effect on response significant at .10 level			
Averaged			
Central experimental differential[a] ($G = 1.0$, $t = .5$,			
$\quad \hat{Y}/pov = 1.32$)		-2.19	
Slopes:			
$\quad \hat{Y}/pov - 1.32$		-12.62	
$\quad G - 1.0$		5.66	
$\quad t - .5$		-7.62	
Interactions:			
$\quad (\hat{Y}/pov - 1.32)(G - 1.0)$		2.73	
$\quad (\hat{Y}/pov - 1.32)(t - .5)$		-17.03	
$R^2 = .2840$			
$n = 228$			
Mean $Y/pov = 1.44$			
Overall experimental response significant at .10 level			
$\hat{Y}/pov$ effect on response significant at .05 level.			

[a] Statistically significant at the .05 level.

Source: Hollister (1973).

Table 5.17

Experimental Response Conditioned by $\hat{Y}/pov$ Earnings of Black Families

	Quarters		
	4	8	12
Pooled			
Central experimental differential ($G = 1.0$, $t = .5$, $\hat{Y}/pov = 1.12$)	4.45	9.40	10.34
Slopes at central point:			
$\hat{Y}/pov - 1.12$	−1.98	1.96	8.48
$G - 1.0^a$		−18.23	
$t - .5^a$		42.35	
Interactions:			
$(\hat{Y}/pov - 1.12)(G - 1.0)$		−43.66	
$(\hat{Y}/pov - 1.12)(t - .5)$		69.37	
$R^2 = .3055$			
$n = 2613$			
Mean $\hat{Y}/pov = 1.04$			
Overall experimental response significant at .01 level			
$\hat{Y}/pov$ effect on response significant at .10 level			
Averaged			
Central experimental differential ($G = 1.0$, $t = .5$, $\hat{Y}/pov = 1.32$)		15.58	
Slopes:			
$\hat{Y}/pov - 1.32$		−56.20	
$G - 1.0^a$		−32.98	
$t - .5^a$		85.25	
Interactions:			
$(\hat{Y}/pov - 1.32)(G - 1.0)$		−186.11	
$(\hat{Y}/pov - 1.32)(t - .5)$		301.29	
$R^2 = .3846$			
$n = 175$			
Mean $\hat{Y}/pov = 1.22$			
Overall experimental response significant at .01 level			
$\hat{Y}/pov$ effect on response significant at .01 level.			

[a] Statistically significant at the .01 level.

Source: Hollister (1973).

Table 5.18

Experimental Response Conditioned by $\hat{Y}/pov$ Hours of Black Families

	Quarters		
	4	8	12
Pooled			
Central experimental differential ($G = 0, t = .5$,			
$\hat{Y}/pov = 1.12$)	− 4.15	− 1.26	− 0.22
Slopes at central point:			
$\hat{Y}/pov - 1.12$	− 9.38	−4.64	1.40
$G - 1.0^a$		−10.22	
$t - .5^a$		16.16	
Interactions:			
$(\hat{Y}/pov - 1.12)(G - 1.0)$		−20.62	
$(\hat{Y}/pov - 1.12)(t - .5)$		27.01	
$R^2 = .2322$			
$n = 2613$			
Mean $\hat{Y}/pov = 1.04$			
Overall experimental response significant at .01 level			
$\hat{Y}/pov$ effect on response significant at .01 level			
Averaged			
Central experimental differential ($G = 1.0, t = .5$,			
$\hat{Y}/pov = 1.32$)		0.98	
Slopes:			
$\hat{Y}/pov - 1.32$		−22.08	
$G - 1.0^b$		−14.74	
$t - .5^a$		28.91	
Interactions:			
$(\hat{Y}/pov - 1.32)(G - 1.0)$		−48.36	
$(\hat{Y}/pov - 1.32)(t - .5)$		78.02	
$R^2 = .3669$			
$n = 175$			
Mean $\hat{Y}/pov = 1.22$			
Overall experimental response significant at .01 level			
$\hat{Y}/pov$ effect on response significant at .01 level.			

[a] Statistically significant at the .05 level.
[b] Statistically significant at the .01 level.
Source: Hollister (1973).

Table 5.19

Experimental Response Conditioned by $\hat{Y}/pov$ Earnings of Spanish-Speaking Families

	Quarters		
	4	8	12
Pooled			
Central experimental[c] differential ($G = 1.0$, $t = .5$, $\hat{Y}/pov = 1.12$)	$-$ .31	$-$ 2.08	$-$ 9.34
Slopes at central point:			
$\hat{Y}/pov - 1.12$	16.45	3.27	-27.97
$G - 1.0^c$		-13.72	
$t - .5^b$		21.12	
Interactions:			
$(\hat{Y}/pov - 1.12)(G - 1.0)$		-50.67	
$(\hat{Y}/pov - 1.12)(t - .5)$		78.08	
$R^2 = .2960$			
$n = 1781$			
Mean $\hat{Y}/pov = 1.07$			
Overall experimental response significant at .01 level			
$\hat{Y}/pov$ effect on response significant at .01 level			
Averaged			
Central experimental differential[a] ($G = 1.0$, $t = .5$, $\hat{Y}/pov = 1.32$)		$-$ 9.26	
Slopes:			
$\hat{Y}/pov - 1.32$		-59.74	
$G - 1.0$		$-$ 8.73	
$t - .5$		-20.19	
Interactions:			
$(\hat{Y}/pov - 1.32)(G - 1.0)$		-42.94	
$(\hat{Y}/pov - 1.32)(t - .5)$		$-$ 1.56	
$R^2 = .1793$			
$n = 127$			
Mean $\hat{Y}/pov = 1.26$			
Overall experimental response significant at .05 level			
$\hat{Y}/pov$ effect on response significant at .01 level.			

[a] Statistically significant at the .10 level.
[b] Statistically significant at the .05 level.
[c] Statistically significant at the .01 level.
Source: Hollister (1973).

Table 5.20

Experimental Response Conditioned by $\hat{Y}$/pov Hours of Spanish-Speaking Families

		Quarters	
	4	8	12
Pooled			
Central experimental			
differential[b] ($G = 1.0$, $t = 5$, $\hat{Y}$/pov = 1.12)	−3.46	−2.60	−4.14
Slopes at central point:			
$\hat{Y}$/pov − 1.12	2.91	−0.17	−12.35
$G − 1.0^b$		−5.45	
$t − .5^a$		11.42	
Interactions:			
($\hat{Y}$/pov − 1.12)($G − 1.0$)		−28.88	
($\hat{Y}$/pov − 1.12)($t − .5$)		41.43	
$R^2 = .1677$			
$n = 1781$			
Mean $\hat{Y}$/pov = 1.07			
Overall experimental response significant at .05 level			
$\hat{Y}$/pov effect on response significant at .01 level			
Averaged			
Central experimental			
differential ($G = 1.0$, $t = .5$, $\hat{Y}$/pov = 1.32)		−6.12	
Slopes:			
$\hat{Y}$/pov − 1.32		−19.71	
$G − 1.0$		−0.77	
$t − .5$		−0.49	
Interactions:			
($\hat{Y}$/pov − 1.32)($G − 1.0$)		−18.57	
($\hat{Y}$/pov − 1.32)($t − .5$)		−10.76	
$R^2 = .1739$			
$n = 127$			
Mean $\hat{Y}$/pov = 1.26			
Overall experimental response significant at .10 level			
$\hat{Y}$/pov effect on response significant at .01 level.			

[a] Statistically significant at the .05 level.
[b] Statistically significant at the .01 level.
Source: Hollister (1973).

$\hat{Y}$/pov $= 1.0$. The calculations would be as follows:

Central experimental differential ($G = 1.0, t = .50, \hat{Y}$/pov $= 1.12$)	=	$-11.00
Adjust central experimental differential to $\hat{Y}$/pov $= 1.0$: $(-.12)(-2.89)$ =		.35
Adjust for $G = .75$:	$(-.25)(-8.45)$ =	2.11
Adjust for $t = .30$:	$(-.20)(15.63)$ =	-3.13
Adjust for interaction G and $\hat{Y}$/pov change: $(-.12)(-.25)(-1.60)$	=	$-.05$
Adjust for interaction t and $\hat{Y}$/pov change: $(-.12)(-.20)(20.11)$	=	.48
Central total experimental differential $G = .75$, $t = .30$, $\hat{Y}$/pov $= 1.0$	=	-11.24

The adjustments are neither always large nor significant, but the average result of controlling for the effects captured in Y can be fairly large, as is witnessed by differences in the R^2 values between Tables 5.12–5.14 and Tables 5.15–5.20. The R^2 values (both hours and earnings) are particularly large for the black subsample, possibly indicating a greater degree of nonrandom sampling for this group. It is interesting that once influence of these variables is taken into account the "pure" experimental effect becomes negative, as expected.

Further Reformulation

Features of the preceding tables suggest further modifications of the regression model. For example, the coefficients measuring the effects of G and t, when statistically significant, have opposite signs. Furthermore, the sign on coefficients of $(t - .50)$ is positive, suggesting that a higher marginal tax rate on earnings will result in *greater* work effort. This seems implausible, and may arise from the fact that few[32] of the experimental families assigned to plans with $t = .70$ actually received payments; they were therefore not influenced by a high marginal tax rate. Many families assigned to these plans also had incomes above breakeven points, were on welfare, or were eligible for welfare. For these reasons Hollister considers some flexible nonlinear (in the variables) models, as well as models that allow for differences between families whose normal earnings placed them below the breakeven level and families whose normal earnings placed them above their breakeven. These models differ from those in the previous two sections in three ways:

1. Additional control variables are added,
2. the experimental variables are reformulated in terms of different functional forms, and
3. a new nonexperimental variable is used (normal earnings $\hat{Y}$ instead of $\hat{Y}$/pov) and interacted with experimental variables.

Furthermore, these models are applied only to the sample for *averaged* results. These results are summarized in Table 5.21. Hollister concludes the following:

1. No inference can be made concerning response to plans having a 70% tax rate since there are too few sample points below breakeven in the corresponding cell.

2. For the white portion of the sample there is little difference in response between plans with a 30 and 50% tax rate. Further, a higher variance[33] in normal earnings (and hours) is associated with a larger negative experimental effect. The response to the tax rate becomes larger with higher levels of normal earnings.

3. For the black subsample in the 50% tax rate plan there is a significantly large, negative coefficient for normal earnings (or hours) interaction. The differential response between the 30% and 50% tax rate is quite pronounced at higher levels of normal earnings (and hours).

4. For the Spanish-speaking subsample the same conclusions hold as for the black subsample, but the response is larger.

Table 5.21
Estimated Percentage Responses[a]

Tax	Hours	Earnings
Whites		
.30	−.18	−.07
.50	−.16	−.08
.70	b	b
Blacks		
.30	+.06	+.14
.50	+.01	+.13
.70	+.09	+.17
Spanish-Speaking		
.30	+.01	−.14
.50	+.09	−.28
.70	b	b

[a] Percentage response derived from net experimental response for group evaluated at experimental group means for predicted variance and predicted earnings or hours, divided by the predicted value for controls from the same regressions.

[b] Number of breakeven families in the sample was less than 10 so the estimate is not reported.

Source: Hollister, 1973.

Generally speaking, Hollister finds a statistically significant negative response to experimental treatment by white and Spanish-speaking families, but not for black families.

IV. THE "POSTOFFICIAL" ANALYSIS

There was lively discussion of the New Jersey results by labor supply economists (Peckman and Timpane, 1975b) and other social scientists (Rossi and Lyall, 1976) shortly after its publication. The subsequent criticism may be grouped into two broad categories: misgivings about the design and sampling methods of the experiment, on the one hand, and shortcomings in model specification, estimation, and statistical testing methods on the other. The main substantive issue of importance, particularly in the more recent publications, is the claim that New Jersey researchers have unwittingly underestimated the labor supply response, particularly that of husbands. Recent reworking of the New Jersey data by alternative techniques has given much higher estimates of labor supply response. In this section we assess this evidence.

Design and Sampling

The *New Jersey Final Report* is uneven in style, content, and technical level. Because authors used different estimation models, the separate findings are not strictly comparable. With hindsight we can also see that the basic design of the experiment and the sampling procedures themselves possess shortcomings. Criticisms of a methodological nature have also attempted to detail the following inadequacies:

1. The structuring of the experiment as a single-treatment design, thereby precluding an analysis of interactions (if any) between the experiment and other welfare programs such as man-power training, day care, and so on;

2. restriction of the target population to work-eligible, low-income male-headed families;

3. specification of the sampling frame in terms of particular urban sites ("test bores" approach) rather than a national probability sample;

4. definition of the policy space in terms of the guarantee level and tax rate to yield only 8 points (plans) to be tested in the guarantee tax rate space (Rossi and Lyall, 1976, p. 14).

Although the preceding points are important for deciding among different policy alternatives to be tested, we will not pursue them further. Our primary interest lies in examining the scientific validity of the labor response results from the guaranteed income experiments. More relevant to our concern are some of the narrower objections against the New Jersey Report results regarding possible bias and inefficiency due to the assignment model, sample selection, or inappropriate estimation techniques. We first consider general objections raised against the New Jersey sampling strategy. We then consider the criticism concerning estimation techniques, examine alternatives proposed, and comment on subsequent reworking of the data.

We have already described the Conlisk–Watts assignment model (Chapter 3) and some of its implications. The budget constraint imposed by government had an important effect. Expensive plans were used less frequently so that four out of the eight plans had fewer than 50 continuous husband–wife families receiving payments. These were further subdivided into four sites and three ethnic–racial groups resulting in very sparse cells. It is no surprise that statistical significance was not always achieved in the final estimation. The assignment model also minimized the trace of the variance–covariance matrix of ordinary least squares regression coefficients. Not only did this introduce the possibility of misspecification bias, but it also renders the sample inflexible for alternative estimation strategies. The constraints used to minimize the sum of the variances of the least squares coefficients (trace of the covariance matrix of least squares coefficients) probably destroyed the random nature of the sample (ignoring for the moment the effect of truncation). Furthermore, minimizing the trace ignores covariances. The existence of covariances tends to reduce efficiency,[34] and a more appropriate criterion might have been the determinant of the covariance matrix of least squares coefficients, particularly since the control variables (covariates) are usually correlated with the treatments in a nonrandom sample. Finally, given that the four dependent labor supply response variables were correlated, a multivariable analysis of covariance would have been preferable, that is, the four variables used simultaneously in the general least squares model.

These criticisms pertain to the selection of the treatment and control samples. The existence of missing data (nonparticipation, nonresponse, sample attrition over time, and unobservable wage rates for the unemployed) and the introduction of aid to families with dependent children (the AFCD-UP welfare program)[35] in New Jersey in January 1969 necessitates a further distinction, that between usable and nonusable sample points for statistical estimation. It is generally agreed that both problems introduce the possibility of serious bias. Because missing data are the result of an essentially nonrandom (self-selection) process, the intact part of the sample may lose its representativity, and in this case no longer reflect the "true" labor supply response. Likewise, the introduction of a welfare program is a potential source of bias—for example, suppose there is no "welfare dominance"; that is, NIT payments are always higher than welfare payments. The treatment sample points will have no incentive to switch to welfare. Although the welfare program does not interfere with the incentive structure for the treatment group, the controls are now in a situation where they can benefit by withdrawing from the labor force. This will tend to *increase*[36] the labor supply differential between treatments and controls. In reality, the effect of welfare on experimental response cannot be predicted with certainty since factors that tend to bias response upward may be counterbalanced by others acting in the opposite direction. For a discussion of the possible effects of welfare programs on NIT experiments see Garfinkel (1973) and Aaron (1975). In any case these issues led some to question the New Jersey results, arguing that failure to address difficulties caused by sample truncation, nonparticipation, and welfare led to an underestimate of the true labor supply response.

The Initial Reworking: Hall's Results

Hall (1975) provides the earliest reworking of the New Jersey data and finds significant but small experimental effects. He uses relatively simple[37] statistical tests for mean differences, and then introduces more complicated models by considering threshold effects in order to discriminate between participants and nonparticipants.

Let θ be the index of family attitudes toward work (including ability to work),

θ_n the critical (threshold) value of θ such that in the absence of a negative tax experiment families will not work at all;

θ_p the critical value of θ such that, among families participating in the program, $\theta > \theta_p$ implies families will not work at all, and

θ^* the critical value that separates families who participate in the experiment from those who do not.

We can define three groups of families and two cases as in Table 5.22. The effect of a NIT program is considered in terms of expected number of hours worked $E(H)$. In the absence of a NIT program:

$$E(H_0) = \text{(fraction of population in group 2)}$$
$$\times \text{(average hours worked in group 2)}$$
$$+ \text{(fraction of population in group 3)}$$
$$\times \text{(average hours worked in group 3)}$$

Table 5.22
Classification of Labor Supply Response by Hall

Group	Case I	Case II
I $(\theta > \theta_n)$	All participants have worked	All participants have worked
2 $(\theta_p < \theta < \theta_n)$	All participants have worked	Those above θ^* participate and do not work; those below θ^* work and do not participate
3 $(\theta < \theta_p)$	All work; those above θ^* participate; those below do not	All work; none participate

Source: Hall, 1975.

Or when the program is available (in case I):

$$E(H_p) = \text{(fraction of population in group 3 with } \theta < \theta^* \\ \times \text{ (average hours worked by these participants)}$$

$$E(H_p) = \text{(fraction of population in group 2 with } \theta < \theta^*) \\ \times \text{ (average hours worked by this group)} \\ + \text{ (fraction of population in group 3)} \\ \times \text{ (average hours in group 3)}$$

Hall's results are presented in Table 5.23 where the eight columns represent the labor supply responses for each plan. It is evident that Hall is in general agreement with the *New Jersey Final Report.* He also finds small, but significantly different from zero, experimental effect(s), namely, a 7% reduction in labor supply.

There are methodological similarities between the *New Jersey Report* and Hall's findings: both use analysis of variance type methods, both attempt to model the effect of the breakeven point by a parameter, and both take advantage of the panel nature of the data. However, Hall ignores the control group, preferring instead to use each experimental respondent as his own control. When behavior is highly correlated over time (serially correlated), individuals' past behaviors are probably more efficient controls than a randomly selected control group. But to ignore the control group entirely is wasteful of data. The main differences between Hall and the *New Jersey Final Report* is in the specification of functional form and the choice of variables. Some of Hall's conclusions do not agree with the *New Jersey Final Report;* Hall views the large ethnic – racial differences in labor supply obtained by the New Jersey researchers as spurious. Since 47% of the black

Table 5.23
Results of Hall's Reworking of New Jersey Data

Item	Combinations of parameters							
	(1)	(2)	(3)	(4)	(5)	(6)	(7)	(8)
Labor supply determinants								
Wage (dollars per hour, w)	1.50	2.00	3.00	2.00	2.00	2.00	2.00	2.00
Nonlabor income (dollars per week, Y_a)	10	10	10	50	10	10	10	10
Guarantee (dollars per week, B_0)	80	80	80	80	40	120	80	80
Tax rate (percent, r)	50	50	50	50	50	50	30	70
Attitude thresholds								
Switch on to program (θ^*)	0	0	0.25	0.17	0.48	0	0	0.21
No work, participants (θ_p)	0.95	0.96	0.97	0.95	0.98	0.94	0.97	0.94
No work, nonparticipants (θ_n)	1.00	1.00	1.00	0.99	1.00	1.00	1.00	1.00
Calculated responses								
Expected hours, no program [$E(H_n)$]	33.7	33.8	33.8	33.2	33.8	33.8	33.8	33.8
Expected hours, with program [$E(H_p)$]	30.6	31.4	32.5	31.0	33.2	30.2	32.1	30.3
Effect of program (hours) [$E(H_n) - E(H_p)$]	3.1	2.4	1.3	2.2	0.6	3.6	1.7	3.5
Percent of families opting for program	100	100	84	93	54	100	100	89
Percent of families continuing to work	99	100	84	92	54	99	100	87
Average reduction in hours of those continuing to work	3.2	2.4	1.6	2.4	1.2	3.6	1.7	4.0
Percent of families stopping work	1	0	0	1	0	1	0	1
Average reduction in hours of those stopping work	2.1	1.6	1.0	1.4	0.8	2.4	1.1	2.6

Source: Hall (1975) model 2, discussed in the text.

and 56% of the Spanish-speaking families were excluded from the category of continuous husband–wife sample, bias was probably introduced.

Labor Supply and Truncation

Hall's model gives more prominence to the effect of the breakeven on the labor supply than did the *New Jersey Final Report;* that is, Hall's analysis takes account of labor force participation rates and, in fact, predicts them. Hausman and Wise (1976; 1977a) consider a different type of "participation." They point out that since eligibility to enroll in the New Jersey experiment depends on total family earnings for the previous year,[38] the sample is truncated. The truncation effect is thought to induce a bias in least squares estimation, even when the population of interest is defined as the "working poor." As pointed out, bias is due to the truncation point acting as a "trapping barrier"; that is, once income exceeds a given point (even if due to the random residual term), that family can never become eligible for the experiment. To investigate the effects of truncation Hausman and Wise (1976) reestimate the labor response using a part of the New Jersey data.[39] These results are reproduced in Table 5.24 where the variables have been transformed to logarithms. The "hours equation" in Table 5.24 indicates that increasing nonwage income by 1% results in a .022% decrease in hours of labor time, whereas increasing wages 1% increases the number of hours worked by .14%. Hausman and Wise note that this is close to preexperimental estimates, and that their estimate of the experimental effect is not much higher than that estimated by the New Jersey researchers. Therefore, they appear to confirm that a guaranteed income induces a very small (but significantly different from zero) withdrawal of labor supply among male heads of intact families. Despite confirming a low response, Hausman and Wise note that it could be substantially higher for those who participate, that is, respondents whose incomes are below breakeven. Because the influence of participation rates is the main theme of a more recent paper (Cogan, 1978), we return to the topic of participation in the next section.

The effect of income truncation by itself, however, does not necessarily introduce bias. We suggest this for the following reasons.

1. Families were accepted in the New Jersey experiment on the basis of their normal (expected) incomes, not the actual (observed) levels. The selection (truncation) procedure therefore selected families more or less independently of the effect of residual error ϵ, thus probably avoiding large bias in the predicted values $\hat{Y} = X\hat{\beta}$. In any case the truncation point was above the poverty level ($1\frac{1}{2}$ times) so that the least squares estimates are probably largely unbiased for families who earned poverty level incomes or less.

2. Although estimates $\hat{Y} = X\hat{\beta}$ of the expected values $E(Y|X)$ are biased when Y is truncated (see Hausman and Wise, 1977a, p. 934), Hausman and Wise do not prove that $\hat{\beta}$ must also be biased.[40] Bias in $\hat{Y}$ need not imply a bias in $\hat{\beta}$ since the least squares regression plane may be shifted in a parallel

Table 5.24
Two Endogenous Variables

Variable	Wage equation estimates (standard error)	Hours equation estimates (standard error)
Constant	.8294	7.4620
	(.3093)	(.9897)
Education	.0155	—
	(.0119)	
IQ	.0045	—
	(.0023)	
Training	.0021	—
	(.0011)	
Union	.2625	—
	(.0342)	
Illness	−.2614	−.0397
	(.0522)	(.0248)
Age < 35	.0110	.0077
	(.0086)	(.0046)
Age 35–45	−.0050	−.0002
	(.0074)	(.0003)
Age > 45	−.0047	−.0024
	(.0032)	(.0018)
Family size	—	.0461
		(.0286)
Time	.0340	.0475
	(.0028)	(.0274)
Log wage	—	.1401
		(.0643)
Log nonwage income	—	−.0223
		(.0066)

Source: Hausman and Wise (1976).

fashion. This would bias only the intercept term (and thus $\hat{Y}$) but not the slopes. It is the slopes that play the main role in tests of significance of experimental effects.

Nonetheless, some observers conclude that the effects of truncation may have been a growth in wage rates and a decline in program participation rates over time. They argue that truncation caused families enrolled in the experiment to have low transitory (rather than permanent) incomes (see, for example, Cogan, 1978, p. 15).

Distinguishing between Participants and Nonparticipants in the Program

One reason for conducting the New Jersey experiment was to estimate the expected cost of a NIT program. Estimates contained in the *New Jersey Final Report* are therefore based on "participants" and "nonparticipants" together, that is, families who received payments or were eligible to receive payments. This procedure has been criticized by Cogan (1978, 1979), who claims that the distinction between participants (those who actually received payments) and nonparticipants (those eligible but did not) should be made explicit in the estimation procedure. To do otherwise, he argues, is to bias (in a downward direction) the estimate of the expected labor supply response.

Cogan (1978) reexamined the sample of husbands and finds a labor supply reduction in the order of five to seven hours per week for nonparticipants. Taking 6.5 hours per week as the "best" point estimate (controlling for the effect of welfare programs) of the reduction in labor supply among participants, Cogan obtains a $6.5 \times .67 = 4.36$ hours per week expected reduction in the labor supply of participants. The figure 67% is the proportion of the eligible husband sample that participated in the experiment. Cogan goes on to say (paradoxically) that "this estimate is similar to the one obtained by ignoring the distinction between program participants and non-participants, but with an otherwise identical empirical equation." However, when the variable indicating welfare status is dropped from the equation, the estimated reduction of labor supply drops to 3.2 hours per week, a figure that is only marginally higher[41] than that reported in Watts *et al.* (1974). This suggests that the effect of welfare rather than the distinction between participants and nonparticipants could be responsible for the higher estimated labor supply response. It is also evident from what follows that Cogan's model (and estimation method) is different from that used by the New Jersey researchers, not necessarily more realistic or better in any sense. Furthermore, Cogan's specification(s) possess considerably less explanatory power (low R^2 values)[42] than those of the New Jersey researchers; consequently, there is a possibility of specification bias due to omitted explanatory variables.[43]

Let

$$H = \alpha_0 X + \alpha_1 D_1 + \alpha_2 D_2 + \epsilon \qquad (5.32)$$

be the labor supply equation where $H =$ the number of hours worked (per week) by an intact-family male head, $X =$ a matrix of explanatory variables, and D_1, D_2 are dummy variables defined as

$$D_1 = \begin{cases} 1, & \text{if individual participates in NIT} \\ 0, & \text{if individual does not participate in NIT} \end{cases}$$

$$D_2 = \begin{cases} 1, & \text{if experimental male head} \\ 0, & \text{if control male head} \end{cases}$$

Equation (5.32) is therefore an analysis of covariance type model in which the variables X serve as covariates or control variables. D_1 and D_2 measure the effect of the experiment for participants and nonparticipants. The expected number of hours worked for the different types of family heads is given as follows. Expected number of hours worked by experimental participants:

$$E(H|D_1 = 1; D_2 = 1) = \alpha_0 X + \alpha_1 + \alpha_2, \tag{5.33}$$

expected number of hours worked by experimental nonparticipants,

$$E(H|D_1 = 0; D_2 = 1) = \alpha_0 X + \alpha_2, \tag{5.34}$$

and expected number of hours worked by controls (necessarily nonparticipants)

$$E(H|D_1 = 0; D_2 = 0) = \alpha_0 X. \tag{5.35}$$

Note that $E(H|D_1 = 1; D_2 = 0)$ is not defined since no one can participate in the program without being an experimental; consequently, the coefficient α_1 has no interpretation by itself. The coefficient α_2 measures the *expected* mean difference in hours worked between nonparticipating experimentals and controls since

$$E(H|D_1 = 0; D_2 = 1) - E(H|D_1 = 0; D_2 = 0) = \alpha_0 X + \alpha_2 - \alpha_0 X$$
$$= \alpha_2 \tag{5.36}$$

and the mean difference between participating experimentals and controls is given by

$$E(H|D_1 = 1; D_2 = 1) - E(H|D = 0; D_2 = 0) = \alpha_0 X + \alpha_1 + \alpha_2 - \alpha_0 X$$
$$= \alpha_1 + \alpha_2 \tag{5.37}$$

Because participation in the program is central in Cogan's work the full model consists of the labor supply equation (5.32) and an additional program participation equation

$$Y = \beta_0 X + \beta_1 T + \beta_2 G + \epsilon \tag{5.38}$$

The dependent variable Y is a latent variable that measures the underlying propensity to participate in the program. Since Y is unobservable, the dependent variable actually used is

$$D_1 = \begin{cases} 1, & \text{if } Y > 0 \\ 0, & \text{if } Y \leq 0 \end{cases} \qquad (5.39)$$

the participation dummy of the labor supply equation (5.32). The model seems to explain actual participation rates quite well (see Table 5.25). Additionally, Cogan's tests determine that there exists no simultaneity between the labor supply and participation equations, so that both equations can be estimated by single-equation methods such as ordinary (generalized) least squares or probit analysis.

The major labor supply findings are summarized in Tables 5.26–5.29.

Table 5.25
Average NIT Program Participation Rates

Tax rate	Guarantee level as a percent of the poverty line			
	50	75	100	125
Complete information				
30	.791	.860	—	—
50	.105	.479	.763	.844
70	—	.084	.515	—
Myopia				
30	.709	.833	—	—
50	.068	.378	.744	.823
70	—	.044	.470	—

Predicted Probabilities of NIT Program Participation[a]

Tax rate	Guarantee level as a percent of poverty line			
	50	75	100	125
30	.759	.907	.974	.995
50	.366	.611	.817	.937
70	.083	.223	.445	.687

[a] The means for these calculations are for quarter six. They are Trenton, .055, Patterson, .125, Jersey City, .10; age, 39.5; education, 9.91; family size, 6, and income $88 per week.
Source: Cogan (1978).

Table 5.26

Ordinary Least Squares of Hours of Work Function (with Experiment Status Dummy Included) (standard errors in parentheses)

Variable	Quarter										
	1	2	3	4	5	6	7	8	9	10	11
Age	-.058	-.032	-.027	-.146	-.149	-.255	-.107	-.253	-.139	-.078	-1.64
	(.091)	(.109)	(.099)	(.103)	(.100)	(.104)	(.114)	(.107)	(.108)	(.117)	(.109)
Log wage	-10.118	-7.760	-7.513	-3.884	-4.150	-2.997	-6.773	-5.082	-5.495	-8.040	-6.285
	(2.730)	(2.817)	(2.640)	(2.876)	(2.621)	(2.781)	(2.945)	(2.557)	(3.046)	(3.166)	(2.677)
Family size	.991	1.598	1.080	.897	1.009	1.221	.557	.947	1.386	2.315	1.070
	(.456)	(.540)	(.486)	(.505)	(.479)	(.494)	(.519)	(.516)	(.529)	(.568)	(.527)
Preenrollment hours = 0	-14.572	-8.385	-9.714	-13.576	-10.028	-8.594	-10.997	-10.124	-12.776	-13.330	-11.055
	(2.477)	(2.882)	(2.633)	(2.705)	(2.612)	(2.678)	(2.992)	(2.809)	(2.783)	(3.043)	(2.855)
Preenrollment hours = 41 − 48	5.546	4.969	6.757	2.177	2.680	3.067	-.311	2.661	1.120	4.696	6.798
	(2.314)	(2.662)	(2.435)	(2.546)	(2.430)	(2.552)	(2.786)	(2.613)	(2.625)	(2.830)	(2.639)
Preenrollment hours > 48	11.260	6.046	6.130	3.334	7.710	8.176	1.965	3.286	.666	2.264	3.645
	(2.674)	(3.062)	(2.727)	(2.832)	(2.716)	(2.821)	(3.064)	(2.914)	(2.892)	(3.079)	(2.915)
Welfare dummy	-8.257	-11.785	-15.177	-9.694	-13.700	-17.062	-9.619	-11.604	-14.464	-10.662	-10.144
	(2.606)	(2.981)	(2.653)	(2.769)	(2.539)	(2.590)	(2.878)	(2.761)	(2.745)	(2.942)	(2.720)
NIT participation dummy	-7.022	-.839	-4.421	-5.361	-6.444	-4.947	2.490	-4.761	-5.440	-4.994	-4.980
	(2.613)	(2.836)	(2.530)	(2.679)	(2.559)	(2.691)	(2.848)	(2.783)	(2.708)	(2.891)	(2.609)
Experimental status dummy	4.260	-3.009	.972	-1.125	1.902	-3.179	-4.471	-3.272	-2.409	-3.700	-1.346
	(2.467)	(2.678)	(2.344)	(2.440)	(2.302)	(2.340)	(2.634)	(2.534)	(2.474)	(2.616)	(2.358)
Constant	42.469	36.199	40.134	44.086	40.996	46.391	46.515	50.075	46.023	38.640	46.145
	(5.311)	(6.106)	(5.775)	(6.232)	(6.018)	(6.293)	(6.926)	(6.683)	(6.841)	(7.493)	(6.884)
R^2	.282	.151	.202	.165	.189	.235	.105	.152	.184	.190	.154

Source: Cogan (1978).

Table 5.27
Ordinary Least Squares Estimates of Hours of Work Differences[a]
(standard errors in parentheses)

Qtr.	$\hat{\alpha}_1$ Experimental status coefficient	$\hat{\alpha}_2$ NIT participation coefficient	Sum = mean difference between hours marked by NIT participants and controls	Significance levels
1	−7.022 (2.613)	4.26 (2.47)	−2.76 (1.95)	1.42
2	−.839 (2.836)	−3.009 (2.678)	−3.85 (2.34)	1.65
3	−4.421 (2.530)	.972 (2.344)	−3.45 (2.14)	1.61
4	−5.361 (2.679)	−1.125 (2.44)	−6.49 (2.25)	2.88
5	−6.444 (2.559)	1.902 (2.302)	−4.54 (2.20)	2.06
6	−4.947 (2.691)	−3.179 (2.34)	−8.13 (2.34)	3.47
7	2.490 (2.848)	−4.471 (2.634)	−1.98 (2.47)	.80
8	−4.761 (2.783)	−3.272 (2.534)	−8.03 (2.30)	3.40
9	−5.440 (2.708)	−2.409 (2.474)	−7.85 (2.31)	3.40
10	−4.994 (2.891)	−3.70 (2.616)	−8.69 (2.53)	3.43
11	−4.980 (2.609)	−1.346 (2.358)	−6.33 (2.92)	2.17

[a] Response estimates conditional on participation.
Source: Cogan (1978).

The second column of Table 5.27 reports the dummy coefficient $\hat{\alpha}_2$. It measures, in the sample, the expected mean difference in hours worked between nonparticipating experimentals and controls[44] (see Eq. 5.36). This coefficient is insignificantly different from zero. This is as expected. Since neither group received payments, once the effect of the control variables is taken into account, the difference in labor supply between the two becomes insignificant (at the 5% level). The difference between participants and controls, however, $(\hat{\alpha}_1 + \hat{\alpha}_2)$ is, at first, not significant but gradually becomes so as participants learn the "rules of the game" better. Again, as expected, the average monthly reduction in hours of work for this group is higher

Table 5.28

Ordinary Least Squares Estimates of Hours of Work Function Without Experimental Dummy
(Standard errors in parentheses)

Variable	Quarter										
	1	2	3	4	5	6	7	8	9	10	11
Age	-.064	-.026	-.027	.145	-.145	-.263	-.121	-.265	-.147	-.884	-.166
	(.092)	(.108)	(.099)	(.103)	(.0997)	(.104)	(.114)	(.107)	(.107)	(.117)	(.109)
Log wage	-9.635	-7.997	-7.408	-4.075	-3.865	-3.444	-7.071	-5.423	-5.791	-8.599	-6.350
	(2.724)	(2.810)	(2.624)	(2.843)	(2.597)	(2.765)	(2.948)	(2.546)	(3.031)	(3.146)	(2.671)
Family size	1.042	1.543	1.091	.876	1.031	1.194	.502	.908	1.361	2.278	1.058
	(.457)	(.538)	(.485)	(.502)	(.478)	(.495)	(.519)	(.516)	(.528)	(.568)	(.526)
Preenrollment hours = 0	-14.796	-8.362	-9.726	-13.582	-10.000	-8.612	-.110	-10.117	-12.721	-13.159	-.110
	(2.481)	(2.883)	(2.630)	(2.702)	(2.611)	(2.681)	(3.001)	(2.812)	(2.781)	(3.046)	(2.852)
Preenrollment hours = 41 – 48	5.520	5.000	6.752	2.161	2.731	2.930	-.392	2.516	1.111	4.793	6.854
	(2.322)	(2.663)	(2.432)	(2.543)	(2.428)	(2.554)	(2.793)	(2.613)	(2.625)	(2.832)	(2.635)
Preenrollment hours > 48	10.821	6.389	6.049	3.403	7.550	8.404	2.292	3.565	.899	2.702	3.841
	(2.670)	(3.048)	(2.717)	(2.825)	(2.708)	(2.820)	(3.067)	(2.909)	(2.882)	(3.068)	(2.892)
Welfare dummy	-8.057	-.118	-15.125	-9.651	-13.638	-.173	-9.516	-11.855	-14.561	-10.651	-10.165
	(2.611)	(2.982)	(2.647)	(2.764)	(2.537)	(2.589)	(2.885)	(2.757)	(2.743)	(2.947)	(2.717)
NIT participation dummy	-3.833	-2.879	-3.776	-6.122	-5.183	-7.055	-.397	-7.025	-7.040	-7.366	-5.769
	(1.854)	(2.180)	(1.992)	(2.108)	(2.052)	(2.202)	(2.291)	(2.164)	(2.153)	(2.359)	(2.210)
R^2	.276	.148	.202	.164	.188	.231	.097	.147	.181	.185	.153

Source: Cogan (1978).

Table 5.29

Estimates of Hours of Work Response Conditional on Program Participation

Qtr.	Coefficient	Standard error	Percent change in hours per week	Average tax rate	Average annual guarantee in 1968 dollars
1	−3.83	1.85	−.10	.47	4104
2	−2.88	2.18	−.08	.46	4135
3	−3.78	1.99	−.10	.47	3869
4	−6.12	2.11	−.16	.43	4466
5	−5.18	2.05	−.14	.47	4529
6	−7.06	2.20	−.18	.47	4542
7	− .40	2.29	−.01	.47	4466
8	−7.08	2.16	−.19	.47	4659
9	−7.04	2.15	−.19	.47	4602
10	−7.37	2.36	−.21	.46	4679
11	−5.77	2.10	−.16	.46	4778

Source: Cogan (1978).

when nonparticipating experimentals are excluded, as was the case in the original *New Jersey Report* analysis. The mean difference in hours worked by participating experimentals and controls, however, does not measure the "true" labor supply response. The labor supply of nonparticipating experimentals must also be included.[45] Cogan therefore considers a labor supply equation containing a welfare dummy variable but omitting the experimental dummy D_2. The new equation is (see Tables 5.7 and 5.8)

$$H = \beta_0 X + \beta_1 D_1 + \beta_3 D_3 + u \qquad (5.40)$$

where D_1 and X are as before [Eq. (5.32)] and

$$D_3 = \begin{cases} 1, & \text{if individual is on welfare} \\ 0, & \text{if individual is not on welfare} \end{cases}$$

The coefficient β_1 measures the expected mean difference in the number of hours worked per week between participants and nonparticipants (including controls) since

$$E(H|D_1 = 1) - E(H|D_1 = 0) = (\beta_0 X + \beta_1 + \beta_3 D_3) - (\beta_0 X + \beta_3 D_3)$$
$$= \beta_1 \qquad (5.41)$$

Cogan proceeds to test variations of Eqs. (5.32) and (5.37), but his principal conclusion is not altered, namely, that a NIT program reduces the number of hours worked per week by 6.5 hours. Expressed in terms of a 40-hour work week, this turns out to be in excess of 16%.[46] This is much higher than the result by Watts *et al.* (1974) or any other researcher (see above).

Cogan's reworking of the New Jersey data represents the last "update" and has tended to be accepted as the latest word on work disincentive effects. The policy implication of Cogan's work is also clear — any income support program that reduces labor supply by as much as 16% is too costly and completely misguided; and other measures (if any) should be adopted to alleviate the condition of the working poor. The overall desirability of a NIT program should probably not be decided only with reference to quantitative measures of work disincentives observed in localized experiments, and we do not propose to do so here. However, given the wide gap between the estimates originally made by Watts *et al.* (1974) and the recent work by Cogan, a relative evaluation of the two methodologies[47] should be interesting.

As previously noted, the *New Jersey Report* modeled the experimental effect(s) by means of continuous, nonlinear spline functions; and most of their estimates were based on panel-type data so that experimental sample points were compared with their own past behavior as well as with those of the control group. This modeling attempt is more sophisticated than that by Cogan, as witnessed by the relatively low R^2 values obtained by Cogan's specification(s) (Tables 5.26 and 5.28). Although the R^2 coefficient does not enter in the estimation of mean differences in dummy regression (analysis of covariance), it remains important nevertheless because it often indicates whether a regression equation is properly specified. Cogan's efforts to avoid bias are concentrated exclusively on that arising from simultaneity. Indeed, Cogan declares that since the participation and labor supply equations are recursive, it follows "the hours worked parameters may be estimated without bias by ordinary least squares" (Cogan, 1978, p. 34).

This is incorrect because bias may also be introduced by (1) errors in the control variables (assuming the dummy variables are properly coded), (2) omitted explanatory variables when these are correlated with those present, and (3) equation specification bias, which may be viewed as a special case of (2). Although it is difficult to take account of errors-in-variables bias, it is probably present in the *New Jersey Report* estimates as well as those by Cogan. However, the New Jersey approach showed a greater awareness of this difficulty by using predicted rather than observed variables.[48] Furthermore (and of greater importance), Cogan's specification of the labor supply equations is very simple — the number of explanatory variables is small, and no interaction terms between the dummy variables and covariates are introduced. Cogan does not discuss these difficulties, which are known to introduce inefficiency and bias in the regression coefficients and, therefore, in the estimated mean response. Consequently, Cogan's "new evidence" is neither conclusive nor definitive, in our opinion; and the superiority of Cogan's methodology is not compelling.[49] Although the distinction between participants and nonparticipants is useful, this is also not new; Watts used it (albeit in different guise) in modeling the breakeven effect. In any case, labor supply responses must be measured for both actual participants and those eligible to participate since the cost of a NIT program is determined by both groups.

NOTES

1. The Watts–Conlisk model introduced not only political factors (see Aaron, 1975, p. 88) but also financial considerations into what should have been a purely scientific (i.e., statistical or probabilistic) decision.

2. The four response variables are not independent (uncorrelated), a fact the New Jersey analysis did not take into account.

3. The difference is expressed in percentage terms since the dependent variable is the log of wages. The mean differential is obtained in the same manner as with dummy variables.

4. Note that Eq. (5.4) represents a semilogarithmic functional relation since only observed wage rates are transformed to logarithms.

5. Zero for controls.

6. Full-time work was defined as 35–45 hours per week.

7. Defined by the expression $\hat{Y}/PL(n)$ where $\hat{Y}$ is previously estimated normal income and $PL(n)$ is the poverty line for a family of size n.

8. This is 68% of the total sample of husbands.

9. W_{m2} is the "wind-down" effect of the experiment on wage rates.

10. Thus the missing data problem is handled by list-wise deletion; that is, an entire observation is deleted if one of the variables has a missing value.

11. Because recipients may view the three-year experiment as temporary, they might not alter their labor supply as much as for a permanent program.

12. The numbers are underlined for ease of reference.

13. Other variables, however, are entered in an "ad hoc" manner (Horner, 1973, p. BIIb-9).

14. No numerical value is offered here owing to the inconsistency between text and values in Table 5.9.

15. The actual analysis is carried out on 693 husband–wife families who reported their quarterly labor force status in eight or more quarters, and for whom there were "reasonably" complete records of the other relevant variables.

16. Essentially, a measure of labor force participation rates.

17. For example, the plan that guarantees 1.00 times the poverty standard (for a given family size) is assigned the value of $G = .25$.

18. For example, the plan with a 30% tax rate (for a given family size) is assigned the value of $t = -.20$.

19. Spanish-speaking and black wives showed no (statistically) significant disincentive effect.

20. This criterion systematically excluded families in which the wife also had full-time employment since this second source of income substantially increased normal family income.

21. This might also depend on cultural factors associated with a given ethnic group.

22. The sample size varies between 117 and 200 young adults.

23. This is equivalent to a misspecified discriminant analysis.

24. This is because the error term ϵ is usually heteroscedastic.

25. Namely, the 75–70 and 50–50 plans.

26. Hollister presents two sets of results—averaged and pooled (see Hollister, 1973).

27. For whites and blacks only. The Spanish-speaking subsample indicates significance only for the averaged hours per week variable.

28. Hollister, however, concludes that the two sets of results ". . . are roughly comparable."

29. This implies that the differential can be tested by the simple usual difference-in-means *t*-tests (or their normal approximations).

30. Averaged estimates are calculated initially for control families only, whereas those used in the pooled estimates use both control and experimental family data. The rationale for this approach, however, is not indicated.

31. This average value of $\hat{Y}/\text{pov}$ is 1.32.

32. Actually only 10 families were in plans with $t = .70$ *and* had normal earnings low enough to be below breakeven but high enough so that their plan was not dominated by welfare (i.e., above the welfare "breakeven income" but below their experimental breakeven income level).

33. Income variance is entered as a variable.

34. In its extreme form the existence of such covariances leads to multicollinearity.

35. The introduction of the AFDC-UP program, initially one of the most generous in the United States, was further complicated by a reduction in the guarantee and in the number of eligible families. Furthermore, a shortage of white families led to an extension of the experiment to Scranton, Pennsylvania, which had a different welfare system from that introduced in New Jersey.

36. Aaron (1975, p. 91), for reasons not clear to us, states that this difference will be reduced.

37. Hall's rationale for the simpler methods is puzzling; he states that simpler models tend to be more powerful.

38. Families having earnings 1.5 times the poverty level or less were eligible to participate in the New Jersey experiment.

39. Male heads for whom complete data were available.

40. Their diagram (Hausman and Wise, 1977a; figure 1) however suggests that $\hat{\beta}$ is also biased, since truncation is depicted to alter the slope β.

41. Since Cogan introduces the estimate as -3.2, it is not clear whether "higher" refers to the entire number or to its magnitude. We assume that the reference is to the magnitude of the estimate.

42. Most R^2 values are less than .15.

43. If these are correlated with the included variables.

44. For some reason Cogan claims this coefficient has no interpretation since "no one could participate in the program without being an experimental."

45. Cogan's statement of this is confusing and indeed contradictory since he writes "The mean difference in hours worked by controls and participating experimentals does not measure the labor supply response among N.I.T. participants" (Cogan, 1978, p. 34).

46. Cogan's original table (Cogan, 1978, p. 34) in fact lists relative reductions in terms of fractional decreases, not percentage decreases, as stated in the column heading.

47. Watts *et al.* (1974) estimates a mean reduction of 1.85 hours per week for white male heads of intact families. Cogan, on the other hand, obtains (for the same quarter) a reduction of 3.78 hours per week—a figure double that of Watts.

48. Normal incomes and wage rates. As seen above, this did not necessarily eliminate bias completely.

49. The time periods for which the *New Jersey Final Report* and Cogan base their estimates are also not the same.

6 The Rural Income Maintenance Experiment

I. INTRODUCTION

The Rural Income Maintenance Experiment (RIME) was the second of four income maintenance experiments, but, unlike the others, it was designed to test labor supply response in a rural setting. The experimental sites were deliberately selected to be representative of the South (the North Carolina site) and the Midwest (the Iowa site), and to typify approximately one-third of the U.S. rural poverty population. The entire sample in Iowa was white; however, in North Carolina, the sample was about evenly divided between black and white families. Both sites contained wage earners as well as farmers.

This chapter considers the labor supply response effects reported by the RIME experiment.[1] The next section describes the sample and its assignment to the two sites and various treatment cells. Subsequent sections describe and assess the labor supply results for farm and nonfarm families.

II. SAMPLE COMPOSITION AND ALLOCATION

A total of 801 families was enrolled in RIME. Table 6.1 presents the distribution of the sample by family type, site, and experimental status.

140

Table 6.1

The RIME Sample By Family Type, Site, and Treatment/Control (Initial Allocation)

Number of families allocated to	Husband–wife (nonaged male)		Female heads (nonaged)		Husband–Wife (at least 1 head aged)		Total
	Treat-ment	Control	Treat-ment	Control	Treat-ment	Control	
North Carolina	170	200	30	33	33	35	501
Iowa	99	118	21	24	21	25	308
Total	269	318	51	57	54	60	809

Within each group (family type) the families were allocated across a design space consisting of 36 cells. The 36 cells result from six experimental statuses (five treatments plus one control), each stratified by three welfare levels and two locations. As in the case of the New Jersey experiment, the sample assignment used the Conlisk–Watts model; consequently, families were not assigned to strata by a random allocation process. For a detailed description of the sampling process the reader is referred to volume I of the RIME Final Report; for convenience, however, the allocation of the sample to experimental strata is reproduced in Tables 6.2–6.4.

Table 6.2

Cell Assignments, Male Heads Under 59 Years of Age

Plan (G/t)	Policy weight	No. of households by poverty level			Row totals
		0–0.5	0.5–1.0	1.0–1.5	
Control	—	26(20,6)[a]	104(77,27)	188(103,85)	318(200,188)
50/50	4	6(4,2)	31(22,9)	0(0,0)	37(26,11)
75/30	6	9(7,2)	0(0,0)	58(33,25)	67(40,27)
75/50	10	2(2,0)	29(26,3)	44(18,26)	75(46,29)
75/70	3	5(3,2)	25(18,7)	0(0,0)	30(21,9)
100/50	10	3(3,0)	0(0,0)	57(34,23)	60(37,23)
Column totals		51(39,12)	189(143,46)	347(188,159)	587(370,217)

[a] Numbers in parentheses are assignments for North Carolina and Iowa, respectively.
Source: Metcalf and Bawden (1976).

Table 6.3

Cell Assignments, Female Heads Under 59 Years of Age

Plan (G/t)	Policy weight	No. of households by poverty level			Row totals
		0–0.5	0.5–1.0	1.0–1.5	
Control	—	7(7,0)[a]	17(11,6)	33(15,18)	57(33,24)
50/50	4	2(2,0)	4(4,0)	0(0,0)	6(6,0)
75/30	6	1(1,0)	0(0,0)	4(4,0)	5(5,0)
75/50	10	2(2,0)	4(4,0)	3(3,0)	9(9,0)
75/70	3	1(1,0)	3(3,0)	0(0,0)	4(4,0)
100/50	10	2(1,1)	0(0,0)	8(5,3)	10(6,4)
100/30		1(0,1)	1(0,1)	3(0,3)	5(0,5)
125/50		1(0,1)	0(0,0)	6(0,6)	7(0,7)
125/70		1(0,1)	3(0,3)	1(0,1)	5(0,5)
Column totals		18(14,4)	32(22,10)	58(27,31)	108(63,45)

[a] Numbers in parentheses are assignments for North Carolina and Iowa, respectively.

Source: Metcalf and Bawden (1976).

Analysis of the sample was carried out in a similar manner to that of the New Jersey experiment. Specifically, a nonlinear regression surface characterized by 16 parameters was fitted employing an analysis of covariance[2] type model, thereby permitting a substantial degree of nonlinearity in the

Table 6.4

Cell Assignments, Head of Either Sex Over 58 Years of Age

Plan (G/t)	Policy weight	No. of households by poverty level			Row totals
		0–0.5	0.5–1.0	1.0–1.5	
Control	—	5(4,1)[a]	19(11,8)	36(20,16)	60(35,25)
50/50	4	1(1,0)	7(4,3)	0(0,0)	8(5,3)
75/30	6	1(1,0)	0(0,0)	11(6,5)	12(7,5)
75/50	10	1(1,0)	6(3,3)	8(5,3)	15(9,6)
75/70	3	2(1,0)	6(4,2)	0(0,0)	8(5,3)
100/50	10	1(1,0)	0(0,0)	10(6,4)	11(7,4)
Column totals		11(9,2)	38(22,16)	65(37,28)	114(68,46)

[a] Numbers in parentheses are assignments for North Carolina and Iowa, respectively.

Source: Metcalf and Bawden (1976).

three underlying stratification (treatment) variables (the guarantee, the tax rate, and the welfare level of the participants) as well as in the covariates (control variables).

The RIME researchers subdivided the data into two major groups—rural nonfarm respondents and rural farm respondents. Each major group was further divided according to family type (see Table 6.1) and the relation of the individual to the family. We first consider the income and work response of the farm families.

III. INCOME AND WORK RESPONSE OF FARM FAMILIES

The Data Base

RIME gathered data from the farm sample by means of quarterly surveys. Information was obtained on cash income, expenses, assets, inventories, production levels, and hours of work to determine the impact of a guaranteed annual income on rural farm families. A number of problems were encountered in gathering these data. There was a low literacy rate and therefore farm records were often not kept (particularly in North Carolina). Additionally, for sharecroppers it was landowners who kept the books, if any were kept at all. Accordingly, RIME researchers undertook a major edit of the data to reduce errors of measurement (Primus, 1976b). As a result, two parallel data bases were created—the first data base containing the "original" data (ORIG) and the second consisting of the edited data (EDIT) from which many "inconsistencies" were removed. In fact, however, both data bases were edited to varying extents.

Data base ORIG consisted of measurements captured from the quarterly periodic interviews with the "obvious" reporting errors and data processing errors removed. For example, if an empirically (technologically) impossible value were recorded—say, a corn yield of 1000 bushels per acre—two basic methods were used to correct the datum. First, the suspect value might be replaced by a more plausible figure—for example, a corn yield of 1000 bushels/acre might be replaced by 100 bushels/acre. Second, the error might be replaced by a number generated by some "standard" (presumably univariate) missing data adjustment technique. However, if a datum seemed "reasonable," from a univariate point of view, no remedial action was taken. Consequently, the editing techniques consisted of the usual computer science patch-up practice of removing univariate outliers without regard for statistical theory or practice.   Therefore data base ORIG does not contain original raw data but has itself been edited to a certain extent.[3]

The data base EDIT removed "a large percentage of inconsistencies" by drawing on outside information (farm budget bulletins), farm practice from previous years, and certain value judgments concerning the quality of the data (see Primus, 1976a, pp. 4–5 for the detailed criteria used).   The difference between the two data bases is fairly large.   Since ORIG already represents an edited ("cleaned") data base, the difference between data actually captured and the final edited data used for analysis is probably even larger, thus rendering the data base, for all practical purposes, virtually useless.

By including differences of the absolute values (ABS) as part of the summary statistics, Primus exaggerates the difference between the two data bases, particularly the impact of editing on the analysis.   Since standard regressions are employed in the analysis of the data, all computation is conducted in Euclidian (L_2) space (i.e., minimization of the sum of squares), which does not admit the non-Euclidian absolute value metric (see Primus, 1976a, pp. 21, 25).   Therefore, the cancellation effect of the sample mean is perfectly valid when comparing the mean (average) differences between the two data bases, given their higher moments.   We consider the effect of data editing on the experimental effects after discussing the farm labor supply results.

Labor Response of Farm Operators

The work behavior of a low-income farm[4] family is assumed to correspond to that of a single individual maximizing a utility function.   Conventionally, overall utility depends on income and the number of (nonwork) leisure hours.   Primus further assumes that "economic" (monetary) returns alone dictate the occupational choice between being a farmer or a wage earner; that is, farm work and wage work are equivalent with respect to nonmonetary benefits or life-styles.   The total sample for analysis consists of farm families from North Carolina and Iowa.   These families have a male head less than or equal to 72 years of age (at the end of the experiment) who farmed each year of the experiment, had constant marital status, and had at least 400 hours of work in any one of the years between 1969 and 1972.   The method of production[5] involved in growing tobacco (North Carolina) and growing corn (Iowa) was different; consequently, separate analyses were performed for each region.   Nerlove's procedure for pooled data is employed, because the data are viewed as cross sections of families traced over a three-year period. Each observation for the model then represents a year[6] of the experiment for each farmer. Before considering the results, we describe the dependent, control, and experimental variables employed.

Eight dependent variables are defined and regressed on a set of independent variables, including interaction terms. The following variables are used:

Dependent (Labor Supply) Variables (Y)

Y_1 is the net farm income defined as gross income minus total expenses, for a given time period (usually a year), where

Y_2 is the gross farm income (used to define Y_1) consists of all income received during a "designated" time period, less the purchase amounts paid for cattle, hogs, or sheep sold during that "designated" time period.

Y_3 is the hours worked, as recalled by the male head during the previous week. This variable depends entirely on the memory of respondents, since they were not required to keep track of their hours worked.

Y_4 is the total hours worked as recalled by all members of family.[7]

Y_5 is the total scaled hours or the number of hours worked by the family as reconstructed from published sources (the term *budgeted hours* also seems to be used interchangeably with *scaled hours*). Variable Y_5 is an aggregate of the variables Y_6 and Y_7, that is, $Y_5 = Y_6 + Y_7$, where Y_6 and Y_7 are defined as follows.

Y_6 is the scaled crop hours: the respondent (male head) is asked the type of crop(s) planted and the acreage covered. By using outside estimates of the number of hours/acre needed to farm a particular crop, a measure is constructed as the total number of hours spent on crops.

Y_7 is the scaled livestock hours: the respondent (male head) is asked the type and number of livestock raised; again, by using outside estimates of the number of hours/animals deemed necessary to raise a particular type of livestock (hogs, cattle, sheep), a measure is constructed to record the total number of hours spent on livestock.

Y_8 is the adjusted scaled hours: variables Y_6 and Y_7 (and thus Y_5) are constructed from published "hours coefficients." These do not take into account differences in farm size or farming method. Consequently, the scaled hours are further adjusted by extra assumptions concerning equipment used (for crops) and by employing a polynomial of the form $21.54 + 2.94x - .001x^2$ to extrapolate advantages of scale for livestock. This procedure yields Y_8.

The following independent variables are used to account for the labor supply variables:

Control Variables

X_1 = HR69 = 1969 scaled hours of appropriate activity (crop hours, livestock hours, or total hours).

X_2 = AGE = age of farm operator.[8]

X_3 = AGE 55 = $\begin{cases} \text{age of farmer operator if age} > 54 \\ 0 \text{ otherwise.} \end{cases}$

X_4 = EDUC = number of years of formal schooling of farm operator.

X_5 = DR = total farm debts/total farm assets.

X_6 = FE = net farm equity.

X_7 = ΔHDWBH = change in the amount of off-farm work performed by the farm operator.

X_8 = D71 = $\begin{cases} 1, & \text{if observation from year 1971} \\ 0, & \text{otherwise.} \end{cases}$

X_9 = D72 = $\begin{cases} 1, & \text{if observation from year 1972} \\ 0, & \text{otherwise.} \end{cases}$

Experimental – Treatment Variables

X_{10} = C/E = $\begin{cases} 1, & \text{if experimental status} \\ 0, & \text{if control status.} \end{cases}$

X_{11} = PN = "measurement" variable, constructed as follows. Let SP = survey data NIT payment amount; PP = predicted NIT payment amount; M = (SP + PP)/2, the mean of the two payment variables. Then

$$PN = \frac{SP - PP}{M}$$

We now consider the labor supply response of farm operators for the RIME Experiment.

Analysis of IOWA Data

The analysis was carried out in two stages, depending on the particular treatment variables considered and the way in which they were incorporated. The core set of regression variables consists of what Primus calls the "basic variables,"[9] whereby each independent variable $Y_i, i = 1, 2, \ldots, 8$, is regressed on the set of controls variables $X_1, X_2, \ldots, X_9$ plus additional treatment variables. There are two sets of results and three models.

Set 1

Primus (1976a) estimates the following three sets of equations (models).

Model I

$$Y_j = \beta_0 + \sum_{i=1}^{10} \beta_i X_i + \epsilon$$

Model II

$$Y_j = \beta_0 + \sum_{i=1}^{10} \beta_i X_i + \beta_{11}(X_1 X_{10}) + \epsilon$$

Model III

$$Y_j = \beta_0 + \sum_{i=1}^{10} \beta_i X_i + \beta_{11}(X_1 X_{10}) + \beta_{12}(X_1^2 X_{10}) + \epsilon$$

for $j = 1, 2, \ldots, 8$. Essentially, these models differ in the manner the experimental effect X_{10} is taken into account. Table 6.5 presents coefficients obtained for the treatment variables only, that is, X_{10}; the dummy

Table 6.5
Iowa Treatment Coefficient Estimates, F-Values, and Predicted Incentives for Models with Simple Treatment Parameterizations for Selected Dependent Variables

	Net farm income (Y_1)	Gross farm income (Y_2)	Head recall hours (Y_3)	Total recall hours (Y_4)	Total scaled hours (Y_5)	Scaled crop hours (Y_6)	Scaled livestock hours (Y_7)	Adjusted scaled hours (Y_8)
Model I								
C/E	−397	−1363	27	97	−173	−23	−152	−230
F	.44	.92	.04	.40	6.66[b]	.42	5.52[b]	8.24[a]
Incentive (%)	−8.1	−6.6	1.1	3.7	−8.4	−2.1	−15.9	−12.6
Model II								
C/E	−1705	988	234	259	21	94	−127	−8.76
C/E*HR69	.66	−1.18	−.10	−.08	−.10	−.11	−.028	−.11
F	.73	.76	.28	.32	4.31[b]	1.01	2.81[c]	5.02[a]
Incentive (%)	−9.6	−6.7	1.2	3.9	−8.3	−2.1	−16.6	−12.3
Model III								
C/E	−4567	6290	321	308	166	−131	−72	−107
C/E*HR69	3.71	−6.27	−.16	−.10	−.24	−.25	.184	−.002
C/E*HR69²	−.00064	.00106	.00001	.00000	.00003	−.00012	.00006	−.00002
F	.95[e]	.66	.25	.32	2.75[b]	.30	2.07[d]	3.19[b]
Incentive (%)	6.4	−9.2	2.1	4.9	−8.9	.2	−20.4	−10.7

[a] Significant at the .01 level.
[b] Significant at the .05 level.
[c] Significant at the .10 level.
[d] Significant at the .20 level.
[e] In the original table, the F-value is reported as 95, presumably a typographical error.
Source: Primus (1976b).

X_{10} = C/E represents the differential in means, for the Y_i, between experimental and control families. To determine the effect of X_{10} = C/E, it is enough to consider model I only, since neither model II nor model III improve the estimate of the experimental effect. Indeed, in model II (see Table 6.5) the significance of the interaction term X_1X_{10} = HR69 · C/E is not given, and model III appears to be misspecified.[10]

The "percent incentive" coefficient of Table 6.5 is defined by Primus as

$$\text{Percentage of expected incentive} = \frac{(\hat{P} - \hat{C})}{\hat{C}} \times 100$$

where $\hat{P}$ = predicted value (of the corresponding dependent variable) for the experimental (treatment) group (computed by using the mean values of the independent variables), and $\hat{C}$ = predicted value (of the corresponding dependent variable) for the *control* groups (also computed by using the mean values of the independent variables). Confining attention to model I, it is clear from Table 6.5 that none of the "observed" dependent variables (see discussion dealing with the data base) are significantly different for experimental and control groups; indeed, not only are the F-values insignificant, they are highly insignificant. Statistical significance is registered only for three of the four constructed variables: total scaled hours (Y_5), scaled livestock hours (Y_7), and adjusted scaled hours (Y_8). Since the total scaled hours (Y_5) variable is defined as an aggregate (linear combination) of the scaled livestock hours (Y_7) and scaled crop hours (Y_6) (which is insignificant), the significance of total scaled hours is probably due mainly to scaled livestock hours. We therefore have only two results:

1. Payments (treatment) families, irrespective of guarantee level and tax rate, reduced (on the average) their scaled livestock (but not crop) hours by 152 hours per year, or 15.9%.
2. Payments (treatment) families, irrespective of guarantee level and tax rate, reduced (on the average) their adjusted scaled hours by 230 hours per year, or 12.6%.

Set 2

The second stage of the analysis consists of adding treatment–guarantee dummy variables as well as interaction terms involving X_{10} = C/E with selected variables, where

$$G50 = \begin{cases} 1, & \text{if guarantee is 50\% of poverty level} \\ 0, & \text{otherwise} \end{cases}$$

$$G100 = \begin{cases} 1, & \text{if guarantee is 100\% of poverty level} \\ 0, & \text{otherwise} \end{cases}$$

$$T30 = \begin{cases} 1, & \text{if tax rate is 30\%} \\ 0, & \text{otherwise} \end{cases}$$

$$T70 = \begin{cases} 1, & \text{if tax rate is 70\%} \\ 0, & \text{otherwise} \end{cases}$$

The overall experimental dummy $X_{10} = C/E$ is nowhere significant, including its interaction terms, with the exception of $X_9 X_{10} = D72 \cdot C/E$. Of the guarantee and tax rate variables defined earlier, only G100 and T70 are significant but then only for a single dependent variable—gross farm income (Y_2). Primus (1976a, p. 46) points out that the sign of G100 agrees with "expectation" but the sign of T70 does not—farmers on the highest tax rate had a higher gross farm income than those who received the average tax rate of 30%! This result is contrary to conventional wisdom respecting monetary incentives and their role in competitive market economies.[11] Actually almost all the significant coefficients are for the nonexperimental control variables (covariates), and these variables account for the relatively high R^2 coefficients of some of the regressions. On the basis of regression results, Primus proceeds to compute his coefficient of expected incentive (defined earlier). However, in view of our comments concerning the significance of treatment effects, it is far from clear whether his incentives coefficients are significantly different from zero.

Analysis of North Carolina Data

Analysis of the North Carolina subsample parallels that of the Iowa portion with two major exceptions. First, because of the virtual absence of livestock farming for the North Carolina sample, the dependent variable $Y_8 =$ "scaled livestock hours" is not used. Consequently, we have only seven dependent variables defined for the North Carolina analysis. Second, the North Carolina sample contains black families, so an extra control variable—"race"—is included in the regression equations. Again, two basic sets of regression results are reported.

Set 1

Three models (equations) are also defined for the North Carolina sample. The results are presented in Table 6.6. Again only model I need be considered since the addition of interaction terms does not improve the global results, as far as the partial F-statistic is concerned.[12] With the exception of gross farm income, statistical significance is again achieved mainly for constructed, rather than observed, dependent variables. Al-

Table 6.6

*North Carolina Treatment Coefficient Estimates, F-Values, and Predicted Incentives
for Models with Simple Treatment Parameterizations for Selected Dependent Variables*

	Net farm income (Y_1)	Gross farm income (Y_2)	Head recall hours (Y_3)	Total recall hours (Y_4)	Total scaled hours (Y_5)	Adjusted scaled hours (Y_8)	Scaled crop hours (Y_6)
Model I							
C/E	−189	−1425	141	148	−266	−83	−290
F	.32	3.17[c]	1.12	.83	3.76[c]	.72	4.84[b]
Incentive (%)	−7.2	−15.8	9.1	7.7	−13.3	−6.5	−15.5
Model II							
C/E	−591	588	238	117	−13	−139	65
HR69*C/E	.26	−1.32	−.06	.02	−.17	.04	−.25
F	.47	2.97[c]	.67	.42	2.62[c]	.43	4.32[b]
Incentive (%)	−7.4	−13.8	9.0	7.2	−12.7	5.9	−15.1
Model III							
C/E	−398	−1104	353	129	−686	−454	−295
C/E*HR69	.033	1.10	−.22	.015	.80	.49	.33
C/E*HR69²	.00005	−.00060	.00004	.00000	−.00024	−.00011	−.00016
F	.28	2.37[c]	.51	.29	3.91[a]	1.11	4.16[a]
Incentive (%)	−6.7	−8.1	.5	7.1	−1.3	2.2	−6.9

[a] Significant at the .01 level.
[b] Significant at the .05 level.
[c] Significant at the .10 level.
[d] Significant at the .20 level.

though gross farm income tends to decline, on the average, by $1425.00 (15.8%) for experimental families, net farm income is not affected by the experiment. This leads one to suspect that the significance of the variable C/E for the equation determining gross farm income is due to variations in costs (expenses). Again, there is no evidence to suggest that the directly observed dependent variables (net farm income and head-recall hours) are significantly affected by payments.

Set 2

Unlike the Iowa data, many experimental coefficients are significant for the North Carolina sample. However, most are of the "wrong" sign. Although economic theory leads one to expect positive coefficients for G50 and T30 and negative coefficients for G100 and T70, the contrary is the case. *All* coefficients of G50 and T30 are significantly positive, whereas only a single significant coefficient for T70 is negative! The dummy variable C/E is not significant for all seven dependent variables, and the only significant interaction term is D72 · C/E for the two recall hours variables. This indicates a significant difference in recall hours between controls and experimentals, but only in 1972. Also the variable "race" is highly significant.

Appraisal and Conclusions

The major problem with estimating the farm work response in RIME lies in the basic data used and the nature of some of the constructed (or partly constructed) dependent variables, such as adjusted and/or scaled hours. Undoubtedly any large-scale survey seeking reliable data on farm labor supply variables such as the number of hours worked, income, and costs of small farm operators, and so on, faces an unenviable task. Furthermore, given the low level of education of poor, small-scale farmers and their mistrust of outsiders, it is probably impossible to obtain highly accurate data. Large outliers are bound to occur for the dependent labor supply measures, and there will be many missing observations as well. But it is not clear that the RIME strategy satisfactorily solved the problems of outlying errors and missing data. To be sure, RIME generated two data bases—the "original" data in ORIG and an edited data base EDIT—but even the "original" data was edited to remove "obvious" reporting errors. Furthermore, missing entries were estimated by a "standard" (?) missing data estimator. It is one thing to notice an "obvious" error but something else to replace it with a good estimate.[13] Thus two objections can be raised against Primus's data editing procedure. First, a univariate outlier is not the same thing as a multivariate outlier. Accordingly, any editing should be performed with the multivariate statistical model in mind—here regression analysis. An outlier is not just any excessively large (or small) number; rather it is a function of *both* observed and estimated values. Second, measurement errors in the dependent variable caused by potential outliers are best taken into account by statistical procedures—for example, non-normal (and non-least-squares) regression models such as the minimum absolute deviation (MAD) estimator. This approach has the advantage of allowing for many different types of estimators/models to be used while at the same time preserving the integrity of the raw data. Should a univariate outlier represent an obvious error (e.g., a crop yield that is empirically impossible), it is probably preferable to treat it as a missing datum and to estimate its value by a maximum-likelihood missing data procedure, rather than "guesstimate" its correct value.[14]

The labor supply results reported by Primus (1976b) are based on the data base EDIT. Because EDIT represents an extensive editing of ORIG, difficulties arise as to the substantive (and logical) interpretation of the findings. That such editing makes a difference is acknowledged by Primus (1976a) himself, and a quick glance at the regressions in Appendix A of the RIME report indicates a large difference between estimates based on the ORIG data and that based on the EDIT data. Indeed, the experimental dummy variable is significant mainly for EDIT rather than for ORIG. This would seem to indicate the decisive role played by the editing procedure. In summary, a major difficulty with interpreting the labor supply response effects from RIME concerns matters prior to specifying and estimating econometric models, namely, data editing.

A second obstacle obscuring interpretation of the RIME results for farm operators lies in the choice of dependent variables. There are also difficulties with the substantive interpretation of the statistical results. Of the eight dependent variables used, four are not observed directly (although some contain observed measurements) but are in fact constructed with the aid of external, published macro data. Additionally, the adjusted scaled hours variable is further altered by a quadratic interpolation procedure, consequently altering its interpretability as a measure of labor supply effect in terms of the observed number of hours worked. Again, this adjustment makes a great deal of difference. For regressions that use adjusted and/or scaled variables, the R^2 coefficient increases (in some cases) three-fold, thus tending to increase the significance levels of the independent variables. And, given the small number of degrees of freedom,[15] the findings must be regarded with reservation. Finally, because of the signs and lack of significance for coefficients reported in the various tables, it is difficult to assert with confidence that any disincentive has occurred (on the average) as a result of the income maintenance experiment for farm operators. Our general conclusion is that the analysis of farm operators, as presented by Primus, can provide no scientific evidence, one way or the other, on labor supply of farm operators under a guaranteed annual income.

IV. INCOME AND WORK RESPONSE OF NONFARM FAMILIES

The Sample and Estimation Approach

We now focus on the labor supply of rural nonfarm families and husbands. A forthcoming chapter on the income and work response of wives and dependents was never included in the final report of the Rural Income Maintenance Experiment and consequently is not considered here.

The sample consisted of two-parent families with a nonaged head whose primary source of income was not from self-employment. Only families meeting these criteria in the year prior to the experiment and during the first year of the experiment were considered. Wage earners who became farmers were excluded on a permanent basis even though they could have returned to wage earner status at a later date. On a more detailed level the following six conditions were used to draw the subsample.

1. Families had to contain the same two parents one year prior to the experiment as well as during the current three-monthly (quarterly) period of observation.
2. The husband had to be less than 63 years of age in the quarter under observation; that is, he could not be retired from the labor force.
3. The husband could not have disabilities during *every* quarter of the experiment if this prevented him from working.
4. The husband was not in formal job training in the year prior to the experiment. Those in job training during 1969 were felt not to have any meaningful preexperimental observations of the dependent labor supply variables.
5. The family did not receive a "random" transfer exceeding $4000 during the quarter of observation, such as life insurance benefits.
6. Finally, the husband must have met *one* of the following three conditions: (a) no farm business income, or (b) wage income greater than gross farm and business income, or (c) wage income less than gross farm and business income, but hours worked for wages averaged 24 or more per week *and* were greater than hours worked in the farm or business.

Condition 6 was used in order to define a wage earner whose primary activity, if any, was in the wage sector, although they were allowed nonwage income as a secondary source of revenues. The sample was thus confined to "traditional" poor families with husband depending primarily on wage income for support.

Table 6.7 shows the distribution of families and quarterly observations between control and experimental status and among the experimental plans. Fifty-six percent of observations were controls and the remainder were assigned to one of the five experiment plans. Of the latter group, 91% were concentrated in three of the five plans: 30 and 50% tax (T) rates combined with a guarantee (G) of 75% of the poverty level (30 and 34% of the sample, respectively) and a 50% tax combined with a guarantee level of

Table 6.7

Wage Earner Sample by Experimental Status

Experimental status	Number of quarterly observations	Quarterly observations (%)	Number of families
Control	1651	56	146
Experimental	1305	44	118
Total	2956	100	264
Experimental plan[a]			
50T/50G	56	4	5
30T/75G	397	30	36
50T/75G	445	34	40
70T/75G	69	5	7
50T/100G	338	26	30
Total	1305	99	118

[a] The experimental plans are shown by tax rate and guarantee level. For example, the first plan — 50T/50G — is read as a 50% tax rate and a 50% (of the poverty line) guarantee level.
Source: Bawden, (1976) RIME final report.

100% of the poverty line (26%). The 50T–50G plan had only 4% of the observations, whereas the 70T–75G plan contained 5%.

The paucity of sample points in the latter two cells is attributable to three things. First, these two cells were assigned the smallest "policy weights." Second, they had the lowest breakeven levels (100 and 107% of the poverty line) and thus were directly "relevant" to only a subset of the entire sample of those below 150% of the poverty line. (No families were assigned to plans with breakeven levels below their preexperimental income levels.) Third, the sample was not stratified by occupation, and the random assignment process led to a higher proportion of farmers than wage earners assigned to the two plans.

The sample is subdivided by region and race in Table 6.8. It shows that half of the sample was composed of North Carolina blacks, with the remainder equally divided between North Carolina whites and Iowa whites. (There were no blacks in the Iowa sample.) Although the sample was stratified by region, it was not stratified by race or occupation. The randomness of the sampling procedure thus left the wage earner sample with twice as many blacks as whites in North Carolina (though the total North Carolina sample was only 55% black). It also left the sample with a relatively large number of experimentals in Iowa (56%) and proportionately

Table 6.8
Experimental Status by Region and Race

Region/race	Number of quarterly observations	Quarterly observations (%)	Number of families
Iowa — white:			
Control	328	11	30
Experimental	425	14	39
Total	753	25	69
North Carolina — black:			
Control	911	31	79
Experimental	543	18	49
Total	1454	49	128
North Carolina — white:			
Control	412	14	37
Experimental	337	11	30
Total	749	25	67
Totals	2956	99	264

fewer experimentals in North Carolina (40%), compared to the total wage earner average of 44%.

RIME differed from the New Jersey experiment in that the basic eligible unit was the household, and adults other than the husband and wife did not count. Therefore the unit of analysis is the central, "straight" family unit consisting of husband, wife, and all dependents less than 18 years of age, or less than age 21 if unmarried.[16]

The basic time unit for analysis is the annual quarter. Data consist of cross-sectional as well as time-series observations. Consequently, a component error term model is used for the panel data; we have

$$\epsilon_{it} = u_i + v_{it} \qquad (6.1)$$

where u_i represents time-persistent individual effects and v_{it} is the random error term obeying the generalized Gauss – Markov assumptions; that is,

$$E(u_i) = E(v_{it}) = 0$$

$$E(u_i u_j) = \begin{cases} 0, & \text{if } i \neq j \\ \sigma_u^2, & \text{if } i = j \end{cases}$$

$$\qquad (6.2)$$

$$E(v_{it} v_{jt}) = \begin{cases} 0, & \text{if } i \neq j \\ \sigma_v^2, & \text{if } i = j \end{cases}$$

so that $\sigma_v^2 = \sigma_\epsilon^2 - \sigma_u^2$. Note that the time-persistent individual effect term u_i is assumed to be serially uncorrelated over time, a not very realistic or useful assumption, particularly when the model used is generalized least squares.

The experimental response is estimated by functional forms

$$Y_{it} = f(C_{it}, X_{it}, C_{it}X_{it}) + \epsilon_{it} \tag{6.3}$$

where Y_{it} is a response variable for the ith unit (family or individual) in quarter t, C_{it} is a set of control variables, and X_{it} is experimental treatment variables.

The response variable Y_{it} is one of the following: total income, earned income (wages plus self-employment income), wage income, hours of wage work, or number of earners per family. Control variables C_{it}, or covariates, are included to take account of potential systematic differences between the various treatments and control families due to nonrandom sample assignment or attrition.[17] Control variables consist of preexperimental values of the dependent variable, Y_{i0}; the usual sociodemographic and economic variables; and a set of time variables and seasonality dummies. Included among the control variables is a measure of "normal income" $\hat{W}$ estimated as

$$\hat{W}_{it} = \hat{\beta}_0 + \hat{\beta}_1 W_{i0} + \hat{\beta}_2 Z_{it} + \hat{\beta}_3 X_{it} \tag{6.4}$$

where W_{it} is the wage rate for sample point i at time t, Z are the control variables, X is the experimental status (plan/control), and W_{i0} is the preexperimental wage rate. Equation (6.4) is estimated separately for both husbands and wives, using a sample of "full-time workers," that is, husbands who averaged at least 35 hours per week and wives who averaged at least 30 hours per week. The normal wage rate is then computed as

$$n(W_{it}) = W_{it}^* - \bar{d}_i \tag{6.5}$$

where

$$W_{it}^* = \hat{\beta}_0 + \hat{\beta}_1 W_{i0} + \hat{\beta}_2 Z_{it}$$
$$= \hat{W}_{it} - \hat{\beta}_3 X_{it}$$

and $\bar{d}_i$ is the average deviation of the ith individual from his predicted wage defined as

$$\bar{d}_i = \frac{\sum_t \hat{\epsilon}_{it}}{N_t} \tag{6.6}$$

where the summation is taken over those quarters (a total of N_t) in which individual i reported working full time, $\hat{\epsilon}_{it}$ being the residual term from Eq.

(6.4).   Then $\bar{d}_i$ is a measure of the extent to which the ith individual exceeds (or falls short) of the average wage for identical persons, as estimated by the wage rate regression equation (6.4).   For those individuals who never worked full time $\bar{d}_i$ is set to zero.   The normal wage rate equations (6.4) are computed separately for blacks and whites, but in what follows we only present the pooled normal wage equation, for both white and black husbands (Table 6.9).   The independent variables are defined as follows.

H/AGE	age of husband in years
H/AGE SQ	age of husband (squared)
H/EDUC	educational attainment of husband in years
H/EDUC SQ	education of husband (squared)
H/AGE*EDUC	interaction of age and education
H/AGE SQ*EDUC	interaction of age (squared) and education
NO. DEPENDENTS	number of children $\leq$ age 18, or $\leq$ age 21 if unmarried
FARM WORKER	a (0,1) binary variable where 1 indicates occupation of a hired farmworker
LARGE TOWN	distance in miles from the nearest town with a population $> 10,000$
MOVED	a (0,1) binary variable where 1 indicates that the family now resides in a county other than its residence at the beginning of the experiment
F/TY $-$ H/WY	family's total income minus husband's wage income, in \$100 per quarter
QUARTER	quarter of the experiment; ranges from 1 to 12
QUARTER SQ	quarter of the experiment (squared)
WINTER	a (0,1) binary variable representing the winter quarter, December–February
SPRING	a (0,1) binary variable representing the spring quarter, March–May
SUMMER	a (0,1) binary variable representing the summer quarter, June–August
H/WR/PRE/DUM	a (0,1) binary variable with 1 representing a nonzero wage rate in the year prior to the experiment
H/WR/PRE	average wage rate of the husband in the year prior to the experiment, in dollars per hour
H/WR/PRE SQ	average wage rate in the year prior to the experiment (squared)
H/WR/P*QTR	interaction of average wage rate in the year prior to the experiment and quarter of the experiment
H/WR/P/QTR SQ	interaction of average wage rate in the year prior to the experiment and quarter of the experiment (squared)
H/WR/PSQ*QTR	interaction of average wage rate in the year prior to the experiment, squared, and quarter of the experiment
EXPERIMENT	a (0,1) binary variable where 1 represents being in the experimental group
EXP*QTR	interaction of experimental status and quarter
EXP*QTR SQ	interaction of experimental status and quarter (squared)
EXP*WINTER	interaction of experimental status and winter quarter
EXP*SPRING	interaction of experimental status and spring quarter
EXP*SUMMER	interaction of experimental status and summer quarter

EXP*FARM WKR	interaction of experimental status and being a hired farmworker
EXP*AGE	interaction of experimental status and age
EXP*EDUC	interaction of experimental status and education
TAX DEV	deviation of negative tax rate from 50%; ranges from -20 to $+20$
GUAR DEV	deviation of guarantee level from 75% of poverty line; ranges from -25 to $+25$

Those independent variables not common to the husbands equations follow.

RACE	a $(0,1)$ binary variable, where 1 indicates black
REGION	a $(0,1)$ binary variable, where 1 indicates North Carolina
REG*QTR	interaction of region and quarter
REG*QTR SQ	interaction of region and quarter (squared)
H/FARMER	a $(0,1)$ binary variables, where 1 indicates that the husband, though predominantly a wage earner, has some farm income
F/TY–W/WY	family's total income minus wife's wage income, in $100 per quarter
EXP*REG	interaction of experimental status and region
EXP*RACE	interaction of experimental status and race

The dependent variable is the natural logarithm of the wage rate.

The experimental variables X_{it} are included to determine whether (1) there was an experimental effect, and (2) if so, whether it varied by tax rate and/or guarantee. The main experimental effect is estimated by a single experimental dummy (EXPERIMENT) whereas the tax rate and guarantee levels are represented by TAX DEV and GUAR DEV, both expressed as deviations from their respective central values as in the case of the New Jersey experiment.

We conclude this section by mentioning a number of factors that bear on the validity of findings, their interpretation, or their generalizability. One issue relates to differences between experimentals and controls in reporting income. The New Jersey experiment found some evidence that experimental families were more likely than control families to report *gross* income (as requested) in the interviews rather than *net* income because experimentals also reported gross income on separate forms in order to receive payments. Thus measured earnings for control families might be biased downward during the early part of the experiment, leading to an upward bias in the measured treatment response. No evidence of such bias could be found in the Rural Experiment, in part because of a reconstructed set of questions asking for income in the interviews.

Other difficulties encountered in the New Jersey experiment include domination of some treatment plans by AFDC-UP, an attrition rate of about 18%, and significant numbers of experimental families receiving no payments because they were above the breakeven level. Neither Iowa nor North Carolina had an AFDC-UP program, so welfare domination was not

Table 6.9
*Wage Rate Equations for Full-Time Iowa
Husbands, for Deriving Normal Wage Rates*

Independent variable	Coefficient	Significance level
H/AGE	0.3177	.10
H/AGE SQ	−0.0037	.10
H/EDUC	0.4707	.30
H/EDUC SQ	0.0027	.83
H/AGE*EDUC	−0.0266	.14
H/AGE SQ*EDUC	0.0003	.12
NO. DEPENDENTS	−0.0453	.08
FARM WORKER	−0.5381	.01
LARGE TOWN	−0.0193	.01
MOVED	0.3337	.01
F/TY−H/WY	0.0015	.77
QUARTER	0.0917	.28
QUARTER SQ	−0.0084	.14
WINTER	0.0966	.04
SPRING	−0.0362	.39
SUMMER	−0.0217	.61
H/WR/PRE	1.1961	.02
H/WR/PRE SQ	−0.0516	.66
H/WR/P*QTR	0.0164	.77
H/WR/P*QTRSQ	0.0039	.13
H/WR/PSQ*QTR	−0.0174	.13
EXPERIMENT	0.1424	.87
EXP*QTR	−0.0111	.80
EXP*QTRSQ	−0.0002	.95
EXP*WINTER	−0.0181	.77
EXP*SPRING	0.0252	.66
EXP*SUMMER	0.0120	.84
EXP*FARM WKR	0.5483	<.01
EXP*AGE	−0.0094	.42
EXP*EDUC	−0.0059	.91
TAX DEV	−0.0001	.98
GUAR DEV	−0.0015	.74
CONSTANT	−5.7262	.20

Note: Mean Dep. Var. = 2.25, S.E. = 0.52, $N = 641$,
$F = 11.04$, $R^2 = .5589$, Rho = .3312.

a problem. The attrition rate in the Rural Experiment was only 9.9% (including involuntary departures, such as death, entering the armed services, and incarceration), but clearly this lower figure does not imply a total lack of selection bias. Finally, only 13% of the quarterly observations of experimental families were above their breakeven level, with half of them being less than 120% of breakeven. Moreover, families were above breakeven only an average of 3.3 of the 12 quarters, and only one family was above breakeven the entire 12 quarters.

Another factor relevent to interpreting the findings relates to the positive income tax. Experimental families had payroll and personal income tax withholdings "rebated" in that these amounts were added to the program payments. Consequently, experimental families faced only the tax rate of their assigned plan. Control families, however, faced a tax rate equivalent to that imposed for OASDI purposes (ranging from 4.8 to 5.2% during the period of the experiment), and those with sufficient incomes also faced the personal income tax. Thus the benchmark for measuring experimental response is not a zero tax rate, but whatever tax rate control families faced.

Further, the design of the experiment limits the extent to which the results can be generalized. The experiment imposed no work requirements; participants did not have to register for work or accept offered employment to receive payments. The work behavior observed, therefore, might not be that which would occur under an income maintenance program with a work requirement. Finally, as mentioned previously, this particular sample had relatively few sample points at the 50% guarantee or the 70% tax rate, so conclusions about response to low guarantees or high tax rates are tentative at best. Similarly, since the rural sample was drawn to be representative of selected states in the South and in the Midwest, extrapolation of results to broader populations should be done with care.

Income and Work Response of the Family

Annual family income, excluding experimental payments, averaged $5861 for the three years of the experiment. Iowans had the highest average family incomes ($6825 as compared to $5520 for North Carolina whites and blacks) and a larger proportion of farm and business income (5% versus 1% for North Carolina) and unearned income (8% versus 6% for North Carolina blacks and 5% for North Carolina whites). Thus wage – salary income made up 87% of total family income in Iowa and 93% (94%) for North Carolina blacks (whites), respectively.

Table 6.10 indicates the percentage contribution to family income for husbands, wives, and dependents (see also Table 6.11), where the number in parentheses indicates expected values on the null hypothesis of independence of rows and columns.

The dependent variables measuring family response income consist of the following:

Table 6.10
Percentage of Family Wage and Salary Income

	NC-B	NC-W	Iowa	Total
Husband	70(80)	80(80)	90(80)	240
Wife	21(12.7)	12(12.7)	5(12.7)	38
Dependents	9(7.3)	8(7.3)	5(7.3)	22
Total	100	100	100	300

Table 6.11
Sources of Family Incomes

Source	Average annual amount	Percentage
Wages and salaries	$5350	91.3
Farm income	125	2.1
Business income	14	0.3
Asset income	23	0.4
Free school meals	74	1.3
Food stamp bonuses	58	1.0
Unemployment insurance	34	0.6
"Welfare" income[a]	31	0.5
Income from formal job training	8	0.1
Education scholarships	7	0.1
Miscellaneous income[b]	137	2.3
Total	$5861	100.0

[a] Principally county-level general assistance, Aid to the Blind, Aid to the Permanently and Totally Disabled, and Aid to Families with Dependent Children for children from a previous marriage. Experimental families were prohibited by the rules of the experiment from receiving income from these sources. See Chapter 1, this volume, for a more detailed discussion.

[b] Includes veterans payments, alimony and child support, life insurance death benefits, gifts from friends and relatives, value of free meals on the job, value of food received from the Food Distribution Program (for North Carolina families in the first year), and all other types of miscellaneous income.

1. Total income: all income, in cash or in kind, except income-conditioned transfers (Public Assistance, general assistance, aid from the Salvation Army, the bonus value of food stamps, housing subsidies, Pensions for Veterans with Non-Service-Connected Disabilities, and free or subsidized meals at school).
2. Earned income: wages and self-employment income from a farm or nonfarm business (the latter includes commissions from selling such items as encyclopedias or Avon products, and piece-rate pay by the job).
3. Wage income: income received according to units of time (hours, weeks, or months), plus related bonuses (e.g., Christmas bonuses).
4. Hours worked for wages: paid vacations and paid sick leave, excluding hours spent in self-employment.
5. Number of wage earners: number of individuals in the family unit who worked for wages sometime during the quarter.

Experimental response is interacted with time and family characteristics to uncover whether it varied over the duration of the experiment, over the seasons, by tax rate and guarantee, by length of the accounting period, and by preexperimental response, Y_0.

Family Total Income

Raw data on total family income (as defined earlier) by quarter is shown in Figure 6.1 for both control and experimental families. Quarter 0 is the preexperimental quarter and is one-fourth of average income for the preceding year (1969); it is therefore unadjusted by season. The graph shows experimental families having slightly higher incomes than control families prior to the experiment, with this situation reversing during the first quarter of the experiment. Thereafter, average income of experimental families remains below that of control families, and the gap widens over the length of the experiment.

This suggestion of a negative experimental response is confirmed by regression analysis. The regression equations, with experimental status depicted by the (0,1) binary variable, are not presented because of constraints on space, but may be found in the RIME final report. Family income response to the experiment was found to be negative, and significant at the .01 level. Experimental families earn $207 less, on the average, than controls, representing a relative decline in family income of 14.6% of the control group's mean ($1,423 per quarter). North Carolina white families also displayed a negative experimental response, but of a smaller magnitude

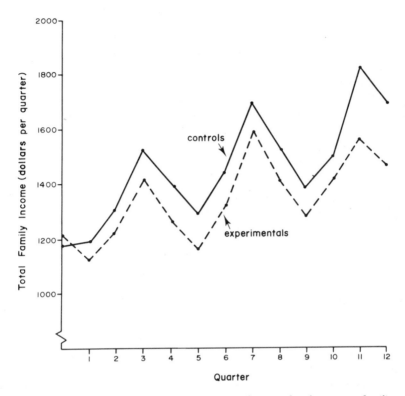

Fig. 6.1. *Average family total income, by quarter, for control and treatment families.*

—$88, or 6.4%, significant only at the .40 level. Iowa families had the largest experimental response in family income—$331, or 18.0% of the control mean of $1841, significant at the .01 level.

Coefficients and significance levels for all of the control variables are also reported. The coefficient for preexperimental (1969) total family income was highly significant in all three equations, and ranged from .60 for the Iowa subsample to .65 for North Carolina whites to .81 for North Carolina blacks. When total experimental response is decomposed into response to tax rate and guarantee, the estimated responses appear to vary more than is implied by the total experimental effect regression coefficients. However, it is not indicated which of the responses to the tax rate–guarantee combinations are significant (if any), and the corresponding table is not discussed here.

Family Wage Income and Hours

Since over 97% of family earned income comprised wages, the experimental responses to earned income and wage income are very similar. Family wage income response to the experiment was $205 for North Carolina blacks and $284 for Iowans. Both are statistically significant at the .01 level. These represent "disincentives" of 15 and 17%, respectively, of the appropriate control group means, and compares with 15 and 18% responses for family total income. North Carolina whites show a negative wage income response of $69, but it does not approach statistical significance.

Family wage income over the duration of the experiment for both controls and experimentals averaged $2875 per year for North Carolina blacks, $2692 per year for North Carolina whites, and $2791 per year for Iowa families. The proportion of family hours contributed by wives and dependents is larger than their contribution to family income, a consequence of receiving lower wage rates. Table 6.12 shows that wives' and dependents' hours make up about a third of total family hours among North Carolina blacks, a fourth among North Carolina whites, and a seventh among Iowans.

Interestingly, the experimental response of hours worked for wages is somewhat different from that of wage income. The basic regression equations for the three subsamples with experimental status represented by a simple binary variable are similar. Table 6.13 reproduces the detailed results for North Carolina white wage earners as an illustration. The overall response to the experiment of hours worked by North Carolina black families was −$69 per quarter, or 9% of the control group mean. This is considerably less than the negative 15% response of wage income.

Conversely, the hours response of North Carolina whites (Table 6.13) is larger than the wage income response, −126 hours per quarter, or 17%, compared to a negative and statistically insignificant response of 5% in wage income. The Iowa hours response is small and not statistically significant,

Table 6.12
Percentage of Family Wage Hours

	NC-B	NC-W	Iowa
Husbands	64	74	86
Wives	26	16	8
Dependents	10	10	6

Table 6.13

Family Hours Equation for North Carolina
White Wage Earners

Independent variables	Coefficient	t-Statistic	Significance level
Experimental dummy	−126.30	2.43	.02
Hours worked/pre exp	0.52	3.48	.01
No. of children age 0−1	−90.72	1.62	.11
No. of children age 1−5	−38.51	1.35	.18
No. of children age 6−17	−10.18	0.56	.58
No. of children age 18−20	81.88	2.35	.02
Husb age	−82.34	0.97	.34
Husb age sq	1.02	1.09	.28
Husb education	−302.43	1.19	.24
Husb education sq	−0.30	0.07	.95
Husb age*education	16.01	1.57	.12
Husb age sq*educ	−0.19	1.63	.11
Wife age	1.71	0.06	.96
Wife age sq	−0.09	0.33	.75
Wife education	−3.12	0.04	.97
Wife education sq	0.71	0.22	.83
Wife age*education	−0.11	0.10	.92
Husb quick test	11.56	0.49	.63
Husb quick test sq	−0.21	0.55	.59
Husb health prevents work	−302.90	4.59	.01
Wife health prevents work	−7.86	0.18	.87
Husb is farm worker	42.82	0.81	.42
Husb has farm income	−176.29	2.36	.02
Distance from large town	0.83	0.37	.71
County unemployment rate	−32.88	0.90	.37
If moves out of county	119.00	1.74	.09
Others income ÷ # others[a]	7.40	1.51	.14
Unearned income[a]	2.41	0.47	.64
Farm income[a]	24.51	1.33	.19
Husb normal wage rate	8.53	0.06	.96
Husb normal wage rate sq	−20.37	0.74	.47
Wife normal wage rate	−421.69	1.34	.18
Wife normal wage rate sq	197.42	1.52	.13
Quarter	−6.32	0.57	.57
Quarter sq	0.38	0.45	.66
Winter	−74.65	2.70	.01
Spring	−8.87	0.43	.67
Summer	100.02	3.42	.01
Constant	2187.07	1.13	.26

Note: Mean Dep. Var. = 673, S.E. = 300, $N = 749$, $F = 5.43$, $\bar{R}^2 = .3143$, Rho = .3373.

[a] Hundreds of dollars.

− 36 hours per quarter, or 5% of the control group mean. This is considerably smaller than the − 17% response of wage income.

Although these differences in response to wage hours and wage income may be surprising, they are not necessarily inconsistent. Differences can occur for a variety of reasons. A negative response in hours worked by wives or dependents will have less of an impact on family wage income than an equal response in hours worked by husbands, because wives and dependents have lower wage rates than husbands. Similarly, a reduction in hours worked by low-wage husbands will have less impact on family wage income than a similar reduction in hours worked by high-wage husbands. A response difference in hours and income can also be due to an experimental response in wage rates — a 10% negative response in hours (by everyone in the family) coupled with a 10% negative response in wage rates (for everyone) results in a 19% negative response in wage income. The close relationship between wage income and number of hours worked per week indicates that both variables should have also been analyzed simultaneously, in one of a number of different models available.

The signs of the coefficients for the tax rate and guarantee level are the same as those for wage income. The negative experimental response of hours worked increased as the tax rate increased for both North Carolina subsamples and decreased as the tax rate increased for the Iowa subsample. Unlike the wage income equations, however, none of the coefficients is statistically significant at better than the .14 level. The guarantee influenced experimental response of hours positively for North Carolina blacks and negatively for the other two groups, the same as for wage income, but the guarantee coefficient for North Carolina blacks is significant at the .05 level. None of the other guarantee coefficients approaches statistical significance. Experimental response of wage hours is derived for each plan and shown in Table 6.14. Because the tax rate and guarantee coefficients are smaller than those for the previous income measures, response is not shown to vary as much by plan.

Income and Work Response of Husbands

The sample of husbands consists of males aged 19 to 62 who were not continuously disabled or ill during the experiment and whose major source of earned income, if any, was wages. The mean age was 42 years; education levels ranged from 1 to 15 years, and the average earned income was $4312.00 per year during the experiment, with wage income representing 98% of earned income in North Carolina and 94% in Iowa. A total of 96% of all husbands worked for wages in any quarter, with 75% working for wages

Table 6.14
*Estimated Response of Family Wage Hours,
by Subsample, by Plan*

Treatment plan	Experimental response					
	N.C. black		N.C. white		Iowa	
	$[a]	%[b]	$	%	$	%
T50/G50	−193	−26	−101	−14	−24	−3
T30/G75	−42	−6	−58	−8	−51	−7
T50/G75	−105	−14	−145	−20	−30	−4
T70/G75	−167	−22	−232	−32	−10	−1
T50/G100	−60	−2	−189	−26	−36	−5

[a] Dollars per quarter.
[b] Percentage of adjusted control group mean, averaged across all plans.

the entire 13 weeks of the quarter.[18] In North Carolina, 5% of black husbands were unemployed the entire 13 weeks of a typical quarter, while 72% worked the entire 13 weeks. In contrast, only 3% of Iowa husbands did not work during a typical quarter, and 85% worked the entire quarter. North Carolina white husbands fell approximately midway between these two groups, suggesting a difference in labor markets between the two regions as well as a small racial difference in North Carolina.

These racial and regional differences are magnified by the data on hours worked per week. Iowa husbands averaged 48 hours per week compared to 41 and 38 hours per week for North Carolina whites and blacks, respectively. The average hourly wage rate for those working was $2.08 per hour, which also masks a sizable regional difference: $2.34 per hour in Iowa and $2.07 and $1.95 per hour for whites and blacks, respectively, in North Carolina.

The distribution of occupations also differs by region. Nearly 40% of Iowa wage earners were in the craftsman-kindred category, a fourth of these being auto mechanics. The rest were distributed among carpentry, plumbing, painting, radio and TV repair, and machine operation. On the other hand, only 20% of the North Carolina sample were in the craftsman-kindred category, with almost half being carpenters and auto mechanics. While a fourth of the Iowa husbands was classified as operatives, with half of these being truck drivers, 40% of North Carolina husbands were operatives, a fourth being truck drivers.

Approximately 10% of the North Carolina sample and virtually none of the Iowa sample were service workers—janitors, barbers, hospital attendants, and kitchen workers.   Twenty-one percent of Iowa men were farm-hands, whereas only 6% of North Carolina wage earners were in this occupational grouping.   Laborers represented nearly 10% of Iowa husbands and about 20% of North Carolina husbands.   The main bulk of the sample was therefore in unskilled or semiskilled occupations.

Husbands' Total Earned Income and Wages

As expected, husbands' incomes showed marked seasonality, as is evident from Figure 6.2.   Although controls initially had a lower mean income ($56 per quarter), earnings of experimental husbands rose relatively less during the experiment, so that by the end of the twelfth quarter there is an apparent gap between their mean earned incomes, indicating a possibly significant

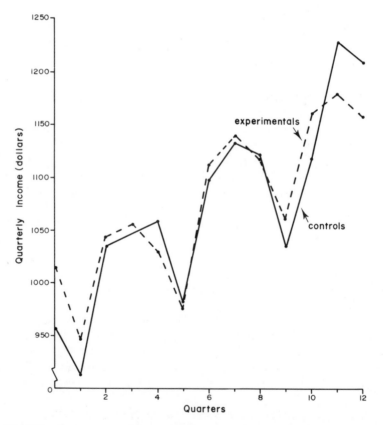

Fig. 6.2.   *Husband's quarterly earned income, for control and treatment families.*

treatment effect. To determine whether the difference is statistically significant, analyses of covariance type regressions are computed for the three husband subsamples—North Carolina black wage earners, North Carolina white wage earners, and Iowa white wage earners. The results for Iowa wage earners are exhibited in Table 6.15, where it is seen that the experimental treatment–control difference is significant. The experimental dummy variable has a coefficient of −199.53, indicating a mean decrease, for treatments (all plans), of $199.53 per quarter, or 13% per quarter with

Table 6.15
Husband's Earned Income Equation for Iowa Wage Earners

Independent variables	Coefficient	t-Statistic	Significance level
Experimental dummy	−199.53	2.44	.02
Earned income/pre	0.74	6.76	.01
Age	−23.33	0.31	.76
Age sq	0.16	0.32	.75
Education	−8.83	0.02	.99
Ed > 8	116.54	0.25	.80
Ed > 11	49.45	0.45	.65
Education*Age	2.13	0.30	.77
Ed > 8*Age	−4.14	0.50	.62
Quick test	−17.90	0.17	.87
Quick test sq	0.23	0.16	.88
# Dep	31.61	1.49	.14
Health prevents work	−686.30	3.97	.01
In job training	−1517.74	7.97	.01
Distance from large town	−12.98	5.34	.01
Is farm worker	−41.52	0.68	.50
Has farm income	−89.74	0.92	.36
Wife income[a]	−16.72	1.58	.12
Unearned income[a]	−0.90	0.15	.89
Dep income[a]	−17.17	2.16	.04
Others income ÷ no. of others[a]	−4.41	0.29	.78
Quarter	25.51	1.44	.15
Quarter sq	0.03	0.03	.98
Winter	−31.29	1.25	.22
Spring	11.06	0.46	.65
Summer	−1.80	0.07	.95
Constant	954.54	0.23	.82

Note: Mean Dep. Var. = 1411, S.E. = 487, N = 753, F = 12.29, $\bar{R}^2$ = .4868, Rho = .3783.

[a] Hundreds of Dollars

respect to the control group mean.   As in the New Jersey experiment, black husbands failed to indicate any drop in labor supply, measured by total earned income, as a result of a guaranteed annual income.

When the experimental response is broken down by tax rate and guarantee, the response is negative and statistically significant at .11 level for North Carolina blacks and at the .02 level or less for the North Carolina whites and Iowa whites, as indicated by Table 6.16.   Only the tax rate has a significant impact on total earnings—negative for North Carolina (both blacks and whites) but positive for Iowa.   The guarantee level does not appear significant for all three subsamples.   The total experimental effects for North Carolina are consistent with the tax rate response, both being negative, indicating that total response is due mainly to the tax rate; the response for Iowa is inconsistent, since total response is negative, although the Iowa response to the tax rate is positive!   It appears, therefore, that the only significant total experimental effect is observed for the Iowa wage earners, a decrease of 13% per quarter, with respect to control means.[19]

Since wages make up the bulk of earned income for wage earners (98% in North Carolina and 94% in Iowa), the experimental response of the two is very similar, and for this reason detailed regression results are not given here.   Wage income response, together with the total earned income response, is summarized in Table 6.17.   Clearly, both sets of results agree

Table 6.16
Experimental Response of Wage Earners by
Tax Rate and Guarantee (Deviations from Mean)

			Significance level	
North Carolina Blacks				
Experimental dummy	−75.4	1.49	.14	
Tax deviation	−7.32	2.21	.03	.11
Guarantee deviation	−0.41	0.15	.89	
North Carolina Whites				
Experimental dummy	−79.2	1.05	.30	
Tax deviation	−17.76	4.01	.01	.01
Guarantee deviation	−1.84	0.50	.62	
Iowa Whites				
Experimental dummy	−125.2	1.36	.18	
Tax deviation	10.66	1.96	.05	.02
Guarantee deviation	−2.37	0.55	.59	

Table 6.17
Total Experimental Response to Payments

	Wage Income			Total Earned Income[b]	
	North Carolina		Iowa	North Carolina		Iowa
Blacks	Whites	(Whites)	Blacks	Whites	(Whites)
−$63.	+$32.	−$150.00	−$44.82	+$42.31	−$199.53
(−7%)[a]	(+3%)	(−11%)	(−5%)	(+4%)	(−13%)
Significant at .15 level	Not significant	Significant at .04 level	Not significant	Not significant	Significant at .02 level

[a] Compared to the control group mean.
[b] Same as in Tables 6.1–6.3.

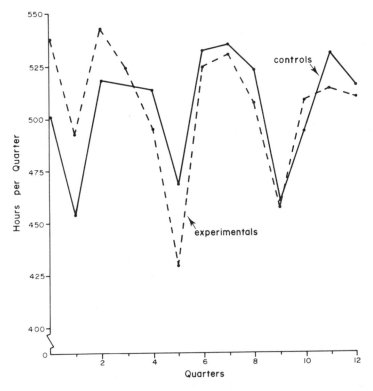

Fig. 6.3. *Husbands' hours worked for wages for control and treatment families.*

closely and may be used as a handy reference for the total earned income – wage income responses.

Husbands' Wage Hours

Since the principal labor supply response is in terms of the number of hours worked, it is important to consider this response variable and compare it to the earned income–wage income variables. Again since most of wage earners' labor time was spent in earning wage income, it is sufficient to consider the husband's wage hours only.[20] During the three years of the experiment, the control and experimental groups indicated a differential trend in the number of hours worked, suggesting a possible disincentive effect on the part of the experimental group (see Figure 6.3). Husbands worked an average of 39 hours per week for wages during the three years of

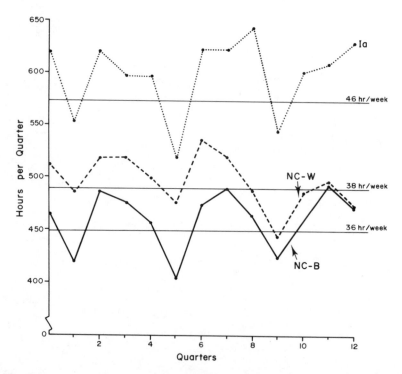

Fig. 6.4. *Husband's hours worked for wages, for subsample, for control and treatment families.*

the experiment, although there was some difference among the three sub-samples (see Figure 6.4).

An analysis of covariance indicates that only black husbands (in North Carolina) reduced their number of hours worked to any significant degree, some 38 hours per quarter (8% of the control mean) (Table 6.18). North

Table 6.18
Husband's Hours Worked Equation for North Carolina Black Wage Earners

Independent variables	Coefficient	t-Statistic	Significance level
Experimental dummy	−38.35	1.97	.05
Hours worked/pre	0.52	8.25	.01
Age	−12.53	1.12	.27
Age sq	0.21	2.14	.04
Education	53.79	1.52	.13
Ed > 8	−134.73	2.44	.02
Ed > 11	16.28	0.38	.71
Education*age	−1.13	1.62	.11
Ed > 8*age	3.11	2.60	.01
Quick test	7.75	0.89	.38
Quick test sq	−0.12	0.76	.45
# Dep	2.49	0.64	.53
Health prevents	−258.83	10.64	.01
In-job training	13.46	0.11	.92
Distance from large town	−2.63	2.58	.01
Is farm worker	−30.28	1.82	.07
Has farm income	31.26	1.17	.25
Farm & business income[a]	−11.42	1.34	.18
Wife income[a]	1.40	0.94	.35
Unearned income[a]	−2.60	0.52	.61
Dep income[a]	0.92	0.70	.49
Others income ÷ no. of others[a]	0.24	0.11	.91
Quarter	−2.21	0.58	.57
Quarter sq	0.27	0.95	.35
Winter	−41.62	7.65	.01
Spring	12.40	2.37	.02
Summer	24.33	4.40	.01
Husb normal wage rate	−72.88	1.18	.24
Husb normal wage rate sq	15.14	1.24	.22
Constant	342.26	0.93	.36

Note: Mean Dep. Var. = 460, S.E. = 154, $N = 1454$, $F = 11.08$, $\bar{R}^2 = .3423$, Rho = .4084.

[a] Hundreds of dollars.

Carolina whites increased their work response by 27 hours per quarter (6% of the control mean), whereas Iowa husbands reduced their number of hours worked by 7 hours per quarter (1% of control means). The reduction on the part of the whites is not statistically significant.

Response to the tax rate and guarantee level is also tested, but only North Carolina whites appear to respond to the tax or guarantee level, with hours worked decreasing as either tax or guarantee increase.

NOTES

1. This chapter is more complete than chapters dealing with the other experiments. The RIME findings are relatively inaccessible because they were not released through commercial publication. For this reason we either describe the RIME results fully or reproduce their findings.

2. Even had the initial sample allocation been random, a social experiment producing both cross-sectional and longitudinal (time-series) data will most certainly yield biased (nonrepresentative) data because of attrition of the sample over time. For this reason covariates or control variables must always be used to correct (as much as possible) for the unbalanced nature of the final data.

3. It is not known how many entries in data base ORIG were altered in this way.

4. Tenants-farmers and landowners-farmers are both considered as "farm operators."

5. Tobacco growing is very labor intensive; growing corn has become highly mechanized.

6. It is not clear why the year rather than the three-month interval was chosen as the unit time period.

7. The original text is unclear. There appears to be a discrepancy or ambiguity between the text and the labeling of the dependent variables in the table of the report (Primus, 1976b, p. 35). The preceding definitions are based on our understanding of the original document.

8. Probably farm operator = male head.

9. Which, in fact, are not so much "basic" variables as simply control variables, or in the parlance of the analysis of covariance, the "covariates."

10. Model II is already curvilinear, that is, the term $X_1^2 X_0 = \text{HR69}^2\text{C/E}$ is added in order to produce a curvilinear (quadratic) regression plane. Actually, model I is quadratic in the interaction term $X_1 X_{10} = \text{HR69C/E}$ while model III is cubic in the term $X_1^2 X_{10} = \text{HR69}^2\text{C/E}$, implying the existence of two inflection points in the response surface, an unlikely situation here. Cubic interaction terms are difficult to interpret and should generally not be used unless there is evidence of their significance.

11. Primus (1976b) further states that "this coefficient is essentially determined by only five observations, thus making it almost impossible to make any conclusions about plan effects."

12. There is, however, a dramatic change in the magnitude and signs of the coefficients of C/E when interactions are added.

13. "Editing" is itself an estimation activity and is not assumption free.

14. For a more complete discussion of the problem of missing data adjustment techniques see Anderson, Basilevsky, and Hum (1983).

15. This is largely due to the fact that both sites (Iowa and North Carolina) are estimated separately, and data from quarterly periodics are aggregated into annual series.

16. It is not clear what happened to dependents less than 18 years of age who were also married.

17. The sample was originally drawn randomly from a predesignated geographic area, and the treatments control assignment was also random.

18. Although not specified in the report, we assume that these figures represent percentages of husbands who worked *only* for wages.

19. The total experimental effect for the entire wage earners' sample appears to be unknown, since a regression sum for all three subsamples combined does not seem to be available.

20. In any case results for nonwage hours are not reported by Bawden.

7 The Seattle–Denver Income
Maintenance Experiment (SIME–DIME)

I. INTRODUCTION

The SIME–DIME experimental sample consists of treatment families subdivided into 11 plans or "treatment" and "control" families (see Table 7.1). In broad outlines the structure of the experiment conforms to the usual situation encountered in statistical experimental design. For details concerning the SIME–DIME experiment the reader is referred to Keeley et al. (1976, 1977a, b, c, 1978), Hurd, M. (1976), and Robins and West (1978). The first analysis of the SIME–DIME data received limited circulation in the form of a Research Memorandum by Keeley *et al.* (1976). This research subsequently appeared in the professional journal literature to a much larger readership (Keeley *et al.* 1978). We consider, in the main, both writings together.

The definition of variables and estimation methodology employed by the SIME–DIME authors was heavily influenced by the needs and objectives of neoclassical theories of labor–leisure choice and "human capital" models, to wit, the estimation of wage rate and income elasticities (effects). Accordingly, regression analysis and allied econometric techniques were used instead of the statistical experimental approaches such as analysis of var-

Table 7.1
*Programs Tested in the Seattle and Denver
Income Maintenance Program, 1971 Dollars[a]*

S	t	r	B_G	B
$3,800.	.50	0.0	$ 7,600.	$10,250.
3,800.	.70	0.0	5,429.	6,350.
3,800.	.70	.025	7,367.	10,850.
3,800.	.80	.025	5,802.	7,800.
4,800.	.50	0.0	9,600.	13,150.
4,800.	.70	0.0	6,867.	8,520.
4,800.	.70	.025	12,000.	19,700.
4,800.	.80	.025	8,000.	11,510.
5,600.	.50	0.0	11,200.	15,700.
5,600.	.70	0.0	8,000.	9,780.
5,600.	.80	.025	10,360.	16,230.

[a] S = NIT annual support level, t = initial NIT tax rate, r = rate of decline of the average NIT tax rate per thousand dollars of income, B_G = grant breakeven level, B = tax breakeven level.
Source: Robins and West (1978).

iance and covariance. Consequently, the experimental nature of the data was virtually ignored and the control (no payments) group was included mainly to increase sample size for the econometric regression estimates. Of course, regression analysis bears a close resemblance to analysis of covariance in the experimental literature. Mathematically speaking, both models are identical, since both are particular instances of the general linear model. As noted in Chapter 4, although both rely on a mixture of continuous (ratio-scale) and discrete "dummy" (nominal) variables, the interpretive roles of the two sets of variates are not the same. Whereas continuous ratio scales act as "covariates" (control variables) in the analysis of covariance—the main interest being to estimate treatment effects, contrasts, and perhaps interactions—the econometric regression equation habitually used for nonexperimental data generally focuses on the continuous variates and treats the dummy variables as controls. Since the objectives of the two procedures are not the same, a discrepancy can arise between the two approaches in terms of the type and number of variables used, the method of estimation, and ultimately, interpretation.

II. THE KEELEY-ROBINS-
SPIEGELMAN-WEST MODEL AND
THE RESULTS

The principal objective of the SIME–DIME researchers (Keeley et al. 1976, 1977a, b, c, 1978) was not to estimate the main effects (and/or interaction terms) of guaranteed income treatments. Nor was it to verify whether significant differences exist between treatments (the payments sample) and controls (nonpayments families). Rather, it was to determine, for the entire sample, whether certain key economic variables such as wage rates and income levels are significant determinants (and therefore efficient predictors) of labor supply. This is the major difference between the analysis of the New Jersey experiment and that of SIME–DIME (and Gary). In fact, it is the key to any further understanding and evaluation of either the methodology or the results of the NIT experiments.

The labor supply model of SIME–DIME (Keeley *et al.*, 1976; 1978) is specified by the linear equation[1]

$$H_e = b_0 + b_1 H_p + b_2 A + b_3 C + b_4 M + b_5 \Delta Y_d(H_p) + b_6 \Delta w$$

$$+ b_7 \text{ (FABOVE)} + b_8 \text{ (BREAK)} + b_9 \text{ (EARNABV)}$$

$$+ b_{10} \text{ (YRS3)} + b_{11} \text{ (DECLINE)} + \epsilon \qquad (7.1)$$

where

H_e is the experimental (i.e., final) number of hours worked per week,
H_p is the preexperimental (i.e., initial) number of hours worked per week,
$\Delta Y_d(H_p)$ is the $Y_{de}(H_p) - Y_{dp}(H_p)$: the change (difference) between experimental (final) disposable income $Y_{de}(H_p)$ and preexperimental
(initial) disposable income $Y_{dp}(H_p)$, both evaluated at preexperimental hours worked H_p;
Δw is the $W(t_p - t_e)$, the change in the net wage rate, where
W is the gross wage rate, t_p the preexperimental tax rate, and t_e the
experimental (final) tax rate.

For a full account of the economic theory underlying the model and a description of the variables, see Keeley *et al.* (1976, 1977a, b). A brief outline of the approach was described in Chapter 4. The preceding variables are the ones of major interest, particularly $\Delta Y_d (H_p)$ and Δw, whose coefficients b_5 and b_6, known as income and substitution effects, respectively, are to be used as predictors of labor supply. As such, $\Delta Y_d(H_p)$ and Δw are viewed as exogenous variables that can be manipulated by welfare agencies, presumably through the main parameters of the guaranteed income. The variables M, A, and C are dummy variables that control for influences resulting from the manpower structure, the assignment mechanism, and other control variables, respectively. The dummy variables FABOVE, BREAK, EARNABV, YRS3, and DECLINE reflect the design or structural features of the experiment and are also treated as control variables. The principal interest and focus, therefore, is on the behavioral characteristics of the sample as described by changes in the wage rates and disposable incomes rather than on experimental parameters.

Before proceeding to estimate Eq. (7.1) Keeley et al. (1976) note two difficulties associated with using the observed wage rate W when defining Δw. These are:

1. Wage rates cannot be observed (do not exist in practice) for unemployed members of the labor force or for nonmembers of the labor force (the nonworkers), and
2. The variable W can itself be further decomposed as

$$W = \mu + \delta \tag{7.2}$$

where μ represents the vector of expected ("normal") wage rates assumed to hold "in the long run" and determined by exogenous explanatory variables X, so that $\mu = f(X)$. The residual term δ reflects short-term random fluctuations, individual circumstances, errors in measurement, and other random influences that act independently of X and that cannot be explained by consistent theory.

Since the term μ rather than W is of interest, Keeley *et al.* (1976) first estimate μ by a linear ordinary least squares regression line for those individuals possessing an observed wage rate. The independent variables used are race (X_1), years of schooling (X_2), experience (X_3), $X_3^2/100$, and a constant term, α_0, yielding the estimated normal wage equation

$$\hat{W}_p = \hat{\alpha}_0 + \hat{\alpha}_1 X_1 + \hat{\alpha}_2 X_2 + \hat{\alpha}_3 X_3 + \hat{\alpha}_4 (X_3^2/100) \tag{7.3}$$

where W_p is the preexperimental wage rate. The least squares results for Eq. (7.3) are presented in Table 7.2 for three subsamples—female family heads, husbands, and wives. Since explanatory variables X are available for both workers and nonworkers, the authors assume that both sets of individuals possess the same least squares coefficients, and then compute (predict) wage rates for the nonworking portion of the sample. The resultant vector $\hat{W}$ of estimated wage rates for both workers and nonworkers is then used to calculate the net wage change $\Delta \hat{W}$ as the product

$$\Delta \hat{W} = \hat{W}(t_p - t_e)$$

as defined in Eq. (7.2). We consider the methodology and least squares results below when we evaluate the main results.

Equation (7.1) is estimated by the nonlinear Tobit procedure (Tobin,

Table 7.2

Wage Equation Estimates[a] (Dependent Variable = Preexperimental Wage Rate)

Independent variable	Female heads	Husbands	Wives
1 = black	.010	−.071	.080
	(.045)	(.051)	(.049)
Years of schooling	.102	.033	.110
	(.013)	(.012)	(.014)
Experience[b]	.045	.061	.036
	(.009)	(.008)	(.008)
Experience 2/100	−.098	−.106	−.073
	(.021)	(.018)	(.020)
Constant term	.816	2.340	.590
	(.183)	(.172)	(.192)
R^2	.112	.048	.116
Standard error of estimate	.613	.950	.598
Sample size	762	1,489	613
Mean of dependent variable	$2.42/hour	$3.30/hour	$2.21/hour

[a] Standard errors are in parentheses.
[b] Defined as (age − years of schooling − 5).
Source: Keeley *et al.* (1976).

1958). Because values of the dependent variable H_e are always nonnegative, the assumption of normality of H_e (and the residual term ϵ) is replaced by the alternative assumption of truncated normality.[2] Since there are also nonnormal truncated distributions (either skewed or symmetric), the Tobit procedure is in fact restricted by the normality assumption and consequently is not as general as it appears. Of course, normality must usually be assumed in practice in least squares regression in order to test significance of the various statistics.

The Keeley *et al.* (1976, 1977a, b, 1978) estimation methodology, as well as the work of Hurd (1976) and Robins and West (1978) concerns itself almost exclusively with estimating the income effect b_5 and the substitution effect b_6 of Eq. (7.1). (See Table 7.3.) It therefore resembles classical econometric work, the main objective of which is usually to verify certain hypotheses of behavior implied by a prior economic theory. In this respect the SIME–DIME analysis largely fulfills its objective, since it is found that both estimates b_5 and b_6 are significantly different from zero and both carry negative signs. This is in accordance with the neoclassical economic theory of "rational man" as well as intuitive "common sense." The objective of

Table 7.3
Results for Experimental Variables (Tobit Estimates)

Treatment variable	Symbol	Female heads		Husbands		Wives	
		6th Quarter	8th Quarter	6th Quarter	8th Quarter	6th Quarter	8th Quarter
Below true breakeven level							
Change in disposable income ($1000s)	$Y_d(H_p) - Y_{dp}(H_p)$	−2.61[b] (1.13)	−1.30 (1.10)	−1.74[b] (.68)	−1.94[c] (.75)	−2.69[a] (1.51)	−2.11 (1.40)
Change in net wage ($/hour)	$-W(t_e - t_p)$	4.97[b] (2.17)	5.43[b] (2.12)	1.10 (1.05)	3.04[c] (1.15)	7.86[b] (3.45)	7.36[b] (3.21)
Above true breakeven level							
1 if above true breakeven	(FABOVE)	−2.74 (7.81)	−.65 (7.86)	−7.00[a] (4.07)	−5.61 (4.52)	−17.48[b] (8.34)	−15.42[a] (7.91)
Earnings at true breakeven ($1000s)	(BREAK)	.93 (1.50)	1.03 (1.47)	.51 (.44)	.37 (.48)	.55 (.88)	.57 (.83)
Earnings above true breakeven ($1000s)	(EARNABV)	−.47 (1.75)	−.28 (1.79)	.99 (.67)	.40 (.74)	1.83 (1.35)	1.72 (1.32)
Other treatment variables							
1 if on three-year financial program	(YRS3)	1.52 (2.32)	−1.50 (2.29)	1.63 (1.34)	5.39[c] (1.46)	3.20 (2.89)	1.77 (2.71)
1 if on declining tax program	(DECLINE)	2.93 (2.19)	1.67 (2.17)	1.90 (1.32)	−2.68[a] (1.43)	1.39 (2.80)	.71 (2.63)
Chi-square test for treatment effects		23.49[c]	26.06[c]	22.73[c]	36.79[c]	18.90[c]	18.97[c]
Standard error of estimate		27.52 (.83)	27.05 (.83)	20.09 (.41)	21.18 (.44)	35.51 (1.16)	33.71 (1.07)
Mean of dependent variable (hours of work per week)		19.05	18.85	33.32	32.89	12.67	13.49
Sample size		1399	1355	1738	1645	1780	1714
Experimentals — below breakeven		764	744	731	691	749	724
Experimentals — above breakeven		87	85	194	180	192	185
Controls		548	526	813	774	839	805

[a] Indicates significant at .10 level.
[b] Indicates significant at .05 level.
[c] Indicates significant at .01 level.
Source: Keeley *et al.* (1976)

the Keeley *et al.* analyses, however, was not limited to this area alone, but was also concerned with the more pragmatic problem of predicting labor supply response(s) with respect to variation in total disposable income and wage rates, which themselves depend on parameters (the guarantee levels and tax rates) of an income maintenance program.

Let S_e, S_p and t_e, t_p be the support levels and tax rates before and after the

Table 7.4

Predicted Labor Supply Responses for ΔS = $2000, Δt = .3 (Asymptotic Standard Errors in Parentheses)

Annual family earnings (1971 dollars)	Female heads				Husbands				Wives			
	ΔH	$E(H\|z_p)$	ΔP_w	P_w	ΔH	$E(H\|z_p)$	ΔP_w	P_w	ΔH	$E(H\|z_p)$	ΔP_w	P_w
0–$1,000	−2.39 (.80)	9.32	−.08	.42	−4.34 (.94)	17.73	−.10	.70	−2.26 (.74)	7.00	−.08	.30
$1000–$3000	−3.64 (1.08)	20.00	−.07	.67	−4.44 (.91)	24.72	−.07	.82	−2.66 (.79)	10.34	−.08	.39
$3000–$5000	−3.71 (1.08)	27.39	−.05	.79	−3.80 (.87)	28.80	−.04	.88	−2.69 (.81)	13.24	−.07	.46
$5000–$7000	−3.68 (1.24)	32.82	−.04	.86	−3.02 (.98)	33.77	−.02	.93	−2.25 (.87)	13.91	−.05	.47
$7000–$9000	−3.38 (1.59)	37.49	−.03	.91	−2.15 (1.22)	36.64	−.01	.95	−1.63 (.97)	12.43	−.04	.44

Note: Predictions are based on eighth-quarter results for the five-year program, assuming that the family is below the true breakeven level. $\Delta H = E(H|Z_e) - E(H|Z_p)$ = change in expected hours per week, $E(H/Z_p)$ = expected hours per week in the absence of income maintenance, $\Delta P_w = F(Z_e/\sigma) - F(Z_p/\sigma)$ = change in the probability of working because of income maintenance, $P_w = F(Z_p/\sigma)$ = probability of working in the absence of income maintenance.

Source: Keeley *et al.* (1976)

program, respectively. Then

$$\Delta Y_d(H_p) = Y_{de}(H_p) - Y_{dp}(H_p) = (S_e - S_p) - (t_e - t_p)E_p. \qquad (7.4)$$

where E_p are initial family earnings. Likewise, we have

$$\hat{W}(t_e - t_p) = \hat{W}(\Delta t)$$

where $\hat{W}$ denotes the normal wage rate of Eq. (7.3). The behavioral respone portion of the labor supply model Eq. (7.1) below the true breakeven is:

$$(\Delta s - \Delta t \, E_p)b_5 - (\hat{W} \, \Delta t)b_6 = Tb \qquad (7.5)$$

where T is a row vector of experimental treatment variables and b is a column vector of treatment coefficients. The coefficients b_5 and b_6 are the income and substitution (wage) effects, respectively, as estimated by Eq. (7.1). Because of characteristics of the Tobit model, Tb yields labor supply response only when $H_e > 0$. Also, using the Tobit conditional expectation function the expected response is given by the expected values.

$$\Delta H = E(H|Z_e) - E(H|Z_p)$$
$$= Z_e F\left(\frac{Z_e}{\sigma}\right) + \sigma f\left(\frac{Z_e}{\sigma}\right) - Z_p F\left(\frac{Z_p}{\sigma}\right) - \sigma f\left(\frac{Z_p}{\sigma}\right) \qquad (7.6)$$

where
$Z_e = Xa + Tb$,
$Z_p = Xa$,
F is the normal distribution function,
f is the normal density function,
X is a row vector of nonexperimental variables, and
a is a column vector of coefficients of nonexperimental variables.
The predicted responses are presented in Table 7.4. They are obtained by substituting the estimated coefficients from the labor supply equation into Eq. (7.6). For all three categories of families we see that ΔH tends to be significantly negative, indicating significant (and large) drops in labor supply resulting from the NIT parameters.

III. APPRAISAL OF THE RESULTS

Besides playing an economic role, disposable income and wage rate estimates are related to experimental parameters and therefore used by Keeley *et al.* (1976, 1978) to predict ΔH, the expected labor supply response. In their summary of the main results Keeley *et al.* (1976) conclude,

"The empirical results indicate that both the disposable income and net wage changes induce husbands, wives, and female heads of families to reduce their labor supply. These results are statistically significant and consistent with economic theory, and are relatively large, indicating that behavior is strongly influenced by changes in incentives. The results can be used to predict the effects of alternative hypothetical income maintenance programs."

The SIME–DIME experiment therefore not only differs from that of New Jersey and the other experiments in terms of analytical methodology and statistical econometric estimation models, but also in terms of empirical findings and substantive conclusions concerning the work behavior of the "working poor" when a guaranteed annual income regime is imposed. In what follows we comment on the estimation techniques used by SIME–DIME and attempt to assess their validity. In keeping with statistical and econometric tradition we evaluate with respect to their efficiency and (possible) bias or inconsistency. The Keeley *et al.* report pays more attention to consistency and bias. Efficiency is treated as a secondary problem, perhaps because both of the variables of interest $[\Delta W$ and $\Delta Y_d\,(H_p)]$ exhibit significant coefficients. Still, inefficient estimates cannot detect weak influences on the dependent variable H_e; they will also reduce the accuracy of prediction, all else remaining constant.

Normal Wage Rates and the Substitution Effect

In the previous section it was seen that Keeley *et al.* (1976, 1978) use calculated wage rates of Eq. (7.3) rather than observed wage rates to define net wage rate changes. There are several difficulties in accepting the validity of this procedure.

First, it is not clear that the computed preexperimental wage rate $\hat{W}_p$ reflects the actual preexperimental wage rate W_p. As defined in Eq. (7.3), $\hat{W}_p$ is a function of years of schooling, experience,[3] and a racial dummy variable. It is difficult to accept that wage rates are determined solely or primarily by these variables. The formulation very likely suffers from omitted variables, which, as is well known, will bias the regression results if the omitted variables are correlated with those explanatory variables included, namely, "years of school," "experience" and the black–white dummy. The low values of the R^2 statistics indicate that this is probably the case (see Table 7.2). Since $\hat{W}_p$ merely reflects variation in "years of schooling," "experience," and "race," and since $\hat{W}_p$ is virtually orthogonal to W_p, it would appear difficult to interpret b_6 as the actual substitution effect. Even if such an interpretation were placed on b_6, it would still be biased and inconsistent because of the omitted explanatory variables. In other words, the change in H_e due to the observed change ΔW will not be very similar to the change in H_e due to the predicted change $\Delta \hat{W}$. And because of the low R^2 values, $\Delta \hat{W}$ will possess large standard errors; prediction will be very inefficient.

Another source of inconsistency arises from misclassification, even in the event that the wage equation, Eq. (7.3), is not misspecified. Hurd (1976) shows that using imputed wages for the nonworkers generally results in inconsistent labor supply estimates because of misclassification when defining class intervals for the cumulative normal distribution. He proposes an alternative maximum-likelihood procedure that apparently eliminates inconsistency due to misclassification when H_e is distributed as a truncated normal distribution.

The Income Effect

With reference to labor supply Eq. (7.1), the preexperimental number of hours worked per week (H_p) is observed with a residual error term. Keeley et al. (1976) propose to remove this bias by regressing H_e on H_p, T and A, where, as in the case of W_p, "permanent" labor supply is separated out from the "transitory" component. Then $\Delta Y_d(H_p)$ is based on a measure of "permanent" labor supply only. The treatment variables T [see also Eq. (7.6)] are therefore purged of error terms (see Keeley et al., 1976, appendix B; Robins and West, 1978, p. 37). This procedure, nonetheless, is not very convincing, because it is not clear how unknown (and unobserved) error terms are in fact removed.

Truncation of the Dependent Variable H_e

Because values of H_e are necessarily restricted to the nonnegative part of the real line, the distribution of H_e will be generally truncated. Keeley et al. (1976, 1978) assume that the appropriate distribution is the truncated normal, thereby allowing the use of the Tobit model. Truncated normality is also assumed by Hurd (1976). Recent work by Poirier (1978) indicates that a more general class of truncated distributions should be considered before adopting the truncated normal. The truncated normal becomes a special case in Poirier's work. Poirier demonstrates that an incorrect assumption concerning the distributional form of the dependent variable results in biased and inconsistent regression coefficients. This may very well be the case with the Keeley et al. estimates of the income effect and substitution effect, since no evidence is presented that H_e does in fact follow a truncated normal distribution. Further, the usual significance tests are no longer appropriate in situations in which the distribution is truncated normal.

Selectivity Bias

The statistical difficulties introduced by selectivity bias have already been discussed in general in Chapter 4. In particular, selectivity bias may arise in estimating the effects of a treatment on future behaviors if one does not account for the fact that the size of the treatment may depend on past observations of the dependent behavioral variable. For example, the behavioral variable may affect assignment between control and experimental groups, or it may affect the size of the treatment received by those in the experimental group. The latter argument is made by Gottschalk (1981) in his critique of the SIME–DIME methodology (see Keeley *et al.* 1978). Assume a three-equation model of the form

$$Y_p = f(X_p) + \delta + \mu_p \tag{7.7}$$

$$Y_e = f(T, X_e) + \delta + \mu_e \tag{7.8}$$

$$T = g(Y_p) + \eta \tag{7.9}$$

[see also Eqs. (4.24)–(4.26)] where Y_p, Y_e represent preexperimental and experimental behavior, respectively; T is treatments, X_p and X_e are preexperimental and experimental values of the control variables (covariates), δ represents an unobserved (but significant) latent variable, and μ_p, μ_e, η are residual terms. Gottschalk then assumes that the treatments T (including presumably the controls as well) vary "with η, the level of the benefit schedule the person is randomly assigned to, and Y_p, the person's preexperimental hours."

Combining Eqs. (7.7) and (7.9), we obtain

$$T = g[f(X_p) + \delta + \mu_p] + \eta$$
$$= h(X_p) + g(\delta) + g(\mu_p) + \eta \tag{7.10}$$

where $h(\cdot) = gf(\cdot)$, say. Therefore because treatments T depend on preexperimental covariates X_p, the unobserved latent trait δ, the residual terms μ_p and η, the assignment to treatments is not random. Consequently, we have selectivity bias (inconsistency). However, this is probably not what occurred in the SIME–DIME (or any other) guaranteed income experiment, since treatments T were *not* made to depend on Y_p, the preexperimental levels of labor supply, as is suggested in Gottschalk's Eq. (7.9). Indeed, it would have been disquieting if the assignment model (see Chapter 3) had been designed to assign individuals to the various treatment plans according to their preexperimental number of hours worked.

Based on the three assumptions represented by Eqs. (7.7), (7.8), and (7.9), Gottschalk defines an alternative estimator that removes the "inconsistency" from the SIME–DIME estimates by including an experimental–control dummy D and Y_p^*, where $Y_p^* = D \cdot Y_p$; that is, Y_p^* is a preexperimental number of hours worked for the noncontrol experimentals. This differs from the Kelley *et al.* (1978) specification in that D is included but Y_p (for both controls and experimentals) is excluded. Thus the main thrust of

Table 7.5
Estimated Wage and Income Effects

	Keeley *et al.* specification			Modified specifications, experimentals on constant tax rate plans plus controls
	Full sample (1)	All experimentals (2)	Experimentals on constant tax rate plans (3)	
Number of observations				
Males	1592.	846.	467.	1213.
Wives	1698.	912.	499.	1285.
Female heads	1358.	831.	469.	996.
Coefficient on ΔY_d (income effects)				
Males	−34.4	−45.7	−83.6	4.6
	(27.3)	(20.8)	(46.5)	(42.7)
Wives	−142.9	−47.2	−31.3	−32.9
	(44.9)	(59.7)	(78.4)	(40.5)
Female heads	−101.1	−107.3	−69.7	53.0
	(39.4)	(53.4)	(69.6)	(40.4)
Coefficient on ΔW (wage effects)				
Males	83.2	96.0	30.0	−57.3
	(37.1)	(77.4)	(63.5)	(60.2)
Wives	168.0	86.6	−109.5	−37.8
	(91.2)	(101.8)	(153.9)	(85.6)
Female heads	125.8	87.5	66.9	−91.2
	(65.9)	(78.1)	(103.2)	(68.7)

Note: Standard errors are shown in parentheses. ΔY_d is the change in disposable income, which is defined by KRSW as the NIT payment at preexperimental hours. ΔW is the change in wage rate, which they define as the change in the effective tax rate multiplied by the preexperimental wage rate.

Source: Gottschalk (1981)

Gottschalk's argument is that control families should *not* have been in-cluded by Keeley *et al.* (1978) in the estimation procedure described in the previous sections of this chapter. A comparison of the Keeley and Gotts-chalk models is presented in Table 7.5. Columns 1–3 contain results by using the Keeley *et al.* model. Column 1 replicates the results in Keeley et al. (1978), column 2 excludes individuals assigned to the control group, and column 3 further excludes people assigned to treatments with nonlinear benefit schedules (see Gottschalk, 1981). Column 4 represents wage and income effects estimated from Gottschalk's model by using a sample of individuals assigned to the linear NIT plans and to the control subsample. *If* Gottschalk's argument is correct, only columns 3 and 4 provide consist-ent estimates of wage and income effects. Evidently, including controls (column 4) has a very large effect on the coefficients, indicating that the Keeley results are sensitive to specification error and that SIME–DIME's claim that a guaranteed income will result in a massive desertion of low-in-come workers from the labor force is suspect. In any case, bias (inconsist-ency) only makes sense if the target population is carefully defined, which is not the case here.

IV. CONCLUSIONS

The Keeley *et al.* analysis (1976, 1978) of SIME–DIME data leaves the reader with a strong impression that much relevant information has not been included. For example, much of the analysis tends to ignore the experimental nature of the data, contrary, for example, to the New Jersey research, where relevant parameters were inserted in the equations in order to model experimental effects (see Chapter 5). Consequently, in the Keeley *et al.* (1976, 1978) study we have no way of inferring even relatively simple differential labor supply behavior between, say, the control and experimen-tal groups. Also the claim that both a significant *and* a large drop in labor supply was observed cannot be substantiated independently of the authors' Tobit procedure, since even simple descriptive statistics such as sample means of labor supply changes are not given. Obviously, the *size* of a behavioral response should not be measured only by the regression coeffi-cients (elasticities), especially by a regression function that in all probability does not explain a substantial proportion of the variance.[4] In addition, the authors' claim that both substitution and income effects are consistent is not very plausible in the context of our discussion. Paradoxically, a recent claim that the Keeley *et al.* estimates are inconsistent has also been made by Gottschalk (1981), who claims that controls should have been omitted *entirely* from the estimation. This recommendation, however, seems questionable in view of the experimental nature of the data. Nevertheless, Gottschalk's reworking of SIME–DIME data supports our suspicion that Keeley *et al.*'s results are not very robust with respect to model specification. Low values of the R^2 statistic are not uncommon in cross-sectional social survey regression estimates. Further, when the main objective of regression analysis is to detect significant explanatory variables (such as wage rate and income in a labor supply equation), low R^2 values do not necessarily invalidate regression estimates. However, such estimates will not be efficient, and many significant variables may be reported as insignificant. When R^2 values are low, regression coefficients must be interpreted with great care, since low R^2 values often (but not necessarily) signal that important explanatory variables have been omitted, thus causing coefficients of the included variables to be inconsistently estimated. Furthermore, when an accompanying objective of the regression estimates is the prediction of behavior, low R^2 values will lead to very inefficient predictions. Both problems are most certainly present in the regression estimates of labor supply in SIME–DIME.

A second general observation concerns the estimation methodology and strategy pursued by the SIME–DIME researchers. "Rigorous" economic reasoning led the authors to adopt a single "optimal" regression model and to use this model to predict labor supply behavior under an income maintenance program. This leaves very little room for constructive skepticism, particularly with respect to alternative statistical or econometric estimation techniques for comparison purposes or assessment of the sensitivity of estimation to choice of model and model specification. For example, a comparison of the Keeley *et al.* (1976) results with those obtained by Robins and West (1978) indicates that substitution and income effects change in magnitude when the role of participation is taken into account.

NOTES

1. In a different version of the equation (Keeley *et al.*, 1977b) the dependent variable is defined as the difference $\Delta H = H_e - H_p$ rather than H_e as in Eq. (7.1). Even though Eq. (7.1) contains H_p on the right-hand side, the two equations will generally not yield the same estimated coefficients and are therefore not interchangeable.

2. A nonnegative random variable can, nevertheless, be well approximated by a normal distribution, particularly in a large sample. If this is the case, then the assumption of truncation is often not necessary.

3. Since experience is defined as "experience" = "age" − "years of schooling" − 5, the "experience" variable mainly reflects "age," which consequently plays the role of an instrumental variable.

4. Keeley *et al.* (1976, 1978) do not report R^2 values for the estimated labor supply equations (7.1).

8 The Gary Income Maintenance Experiment

I. INTRODUCTION

The Gary Income Maintenance Experiment was conducted between 1971 and 1974 in Indiana. It focused on a black urban sample with a high proportion of female-headed families. Of 1800 eligible families, 1000 were female headed and only 800 had both wife and husband present. Eligibility criteria included the following: the head of the household must be black; at least one dependent under age 18 must be present; and family income must generally not exceed 2.4 times the poverty level at time of enrollment.[1] However, families with relatively high incomes were also enrolled, but to a much smaller extent[2] (Kehrer et al., 1979, p. 29) than in New Jersey. Consequently, sample restriction through income truncation was carried out at a much higher level in Gary than in New Jersey. The sample was stratified by income levels. Experimental randomization occurred within each income strata, but between strata the experimental-control allocation was carried out according to the Conlisk–Watts model. The Conlisk–Watts allocation procedure apparently led to preexperimental differences between the control and experimental groups[3] (Kehrer et al., 1979, p. 21), but these differences turned out to be quite small (Hausman and Wise, 1977b). The control group received a fixed (nominal) payment for answering questionnaires; the treatment group was assigned to one of four payment plans defined by combinations of two tax rates (40%, 60%) and two guarantee levels ($3300, $4300 for a family of four). The guarantee level varied with family size (see Table 8.1); semiannual adjustments to the guarantee were made to take into account price inflation. Income tax liabilities were fully reimbursed to families with incomes up to the breakeven point.

Families with a male head present (almost all of which were intact husband–wife families) had low incomes but were generally not extremely poor. Typically, husbands were full-time unionized workers with a history of continuous employment and earned enough to keep their family out of complete poverty (however, 10% were below the official poverty line). Wives generally did not work outside the home (only 13% did so). Families in which both the husband and wife were employed enjoyed sufficiently high income to be disqualified for NIT payments. Families headed by females were generally much poorer than husband–wife families; over 80% of female-headed families received welfare benefits from the Aid to Families with Dependent Children (AFDC) program prior to the experiment, and

Table 8.1

Gary Income Maintenance Experiment Payment Schedule, by Family Size

Family size	$4300 Guarantee Level		$3300 Guarantee Level	
	Annual guarantees	Monthly guarantee	Annual guarantee	Monthly guarantee
1	$ 1,433.00	$ 119.41	$ 1,100.00	$ 91.66
2	2,866.00	238.83	2,200.00	183.33
3	3,582.50	298.54	2,750.00	229.16
4	4,300.00	358.33	3,300.00	275.00
5	4,872.20	406.01	3,740.00	311.66
6	5,302.10	441.04	4,070.00	339.15
7	5,558.70	465.72	4,290.00	357.50
8	5,732.00	477.63	4,400.00	366.66
9	5,817.97	484.83	4,466.00	372.16
10	5,903.95	492.00	4,532.00	377.66
11	5,989.93	499.16	4,598.00	383.16
12	6,032.93	502.74	4,631.00	385.91
13	6,075.91	506.33	4,664.00	388.66
14	6,118.91	509.91	4,697.00	391.41
15	6,161.89	513.49	4,730.00	394.15
16	6,204.89	517.07	4,763.00	396.91
17	6,247.87	520.66	4,796.00	399.66
18	6,290.86	524.24	4,825.00	402.41
19	6,333.85	527.82	4,862.00	405.16
20	6,376.85	531.40	4,895.00	407.91

Source: Kehner *et al.* (1975).

about three out of four female-headed families who switched from the AFDC program to NIT payments were below the poverty line. Of those not on AFDC prior to the experiment, only 38% were below the poverty line. Only 13% of the AFDC female heads were employed, whereas 40% of non-AFDC female heads were employed.

The estimation of labor supply played a lesser role in the overall objectives of the Gary experiment; the Gary experiment had a decidedly more "sociological" or "noneconomic" dimension. Still, labor supply response remained an important question and a number of studies were conducted using the Gary Experiment's data. Compared to the amount undertaken by the New Jersey experiment, however, the volume is quite small. The entire research is contained in a few documents (Burtless and Hausman, 1977, 1978; Hausman and Wise, 1979; Moffit, 1977, 1979). The approach employed in analyzing the Gary experiment is strictly "econometric;" labor supply functions are derived in accordance with neoclassical utility theory and the statistical problem conceived in terms of estimating the income and substitution effects of a labor supply regression equation. Therefore the methodology is similar in spirit to SIME–DIME but somewhat different from that of New Jersey, where prime interest lay in analyzing experimental effects by means of analysis of covariance. At the same time, the Gary researchers focused on concerns not considered by previous investigations, such as truncation bias, convex budget constraints, model sensitivity, and so on, and, in the process, extended the range of refinements to the basic neoclassical model of labor supply as well as estimation issues. Much of this work is becoming the standard approach in statistical analyses of socioeconomic projects.

II. LABOR SUPPLY RESPONSE

Adult Married Males

We first consider the study by Burtless and Hausman (1978) on a sample of 380 married adult males (247 experimentals and 133 controls). Their analysis stressed neoclassical economic theory and placed importance on the "indirect utility function." Specifically, Burtless and Hausman adopt a stochastic specification of the neoclassical labor supply model and incorporate NIT features so as to define a piecewise linear or "kinked" budget constraint. From an estimation perspective Burtless and Hausman pay close attention to the issue of income truncation in the sample.

Burtless and Hausman (1978) define a log-linear labor supply equation of the form:

$$H_i = k_i W_i^\alpha Y_i^{\beta_i} \tag{8.1}$$

where for the ith individual H_i is the number of hours worked, W_i the wage rate, Y_i the nonlabor income, and k_i a constant term controlling for individual characteristics and further specified as

$$k_i = \exp(Z_i \delta + \epsilon_{2i}) \tag{8.2}$$

where Z_i is a vector of individual characteristics for the ith individual.

The income elasticity β_i is allowed to vary (in the population) from one individual to another; that is, β_i is defined as

$$\beta_i = \mu_\beta + \epsilon_{1i} \tag{8.3}$$

where μ_β and ϵ_{1i} are the "common effect" and the "individual effect," respectively. However, the substitution (wage) effect α is assumed equal (constant) for all individuals. The authors note that sufficient data points are available to allow both income and substitution effects to vary for individuals, but only allow β_i to vary randomly due to econometric "convention." Finally, the residual terms ϵ_2 and ϵ_1 are assumed to be normal $N(0,\sigma_2^2)$ and truncated normal $TN(0,\sigma_1^2)$ random variables, respectively. Taking natural logarithms on both sides of Eq. (8.1), we have

$$\begin{aligned} \log H_i &= (Z_i \delta + \epsilon_{2i}) + \alpha \log W_i + \beta_i \log Y_i \\ &= Z_i \delta + \alpha \log W_i + \beta_i \log Y_i + \epsilon_{2i} \\ &= \log H_i^* + \epsilon_{2i} \end{aligned} \tag{8.4}$$

where

$$\log H_i^* = Z_i \delta + \alpha \log W_i + \beta_i \log Y_i \tag{8.5}$$

represents the desired (but unobserved) number of hours of work. The subsequent estimation procedure has two important main features:

1. Because $\log H_i = \log H_i^* + \epsilon_{2i}$, it is assumed that experimental respondents are expected, on the average, to maximize their desired hours of work H_i^*; that is, actual hours worked H_i tend to approach desired hours H_i^*.

2. The income elasticity is defined as $\beta_i = \mu_\beta + \epsilon_{ii}$ and the random error term ϵ_1 assumed to follow a truncated normal distribution $TN(0,\sigma_1^2)$. This implies that β is also distributed as a truncated normal distribution. This specification accords with Hausman and Wise (1977a), who believe the income truncation effect must be taken into account to avoid bias. Because the substitution effect α is assumed constant for the entire population, it is not affected by truncation.

Estimation consists of a nonlinear maximum likelihood procedure and can be summarized as follows: Let $f(\beta)$ be the truncated normal density of β; $F(\beta)$ the cumulative distribution associated with $f(\beta)$, and $\phi(\cdot)$ the standard normal density. Then the probability $P(NC)_i$ of observing H_i for the ith treatment (noncontrol) male head (assuming H_i^* is maximized) is given by [see Eq. (8.4)]

$$P(NC)_i = \int_{-\infty}^{\beta_i^*} \frac{1}{\sigma_2} N\left(\frac{\epsilon_{2i}}{\sigma_2}\right) f(\beta)\, d\beta + \int_{\beta_i^*}^{0} \frac{1}{\sigma_2} N\left(\frac{\epsilon_{2i}}{\sigma_2}\right) f(\beta)\, d\beta \qquad (8.6)$$

for the two budget segments (see Burtless and Hausman, 1978). Evaluation of the integrals in Eq. (8.6) is equivalent to evaluating the cumulative standardized normal distribution when β_i are defined only for negative values.[4] The probability of observing actual hours worked by controls, $P(C)_i$ is similarly defined. Consider Figure 8.1, where H denotes the "kink point" of the convex budget curve.[5] The convex budget curve is different from the usual situation because there exists a range for β, say a lower value $\beta_{\ell i}$ and an upper value β_{ui}, for which the utility maximizing point is at the kink H. Thus if individual i's value β_i is much less than zero, the global maximum H_i^* will be on the first segment associated with net wage W_1 and nonlabor income Y_1 (see Figure 8.1). On the other hand, if his income elasticity β_i is near zero the utility maximum will be along the second segment corresponding to net wage W_2 and nonlabor income Y_2. The lower and upper values are computed from the (uncompensated) labor supply function, since from Eq. (8.4) we have for the ith control individual

$$\beta_{\ell i} = (\log \tilde{\tilde{H}}_i - Z\delta - \alpha \log W_{1i})/\log Y_{1i} \qquad (8.7)$$

and

$$\beta_{ui} = (\log \tilde{\tilde{H}}_i - Z_i\delta - \alpha \log W_{2i})/\log Y_{2i} \qquad (8.8)$$

All values of β_i that lie between $\beta_{\ell i}$ and β_{ui} lead to a utility maximum

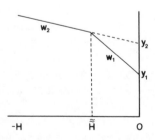

Fig. 8.1. *The "kinked" budget constraint.*

at the kink point $\tilde{\tilde{H}}_i$. The probability that the observed level of hours H_i corresponds to a utility maximum at the kink point is given by

$$\frac{1}{\sigma_2}\phi\left(\frac{\log H_i - \log \tilde{\tilde{H}}_i}{\sigma_2}\right)\int_{\beta_{\ell i}}^{\beta_{u i}} f(\beta)\, d\beta \tag{8.9}$$

so that for the ith control the probability of observing actual hours worked H_i is

$$
\begin{aligned}
P(C)_i &= \int_{-\infty}^{\beta_{\ell i}} \frac{1}{\sigma_2}\phi\left(\frac{\log H_i - \log H_{1i}^*}{\sigma_2}\right) f(\beta)\, d\beta \\
&+ \frac{1}{\sigma_2}\phi\left(\frac{\log H_i - \log \tilde{H}_i}{\sigma_2}\right)[F(\beta_{ui}) - F(\beta_{\ell i})] \\
&+ \int_{\beta_{ui}}^{0} \frac{1}{\sigma_2}\phi\left(\frac{\log H_i - \log H_{2i}}{\sigma_2}\right) f(\beta)\, d\beta
\end{aligned}
\tag{8.10}
$$

where H_{1i}^* and H_{2i}^* correspond to the budget segments defined by W_{1i}, Y_{1i} and W_{2i}, Y_{2i}. The log likelihood function is then

$$L = \sum_{i=1}^{n_1}\log P(NC)_i + \sum_{i=1}^{n_2}\log P(C)_i \tag{8.11}$$

wher: n_1 and n_2 are, respectively, the experimental and control sample sizes.

Th: Burtless–Hausman results are presented in Tables (8.2) and (8.3). Table (8.2) reports the mean parameter estimates of labor supply Eq. (8.4). Since NIT payments constitute nonlabor income, the experimental effects are reflected in the (random) regression coefficient β_i. The mean response is therefore measured by $\bar{\beta}$, the mean value of the β_i. Since regression is carried out on logarithms of the observed data, the coefficients α and β are "elasticities" measures. Therefore, a statistically significant value for β in Table 8.2 is interpreted to mean that a 1% increase in nonlabor income will lead to a .0477% *decrease* in labor supply.

Table 8.3 presents a breakdown of the response variable H according to the experimental parameters (tax rate and guarantee) and hourly wage rate. It can be seen that experimental adult male heads reduced their labor supply by 6–8% compared to controls. Burtless and Hausman report that the tax rate had no influence on labor supply behavior, although the guarantee level did; the higher guarantee tended to reduce labor supply to a greater extent. This conclusion is similar to that reached in the New Jersey experiment. Indeed, in spite of the fact that very different models were used, the labor supply reductions of adult married family heads (ignoring for the moment the racial–ethnic differences in New Jersey) are very similar in both experiments, lying in the range of 3–8%.

Table 8.2
*Estimates of Labor Supply and Indirect
Utility Function*

Variable	Parameter estimates
Constant	3.75043
	(.02555)
Primary education	(.01078)
	(.00558)
Adults *(N)*	.03300
	(.01272)
Poor health	−.02224
	(.00438)
Age	−.00869
	(.01347)
Wage elasticity, $\bar{\alpha}$	.00003
	(.01632)
Mean income elasticity, $\bar{\beta}$	−.04768
	(.00465)
Variance of β distribution, σ_1^2	.06751
	(.00399)
Variance of ϵ_{2i}, σ_2^2	.00135
	(.00022)

Note: Observations $(N) = 380$; log of the likelihood
function $= -196.27$. Asymptotic standard errors in
parentheses.
Source: Burtless and Hausman, 1978.

Burtless and Hausman go to great lengths to describe what they perceive
as the essentials of a relevant economic theory of labor supply; however, they
do not link the analysis to the actual experimental design, and the empirical
content could also be more detailed. Very little indication is given of how
the numbers of Table 8.3 are obtained, or why elasticities are at all important in measuring experimental response. Additionally, a possible drawback of the maximum likelihood model (8.11) is that it does not generate a
summary measure of the explanatory power of the model,[6] and it is difficult
to be convinced that only six explanatory variables (those listed in Table 8.2)
can achieve any meaningful degree of explanatory power. Although the
explanatory power of a model is not very important for significance testing
of experimental–control differences, a very low percentage of variance
explained may serve to indicate omitted "explanatory" (i.e., control) variables. This in turn leads to bias and statistical inefficiency. Given that the
standard deviations of the coefficients in Table 8.2 are only asymptotic and

Table 8.3
Location of 15 Budget Lines in Gary Experiment

Financial plan and gross wage/hr ($)	w_1 ($)	w_2 ($)	y_1 ($)	y_2 ($)	Hours at kink point	Expected hours	Change from control (%)	95% Confidence range of expected hours	Probability of below breakeven point
Control:									
2.25	2.07	1.67	2.72	27.82	43.16	43.55	—	36.8, 45.38	—
4.25	3.92	3.15	2.72	27.82	22.85	40.37	—	36.8, 45.38	—
6.25	5.76	4.63	2.72	27.82	27.82	40.34	—	36.8, 45.38	—
40% tax/low guarantee:									
2.25	1.35	1.67	78.63	27.82	159.59	38.68	-11.8	34.15, 44.95	1.0
4.25	2.53	3.15	78.63	27.82	81.77	38.68	-4.3	34.15, 44.95	1.0
6.25	3.75	4.63	78.63	27.82	57.45	38.68	-4.2	34.15, 44.95	1.0
60% tax/low guarantee:									
2.25	0.90	1.67	78.09	27.82	65.42	38.69	-11.8	34.17, 44.96	1.0
4.25	1.70	3.15	78.09	27.82	34.63	39.62	-1.9	34.16, 43.48	.21
6.25	2.50	4.63	78.09	27.82	23.55	40.23	-.3	34.16, 45.38	.02
40% tax/high guarantee:									
2.25	1.35	1.67	102.63	27.82	234.97	38.27	-12.9	33.50, 44.85	1.0
4.25	2.53	3.15	102.63	27.82	120.39	38.27	-5.3	33.50, 44.85	1.0
6.25	3.75	4.63	102.63	27.82	84.59	38.27	-5.3	33.50, 44.85	1.0
60% tax/high guarantee:									
2.25	.90	1.67	102.09	27.82	96.66	38.29	-12.9	33.50, 44.84	1.0
4.25	1.70	3.15	102.09	27.82	51.17	38.29	-5.3	33.50, 44.84	1.0
6.25	2.50	4.63	102.09	27.82	34.86	39.38	-2.4	33.50, 45.38	.23

Note: Mean = -6.53
Source: Burtless and Hausman, 1978.

that the sample size did not exceed 400 individuals, any available information on the precision of the estimates is an important ingredient in evaluating the empirical results presented in Tables 8.2 and 8.3. Despite these observations we regard the efforts of Burtless and Hausman as a valuable contribution to the literature.

Married Men, Female Heads, and Wives

To avoid the endogeneity of the tax rate and to estimate the choice-of-segment function[7] (of the budget constraint), Burtless and Hausman (1978) use a maximum likelihood specification. Kehrer *et al.* (1979), however, choose a more straightforward approach; their method is to approximate the budget constraint rather than represent it in all its detail. In essence, the budget constraint is "smoothed out" by averaging all the marginal tax rates along it. The cumulative tax rate in each segment of an individual's constraint is weighted by its fraction of hours worked and then summed to obtain a weighted average tax rate. While this procedure only approximates the entire budget constraint and thus provides only an approximation of the "true" labor supply function, it has the advantage of modeling (approximately) the response to the entire budget constraint rather than a local segment.

The labor supply equation is specified as

$$H = \beta_0 + \gamma_1 W(1 - r - t) + \gamma_2(N + B_0) \qquad (8.12)$$

where

H is the number of hours worked per month (including zeros),

W the gross hourly wage rate (preenrollment wage rates, those for unemployed workers being estimated),

r the average tax rate on non-NIT income,

t the average tax rate on NIT income (i.e., average NIT tax rate),

N the nonwage income (includes wives' and other family members' incomes, if any), and

$B_0 = (G - tN)$, the NIT benefits at zero hours worked.

Equation (8.12) therefore specifies hours worked per month under a NIT program as a linear function of the net wage rate $W(1 - r - t)$ and the value of nonwage income $(N + B_0)$. Because the coefficients γ_1 and γ_2 depend on both experimental and nonexperimental variables, Eq. (8.12) is rewritten in the form

$$H = \beta_0 + \beta_1 W(1 - r) + \beta_2(-Wt) + \beta_3 N + \beta_4 B_0 \qquad (8.13)$$

where β_2, β_4 reflect experimental effects and β_1 and β_3 are associated with nonexperimental sources of income.

The data for estimating Eq. (8.13) consist of a preenrollment interview as well as seven interviews conducted throughout the experiment. Groups thought to be atypical, such as the aged, the young, the self-employed, and the disabled, are excluded from analysis. Families that left the experiment early are included in the sample (naturally, only for periods before their departure), as are members of families who changed marital status during the experiment.[9]

Because systematic preenrollment differences were observed between controls and experimentals, both preenrollment and experimental data are used to estimate Eq. (8.13). Two methods are employed. The first method is to include a dummy variable D.

$$D = \begin{cases} 1, & \text{if during-experiment observation} \\ 0, & \text{otherwise} \end{cases} \tag{8.14}$$

The alternative method is to include in Eq. (8.13) H_p; the value of the dependent variable observed for the preenrollment period. The second method employs only the during-experiment data, because the effect of preexperimental differences is captured by the variable H_p. Also included in the equation are such control variables as the number of adults in the family, the total number of children, the presence (or absence) of children in various age categories (dummy variables), the local unemployment rate, a seasonal dummy, and the presence (or absence) of a separate family living in the household. The final "basic" model estimated is

$$\begin{aligned} H = \beta_0 &+ \beta_1 W(1-r) + \beta_2(-Wt) + \beta_3 N + \beta_4(B_0) + \beta_5(-Wt)(D) \\ &+ \beta_6(B_0)(D) + \beta_7(D) + \beta_8(Z) + \epsilon \end{aligned} \tag{8.15}$$

where D is the dummy variable defined as (8.14) and Z comprises the listed control variables.

Unlike New Jersey, the Gary Experiment estimated labor supply functions using the same models on separate subsamples of male heads, female heads, and wives. In addition, alternative estimation techniques (and equation specifications) were used to investigate the robustness of the various models. Consequently, the labor supply results from the Gary experiment may be compared for the three subsamples of respondents, and the effect(s) of various specifications on the estimates also examined. We now consider the findings from the Gary experiment in greater detail; in certain cases we also fill in statistical details not explicitly indicated by the authors.

III. FINDINGS OF THE GARY EXPERIMENT

The Overall Experimental Effect

The first model considered is essentially the one-treatment analysis of covariance model

$$L = T\alpha + X\beta + \epsilon \qquad (8.16)$$

where

L = some measure of labor supply,

$$T = \begin{cases} 1, & \text{if experimental} \\ 0, & \text{if control} \end{cases} \qquad (8.17)$$

Z = matrix of demographic and socioeconomic control variables (covariates)

As indicated earlier, two versions of model (8.15) are estimated, depending on the method used for controlling systematic preenrollment experimental–control differences arising from nonrandom sampling. The first, or the "net," version is specified as

$$L = T\alpha + TD\beta + D\delta + Z\delta + \epsilon \qquad (8.18)$$

where variables are as defined previously in this section.[10] Equation (8.18) is estimated using both preenrollment and experimental data. The coefficient δ measures the mean difference in the labor supply response variable L between preenrollment controls and experimentals. This being the case, α is then the "net" mean difference in labor supply between the control group and the payments (treatment) group. Therefore α yields a measure of the overall experimental effect (if any) corrected for preenrollment differences.

The second version introduces the preenrollment labor supply as a "lagged" dependent variable L_p. This version of the model,

$$L = T\alpha + L_p\delta + Z\gamma + \epsilon \qquad (8.19)$$

is estimated with during-experiment data only, and α has the same interpretation as before. Table 8.4 presents estimates of L for both versions (8.18) and (8.19), and for two labor supply measures:

1. L = EM = employment status where

$$L = \begin{cases} 1, & \text{if employed} \\ 0 & \text{otherwise} \end{cases} \qquad (8.20)$$

2. $L = H$ = hours worked per month,

as in Eq. (8.12) and (8.15). Because of the nature of the two labor supply response variables different estimation procedures are necessary. The employment status equations are estimated by Probit regression, since EM is dichotomous, whereas the hours worked equations are computed using the Tobit model, because values of H are "bunched up" at $H = 0$ for unemployed members of the sample. Table 8.4 shows statistically significant labor supply reductions for husbands and female heads, but not for wives. For husbands, employment status reductions of 2.7–4.9% of the control mean and unconditional hours reductions of 2.9–6.5% are reported, depending on the model used. For female heads the labor supply reductions are much higher—between 26 and 27% (of the control mean) for employment status and 26–30% (of the control mean) for unconditional hours worked per month.[11] Wives, on the other hand, showed an increase in employment status between 2.1 and 2.8% and an increase in the unconditional hours worked per month of 1.0–5.0% (of the control means), although none of the coefficients measuring labor supply response were significant at the 95% level.[12]

The Basic Model

The analysis of covariance model of the preceding section contains a single experimental treatment variable T and does not distinguish between NIT tax rate and the guarantee level. In order to measure the independent impact of these two factors, Kehrer *et al.* (1979) estimate the "basic" model (8.15) by Tobit analysis, since the dependent response variable now consists only of the number of hours worked per month. In Eq. (8.15) the existence

Table 8.4
Estimated Mean Experimental–Control Labor Supply Differences

Dependent variable	Husbands		Wives		Female heads	
	Net	Lagged	Net	Lagged	Net	Lagged
Employment status						
(1 if employed, 0 if not)	−.042[a]	−.023	.004	.003	−.055[a]	−.053[b]
Percent of control mean	−4.9	−2.7	2.8	2.1	−26.8	−25.8
Unconditional hours per month	−9.53	−4.24	1.18	.32	−9.35	−8.23
Percent of control mean	−6.5	−2.9	5.0	1.0	−30.0	−25.9

[a] Coefficient significant at .95 level.
[b] Coefficient significant at .99 level.
Source: Kehrer *et al.*, 1979.

of any systematic preenrollment difference is controlled for by the dummy variable D in contrast to the "lagged" version. The results for the income and net wage effects (both NIT and non-NIT) are given in Table 8.5. As in the case of the Burtless and Hausman model, the (NIT) net-wage rate measures the effect of the tax rate, while the (NIT) income effect measures the impact of the guarantee level. The estimated "budget-line" coefficients of Eq. (8.15) are given in Table 8.5. For husbands neither the income effect nor the wage effect (NIT) are significant at the 5% or 10% level, although the non-NIT effect is highly significant even at the 1% level. The husband's income elasticity, indicating a 5% reduction in labor supply for a 1% increase in the guarantee level, although statistically insignificant, is comparable to the value found by Burtless and Hausman (1978) discussed earlier. Similarly, both the NIT income effect and the net wage effect for wives are statistically insignificant, although (perhaps paradoxically) the non-NIT income and net wage effects are highly significant and much larger in magnitude (see Table 8.5).

Table 8.5
Mean Coefficients in Tobit Hours per Month Regression[a]

	Husbands		Wives		Female heads	
	Coefficient	Elasticity	Coefficient	Elasticity	Coefficient	Elasticity
NIT						
Income effect[b]	−5.85	−.05	4.07	.07	−6.35[c]	−.23
	(1.42)		(.58)		(1.91)	
Net wage effect	−3.60	−.01	12.67	.16	−4.61	−.12
	(.36)		(.65)		(.49)	
Non-NIT:						
Income effect[b]	−24.53[d]	−.13	1.61[d]	.45	−4.94[d]	−.20
	(15.38)		(3.00)		(4.98)	
Net wage effect	−.621	−.01	5.55[e]	.46	−4.38[d]	−.27
	(.33)		(3.15)		(2.46)	

Note: Unsigned t-statistics are in parentheses.

[a] All coefficients evaluated at the mean value of the Tobit index. That is, if β is the vector of coefficients, X is the vector of independent variables, and F is the cumulative normal distribution function, then the coefficients in the table are $\beta F(\overline{X}\beta/\sigma)$. $F(\overline{X}\beta/\sigma)$ equals .99, .15, and .21 for husbands, wives, and female heads, respectively.

[b] Divided by 100.

[c] Significant at the .10 level.

[d] Significant at the .05 level.

[e] Significant at the .01 level.

Source: Kehrer *et al.,* 1979.

The specification of model (8.15) is relatively simple, containing no interaction terms between NIT and non-NIT income and net wage variables. Furthermore, husbands' and wives' labor supply are not determined simultaneously and the number of control variables in the matrix Z is relatively small. Consequently, the preceding results could well be spurious, although even the observed number of hours worked for both husbands and wives does not indicate any substantial increase.[13] It is only for female heads that we observe large and significant decreases in labor supply. The number of hours worked drops by .23% for every 1% increase in NIT payments (the income effect). Again, the non-NIT net wage effect is significant and of high magnitude (elasticity equals $-.27$), while the NIT net wage effect is not statistically significant.

Model Sensitivity Tests

To determine the robustness of the estimates in Tables 8.4 and 8.5 Kehrer *et al.* (1979) reestimate Eq. (8.15) and (8.18) by ordinary least squares and generalized least squares. The generalized least squares is an error-component model with a constant "individuals effect" form and nonautocorrelated random residual effect. Also preenrollment treatment differences are estimated by both a dummy variable and a lagged hours-worked variable and data are averaged (over time periods) as well as pooled, the midyear of the experiment being used to estimate the regression equations. The results are found to remain stable, within narrow intervals, so the experimental results appear to be robust with respect to the preceding model specifications. Husbands reduce their labor supply from 3% to 6% measured relatively to controls, wives show no significant reduction, and female heads reduce their labor supply by 25 – 30%, according to Kehrer *et al.* (1979). As already pointed out, however, estimation precision is partly illusory, since it is based on a comparison of *point* estimates of the various models. Had *interval* estimates (confidence intervals) been used as the basis of comparison among the models, the conclusions would have indicated wider differences.

The Effect of Social-Demographic Variables

Horner (1977) considers the effect of age, experience, education, and wage rates on the labor supply response of prime-age husbands to test the effect of social and demographic variables. Two basic models are considered: Model

1 has the general form

$$
\begin{aligned}
H = {} & \beta_0 + \beta_1 \Delta Y + \beta_2 \Delta W + \beta_3 A(\Delta Y) + \beta_4 A^2(\Delta Y) + \beta_5 A(\Delta W) \\
& + \beta_6 E(\Delta Y) + \beta_7 E(\Delta W) + \beta_8 Y_p + \beta_9 W_p + \beta_{10} A + \beta_{11} A^2 \\
& + \beta_{12} E + \beta_{13} H_p + \epsilon_1
\end{aligned}
\tag{8.21}
$$

where

ΔY, ΔW are the changes in income and wage rate effected by the NIT program,

Y_p is the preexperimental income,

W_p the preexperimental wage rate,

H_p the preexperimental hours worked per month,

A is age, and

E is education

Since Eq. (8.21) contains interaction terms such as $A(\Delta Y)$ and the like, it is not linear in the variables.

Model 2 is specified as

$$
\begin{aligned}
\Delta H = {} & \gamma_0 + \gamma_1 \frac{\Delta Y}{W_e} + \gamma_2 \frac{\Delta Y}{W_e}(A) + \gamma_3 \frac{\Delta Y}{W_e}(A^2) + \gamma_4 \frac{\Delta Y}{W_e}(E) \\
& + \gamma_5 Y_p + \gamma_6 W_p + \gamma_7 A + \gamma_8 A^2 + \gamma_9 E + \gamma_{10} H_p + \epsilon_2
\end{aligned}
\tag{8.22}
$$

where ΔY, Y_p, H_p, W_p, A, and E are defined as above, and ΔH = change in hours worked between the experimental and preexperimental periods, and W_e = the effective wage rate faced by individuals during the experiment. Horner also employs other variables, such as experience (in years), years of education, and a dummy variable

$$
E(\mathrm{HS}) = \begin{cases} 1, & \text{if completed high school} \\ 0, & \text{otherwise} \end{cases}
$$

but regressions containing these variables are not presented. Horner's main results with Eqs. (8.21) and (8.22) are given in Table 8.6. The first and third regressions estimate labor supply functions, which include the basic treatment terms of Table 8.6 but do not include interactions. The signs of the coefficients are "as expected" and accord generally with results found by other researchers using the Gary sample. However, the results of model 1 are not statistically significant at the 95% level. Using a one-tailed test, the "Cobb–Douglas" treatment term is significant at the 5% level.

Regressions 2 and 4 contain both age and education interaction terms; these results are felt to estimate models 1 and 2 best. They were chosen from a variety of alternatives based on hypothesized interactions and their statistical significance in explaining the treatment effect. In all regressions (including those not presented), the age–income change and experience–

Table 8.6

Coefficient of the Treatment Terms for the Primary Labor Supply Regression (Standard Errors in Parentheses)

	Model I		Model II	
Variable	No interactions	Age and education interactions	No interactions	Age and education interactions
ΔY	−0.8599 (0.6993)	−0.3502[b] (0.1086)	—	—
ΔW	−0.8432 (1.0360)	−0.8430 (0.9955)	—	—
$\dfrac{\Delta Y^c}{W_e}$	—	—	−0.0221[a] (0.0115)	−0.6183[a] (0.1896)
$\dfrac{A\,\Delta Y^d}{100}$	—	1.8285[b] (0.5411)	—	—
$\dfrac{A^2\,\Delta Y^d}{10{,}000}$	—	−2.3806[b] (0.6611)	—	—
$E\,\Delta Y$	—	2.8798[b] (1.0828)	—	—
$A\dfrac{\Delta Y^d}{\Delta W}$	—	—	—	0.0314[d] (0.0095)
$A^2\dfrac{\Delta Y}{\Delta W}$	—	—	—	−0.0401[d] (0.0116)
$E=\dfrac{\Delta Y}{\Delta W}$	—	—	—	0.0629[d] (0.0208)
F value for adding treatment terms[e]	2.22 (2.04)	5.69[d] (2.26)	3.69 (3.89)	6.56[d] (2.51)
Regression R^2	.234	.291	.207	.288

[a] Significant at the .95 level.
[b] Significant at the .99 level.
[c] A two-tailed test of significance is applied to coefficients of ΔW. A one-tailed test is used for all other variables.
[d] These terms are age interactions in regressions 2 and 5 and experience interactions in regressions 3 and 6.
[e] The number in parentheses is the F level for .05 significance.
Source: Horner, 1977.

income change interactions were by far the most important. The interaction of a dummy variable indicating whether or not the respondent completed high school with the treatment-related income change was also significant. However, the wage rate–income change and years of education–income change interactions were generally not statistically significant. In addition, none of the life-cycle–human-capital variables was statistically significant when interacted with the change in wage rate.[14]

According to model 1, the estimated decrease in labor supply for a twenty-year-old is 12.6 hours for non-high-school graduates, and 8.5 hours for high school graduates. From age 35.6 to 41.0 for nongraduates and 27.6 to 49.1 for graduates, a small but statistically insignificant increase in labor supply is indicated. As age increases beyond 40 years, the disincentive effect again increases, until, at age 60, non-high-school graduates and graduates, respectively, reduce their labor supply by 17.7 hours and 13.5 hours. The results for model 2 are similar, although the differentials with respect to age are somewhat less.

While the predicted decreases in hours worked are fairly high for very young and old workers, the shape of the relationship for younger workers is based on relatively few observations. Only 16 (7.8%) of the observations were heads 25 years of age and under. However, 54 (26.3%) of the heads were 46 years of age or older.

The most significant finding of Horner's results is that one's position in the life cycle is an important determinant of the response to the negative tax program. A major decrease in work effort takes place among both young and older, low-income, black male family heads. During the prime-age working years, no such decrease occurs. Indeed, the regression estimates that an increase will occur; however, the increase evaluated at its maximum is not significantly greater than zero.

Interaction of education with the treatment indicates that completion of high school is an important determinant of response to the program. On average, those who did not complete high school decreased their work effort by 2.9 more hours than graduates, for every $100 of subsidy per month. The results for model 2 confirm model 1, and the predicted differential is in the same range for the two models. The years of education–treatment interaction term (not shown) was not significant when using a variety of alternatively specified models. None of the control variables was statistically significant except preexperimental work, H_p. The coefficient for H_p is negative, indicating that the lower the value of H_p, the greater the positive change in hours worked regardless of treatment or control status.

Table 8.7 presents the income, wage, and income-compensated substitution elasticities implied by models 1 and 2 for different education status and age subgroups. The elasticities are calculated at the mean levels of preexperimental income and wage rates. The income elasticities become quite large at the age extremes, especially for those without a high school education. A 1% change in income results in a more than 1% change in hours worked at very high and low working ages. However, for those between

Table 8.7
Income, Wage, and Substitution Elasticities, by Education Status and Age

	Non-high school			High school		
Age	Income	Wage	Substitution	Income	Wage	Substitution
			Model I			
20	−1.155	−0.0890	0.1899	−0.774	−0.0890	0.0979
30	−0.218	−0.0890	−0.0362	+0.180	−0.0890	−0.1325
40	+0.01	−0.0890	−0.0931	+0.398	−0.0890	−0.1850
50	−0.449	−0.0890	0.0194	−0.068	−0.0890	−0.0725
60	−1.616	−0.0890	0.3012	−1.235	−0.0890	0.2093
			Model II			
20	−1.085	0.264	0.4147	−0.632	0.154	0.242
30	−0.268	0.0652	0.1024	0.185	−0.045	−0.071
40	−0.028	0.0068	0.0107	0.425	−0.103	−0.162
50	−0.366	0.0890	0.1398	0.0871	−0.021	−0.033
60	−1.281	0.312	0.490	−0.828	0.201	−0.316

Source: Horner, 1977.

thirty and fifty years of age (67% of the sample), the income elasticities are considerably smaller. It should be noted that the average change in income effected by the experiment ($81.00 per month) is only 14.3% of preexperimental family income ($566.00 per month).

The wage elasticities are invariant with age and education in model 1 and are of such magnitude that the income and substitution effects of a wage change nearly offset each other. In model 2 the wage effect does differ by age and education; the calculated wage elasticities are more positive and indicate a somewhat larger (more positive) substitution effect for older and younger workers than for prime-aged workers.

School Enrollment and Labor Supply of Teenagers

McDonald and Stephenson (1979) consider the labor supply of teenagers by analyzing a sample of 266 black urban teenagers. They seek to determine whether or not a NIT program will alter the probability of enrolling in high school. Thus their sample consists of all teenagers who are potential high school students, in the age range of 16–18 years old, and who had completed 8–11 years of schooling.[15] Since schooling in Indiana is only compulsory to age 16, teenagers can choose to continue education or to join the labor force under a NIT, all else being constant.

To determine whether a NIT has a significant impact McDonald and Stephenson specify two linear[16] logit regression models

$$Y_{(k)} = X\beta + \epsilon, \qquad k = 1, 2 \qquad (8.23)$$

where

$$Y_{(1)} = \begin{cases} 1, & \text{in labor force} \\ 0, & \text{otherwise} \end{cases}$$

$$Y_{(2)} = \begin{cases} 1, & \text{enrolled in school} \\ 0, & \text{otherwise} \end{cases}$$

Table 8.8
Logistic Function Results (t-values in Parentheses)

	Labor force status		School enrollment	
	Male	Female	Male	Female
Male-headed household	.67	.56	.14	−.18
	(1.25)	(.86)	(.26)	(.79)
Number of potential earners	−.66	−.36	.23	−.23
(age 16 and over)	(2.54)	(.93)	(.99)	(.80)
Age	.79	.43	−1.40	−.97
	(3.03)	(1.47)	(4.28)	(2.97)
Family earnings minus own	−.73	−.47	.03	.26
earnings ($100 last week)	(1.90)	(.90)	(.08)	(.53)
Family AFDC payments	.01	.12	.08	.07
($100/month)	(.04)	(.32)	(.17)	(.19)
Family social security	−.17	−.27	.28	.52
payments ($100/month)	(.80)	(.71)	(1.26)	(1.67)
Family food stamp payments	−.03	.64	−.47	1.52
($100/month)	(.33)	(.98)	(.54)	(1.13)
Mother's education (years)	.12	−.03	−.01	.11
	(1.16)	(.28)	(.08)	(1.18)
Teenager's education	−.16	.13	.88	.78
(years)	(.74)	(.39)	(3.37)	(2.81)
Size of family	.19	−.07	−.09	.16
	(1.98)	(.64)	(.97)	(1.51)
Experimental	−.58	−.53	.33	.17
	(1.51)	(1.22)	(.77)	(.36)
Constant	−13.79	−8.36	16.44	7.54
	(3.20)	(1.86)	(3.35)	(1.90)
Log of likelihood function	−34.22	−28.02	−29.46	−28.90
N	137	129	137	129

Source: McDonald and Stephenson, 1979.

Equation (8.23) is estimated separately for the preceding two dependent variables as well as separately for males and females (see Tables 8.8 and 8.9). It is not clear why the two dependent variables are used separately, since they are obviously highly intercorrelated. The decision to participate or not participate in the labor force is dependent, to a large extent, on the decision to continue schooling (so that a multivariate logit regression could have been used). The data are from the second year of the experiment (the third periodic interview), in order to exclude as much as possible the "start-up" and "wind-down" effects of the experiment. The NIT treatment effect(s) is measured either by dummy variables (see Tables 8.8 and 8.9) or by actual guarantee levels and tax rates for those teenagers whose families were below the breakeven income level. These variables are not explicitly discussed by McDonald and Stephenson, however, so their exact role and

Table 8.9
Teenagers Logit Coefficients (t-values in Parentheses)

	Labor force status			School enrollment		
	1	2	3	4	5	6
Male						
Experimental	−.578 (.151)	—	—	.330 (.77)	—	—
Experimental, under breakeven	—	−1.019 (1.92)	—	—	1.853 (2.33)	—
Over breakeven (experimentals and controls)	—	−.235 (.50)	−.247 (.52)	—	.182 (.32)	.637 (.78)
Guarantee/1000 (under breakeven experimentals)	—	—	−.459 (1.15)	—	—	.617 (1.49)
Tax (under breakeven experimentals)	—	—	1.416 (.51)	—	—	−.602 (.19)
Female						
Experimental	−.525 (1.22)	—	—	.168 (.36)	—	—
Experimental, under breakeven	—	−.224 (.47)	—	—	−.132 (.22)	—
Over breakeven (experimentals and controls)	—	−.357 (.51)	−.515 (1.00)	—	.617 (.94)	.858 (1.26)
Guarantee/1000 (under breakeven experimentals)	—	—	−1.009 (1.74)	—	—	.618 (1.76)
Tax (under breakeven experimentals)	—	—	6.699 (1.77)	—	—	−5.104 (2.00)

Source: McDonald and Stephenson, 1979.

definition are not clear. The results for males indicate that labor force participation is reduced and school enrollment is increased at statistically significant levels for below breakeven experimentals compared to "below breakeven" controls—in probability terms $-.11$ and $+.18$, respectively, at the mean point. The separate effects of the guarantee and the tax rate are insignificant. For females the results are more paradoxical. While the total experimental effect is zero, the separate effects of the guarantee and the tax rate attain statistical nonzero significance. Considering the value of the function at the mean point, the results indicate that an additional guarantee amount of $1000.00 lowers labor force participation by a probability of .07 (and increases school enrollment by .05); an increase in the tax rate of .2 increases labor force participation by a probability of .10 (and lowers the probability of school attendance by .08). The nonsignificance of the total experiment effect, but significance of its constituent parts, is very puzzling. The authors offer no explanation of these results.

NOTES

1. The precise role played by family income is not very clear. Thus the reader is never sure whether eligibility depended on actual or normal family income, and if on the latter, exactly how normal income was determined.

2. Families who earned in excess of 2.4 times the poverty level were undersampled by a factor of approximately 3.

3. It is not specified whether such differences were statistically significant.

4. This amounts to imposing an a priori restriction on the values of β_i, because according to "economic theory" an increase in nonlabor income does not lead to an increase in H, the number of hours of market labor, all else being constant. The estimation procedure is biased if the restriction is in fact incorrect.

5. It is assumed that experimentals possess a concave budget curve while controls exhibit a convex budget curve, which motivates distinct definitions for the probabilities $P(NC)_i$ and $P(C)_i$.

6. Since the Burtless–Hausman model is "behavioral," unlike that used in the New Jersey analysis, a measure of explanatory power is important.

7. Others have used instrumental variables to control for this endogeneity.

8. The husband's nonwage income is increased by the value of his wife's wage rate multiplied by 95 hours per month, the average number of hours worked per month by all wives in the sample.

9. These decisions are apparently based on previous work by Wolf (1977) and Hausman and Wise (1979), indicating that the Gary experiment had no effect on marital dissolution; and that sample attrition will not bias estimation results if Eq. (8.13) contains control variables. The control variables presumably correct for any bias that may result.

10. It is not clear why covariates are not interacted with the dummy D.

11. Note that the interpretation of these intervals is somewhat ambiguous since only *point* estimates of α are given. The response *intervals* are due to the fact that two different models

are used, and *not* because of sampling variance. Had sampling interval estimates been given, differences between one model and another would have been much greater.

12. While significance levels for husbands are indicated at the 90% level in the basic model, only 95% and 99% significance levels are indicated for wives (as well as husbands and female heads) in Table 8.4.

13. The mean number of hours worked per week by the working sample (wives) is actually *lower* for the control group than it is for the experimental group.

14. Horner does not discuss difficulties usually encountered with nonlinear equations, such as statistical inefficiency arising from multicollinearity. Also most significance tests are one-tailed (see Table 8.6).

15. To "control" for academic ability and motivation McDonald and Stephenson omit from the sample teenagers who completed less than eight years of school, since these would have failed at least one year (presumably due to lack of ability and/or motivation). This factor, however, is already controlled for by the control group teenagers. In any event a dummy variable could be included to check for systematic differences between controls and experimentals as far as academic ability and interest are concerned. This strategy has the advantage of increasing degrees of freedom.

16. The model is not stated explicitly but is implied from the table of results (see Table 8.8). We assume the model to be linear in the variables (and in the coefficients).

9 Conclusions

The American income maintenance experiments, taken together, reflect their time and place. They were the result of a sincere and concentrated effort to understand the nature of poverty and to design better income transfer programs for work-eligible individuals and their families. The policy debate had tentatively settled down for the time being on such issues as the extent of the work disincentive, the cost of a national NIT, and whether a guaranteed income could be delivered at effective cost and with minimal intrusion into individual privacy. There was little more to be gained by further discussions on a scientific level without "getting the facts."

This book has been concerned with what the "facts" are, how the various researchers "got the facts," and the amount of confidence we should place on all these "facts," taken together. Consequently, we have been concerned less directly with criticism of the experiments with respect to their implementation or operations and virtually not at all with the relationship between the experiments and the political process [e.g., see Rossi and Lyall (1976)]. Nor have we addressed directly whether the experiments should have occurred at all, given both the extremely costly nature of large-scale social experiments and their potential benefits. Others have examined in detail the scientific, political, and policy preconditions for large-scale social experiments [e.g., see Riechen and Boruch (1974)]. Even on the most narrow view whether the marginal benefits of having exogenous variation in the income maintenance experiments justified their enormous cost, we did not take a firm stance. There is, however, some consensus that the gain in knowledge was indeed worth the money (Keeley 1981, p. 172), and we are part of this consensus.

We have restricted our attention in this book, to repeat, to a survey and assessment of "the facts" themselves, and the techniques by which the facts were produced at the analysis stage of the experimental process. Just what are the facts then?

The four income maintenance experiments, conducted in diverse parts of the United States, and for different racial–cultural subsamples in both urban and rural settings, failed to detect any large desertion of prime-age males from the labor force. However, all experiments detected some experimental reaction to payments (treatments); the magnitude of the response effect tended to be between 3 and 8% (taken as *point* estimates, *interval* estimates are much wider). The exception was the Keeley et al. analysis of the SIME–DIME data, which found a much larger effect. We suggested (in Chapter 7) that these results contain many statistical short-comings, and therefore the "large and significant" withdrawal from the labor force reported by the authors should, in our opinion, be heavily discounted.

Secondary earners (mainly wives) exhibited a larger tendency to reduce their labor supply, although the percentage reductions are much more variable and, in fact, represent much smaller absolute reductions because of the relatively small number of working wives. Nevertheless, an overall reduction was found for both males and females, although smaller in magnitude than was perhaps expected.

Among the New Jersey black subsample, prime-age married males actu-ally exhibited a statistically significant *increase* in labor supply, though not large. Black wives also appear to have increased their earnings slightly, although other labor supply measures decreased. The behavior of the blacks was certainly not predictable from economic theory and reveals the danger of too much a priori specification and restriction.

Readers interested in examining the overall experimental results reported by the four projects may consult the detailed tables and discussions pre-sented in Chapters 5 through 8. In what follows, we give our views concerning the more theoretical aspects of statistical estimation carried out by the experiments as a whole. By necessity (and the extreme advantage of hindsight), some of our criticisms will be negative, but this should not be interpreted as a denial of the usefulness of the experiments. On the contrary, given the magnitude of the endeavors and the quantity and quality of the data, most of the econometric and statistical analysis undertaken is truly impressive. Accordingly, it is important and appropriate that we express our unabashed admiration at the outset.

Having stated that the overall effect in the experimental samples did not appear to be large, we would like to caution against hasty conclusions that a national NIT program would have no or little effect on labor supply. Many critics have alluded to the "temporary" nature of the experiments and the difficulty of drawing inferences about responses to permanent, universal changes based on estimates from a temporary, dispersed treatment program. Furthermore, structural changes in the economy may also modify the nature of estimated responses; for example, high temporary or permanent unemployment in an economy may influence people both to keep their jobs and not to reduce labor supply. But these reservations were recognized at the beginning of the experiments; they were not necessarily unexpected and certainly were not the result of viewing the econometric and statistical analyses. Rather, our main caution against extreme optimism or pessimism stems from a difficulty in accepting certain statistical practices used, and the methods by which the results were reported. The "final numbers" that emerged from the experimental findings therefore need not be representative of the target population; that is, the working poor. In short, our reservations are ex post ones.

First, we pointed out in Chapter 3 that the Conlisk–Watts algorithm did not necessarily result in a representative sample, largely because of the "policy weights" and the budget constraint. Therefore the labor supply equations may represent biased estimates of the labor supply behavior of the working poor under a guaranteed income plan available to the U.S. population. Moreover, if the temporary nature of the experiment caused a more cautious response on the part of experimentals, we will simply have to wait for further results from SIME–DIME, which retained a sample for a 20-year period, before drawing any inferences about "long-run equilibrium" labor supply effects with confidence.

The RIME experiment used highly "adjusted" data for farm operators in order to reduce errors in variables. We believe (see Chapter 6) that this procedure probably led to even larger measurement error and therefore contributed to bias over and above the two reasons cited earlier. The use of normal wages and normal income measures may have also exacerbated the problem of errors in variables; for example, the SIME–DIME estimates produced adjusted (normal) wage and income measures that were virtually uncorrelated with the observed wages and incomes. All of these factors most probably resulted in biased and inconsistent estimates of labor supply.

Second, the dependent variables (such as employment, hours worked, wage rates, etc.) were analyzed independently, in spite of the fact that theory would expect these variables to be intercorrelated. Consequently, a potentially rich source of information was lost, resulting in relatively less efficient estimators. Therefore, some of the labor supply reductions reported as insignificant may turn out to be significant once interdependence of various labor supply variables is taken into account. Additionally, relatively small experimental effects might go undetected if multicollinearity were present.

And multicollinearity could easily be introduced even for cross-sectional data through quadratic and interaction terms among the continuous control covariates—a not uncommon practice by the researchers. Even more surprising perhaps, in light of the extensive econometric background of the researchers involved in the analysis, simultaneity between the husbands' and wives' labor supply decisions was not fully considered (e.g., by simultaneous equations methods).

Finally, basic (and elementary) statistical information was often not included in the final reports of the experiments. One important piece of information omitted particularly stands out. None of the experiments indicated whether or not the normality assumption was satisfied. This condition is indispensable for using the t, F, and chi-squared tests. Consequently, it becomes impossible to conduct an independent assessment of the labor supply results. Needless to say, least squares estimators are not always robust with respect to nonnormality of the error term. Thus the significance (or nonsignificance) of labor supply behavior reported by the experiments is brought into question.

It is absolutely necessary and proper to repeat what we said earlier. Although we criticized the econometric and statistic procedures of the many researchers who worked on the income maintenance experiment data, our message should not be interpreted as unappreciative. Perhaps this is the best way to conclude. We seriously doubt that others (including ourselves) could have fared any better given the circumstances. Furthermore, a great many (including ourselves) might have done much, much worse.

References

Aaron, H. J.
    1975   "Cautionary Notes on the Experiment." *In Work Incentives and Guarantees: The New Jersey Negative Income Tax Experiment* (J. A. Pechman and P. M. Timpane, eds.) The Brookings Institution, Washington D.C.

Ahlberg, J. H., Nelson, E. N., and Walsh, J. L.
    1967   *The Theory of Splines and Their Applications.* Academic Press, New York.

Amemiya, T.
    1973a "Multiple Regression and Simultaneous Equation Models When the Dependent Variables are Truncated Normal." Technical Report No. 82, Institute for Mathematical Studies in the Social Sciences, Stanford Univ. Press, Stanford, California.

Amemiya, T.
    1973b "Regression Analysis When the Dependent Variable is Truncated Normal." *Econometrica* **41,** 997–1016.

Anderson, A., Basilevsky, A., and Hum, D.
    1983   "Missing Data: A Review of the Literature," *In Handbook of Survey Research,* (P. Rossi, J. Wright, and A. Anderson eds.) Academic Press, New York.

Ashenfelter, O.
    1978   "The Labor Supply Response of Wage Earners." *In Welfare in Rural Areas* (J. Palmer and J. Pechman eds.) The Brookings Institution.

Ashenfelter, O., and Heckman, J.
    1974   "The Estimation of Income and Substitution Effects in a Model of Family Labor Supply." *Econometrica* **42,** 73–85.

Avery, R.
    1973. "The Effects of the Welfare 'Bias' on Family Earnings Response to the Experiment." *In The Final Report of the New Jersey Graduated Work Incentives Experiment, Vol. I: Central Labor Supply Response, Part* B.

Barnow, B. S., Cain, G. G., and Goldberger, A. S.
    1980   "Issues in the Analysis of Selectivity Bias." *In Evaluation Studies* (E. W. Stromsdorfer and G. Farkas, eds.) Review Annual, Sage Publications, Beverly Hills, California.

Barth, M. C., Orr, L. L., and Palmer, J. L.
    1975   "Policy Implications: A Positive View." *In Work Incentives and Guarantees: The New Jersey Negative Income Tax Experiment* (J. A. Pechman and P. M. Timpane, eds.) Brookings Studies in Social Experimentation, Brookings Institution, Washington, D.C.

Baumol, W. J.
    1973a "An Overview of the Results on Consumption, Health and Social Behavior." *The Final Report of the New Jersey Graduated Work Incentives Experiment, Vol.* III: *Responses with Respect to Expenditure, Health and Social Behavior, Part D.*

Baumol, W. J.
    1973b "An Overview of the Results on Consumption, Health and Social Behavior." *The Journal of Human Resources* **9,** 253–64.

Bawden, D. L.
    1970   "Income Maintenance and the Rural Poor: An Experimental Approach." *American Journal of Agricultural Economics,* Vol. **52,** pp. 438–41.

Bawden, D. L.
    1976   Chapters 1–4 in *Final Report of Rural Income Maintenance Experiment.* Institute for Research on Poverty, Vol. III. University of Wisconsin, Madison, Wisconsin.

Bawden, D. L., and Harrar, W.
    1978   "Design and Operation." *In Welfare in Rural Areas* (J. Palmer and J. Pechman, eds.) The Brookings Institution.

Box, G. E. P., and Draper, N. R.
    1959   "A Basis for the Selection of a Response Surface Design." *Journal of the American Statistical Association* **54,** 622–54.

Burdick, D. S., and Naylor, T. H.
    1969   "Response Surface Techniques in Economies." *Review of the International Statistical Institute* **37,** 18–35.

Burtless, G.
    1977   "The Effect of Taxation on Labor Supply: Evaluating the Gary Negative Income Tax Experiment." Working Paper A-27, Mathematica Policy Research. Princeton, New Jersey

Burtless, G., and Hausman, J. A.
    1978   "The Effect of Taxation on Labor Supply: Evaluating the Gary Negative Income Tax Experiment." *Journal of Political Economy,* **86,** 1103–29.

Buse, A., and Lim, L.
    1977   "Cubic Splines as a Special Case of Restricted Least Squares." *Journal of the American Statistical Association* **72,** 64–8.

Cain, G. G.
    1973   "The Effect of Income Maintenance Laws on Fertility; Results from the New Jersey–Pennsylvania Experiment." *The Final Report of the New Jersey Graduated Work Incentives Experiment, Vol.* III: *Responses with Respect to Expenditure, Health and Social Behavior, Part D.*

Cain, G. G., and Watts, H. W. (eds.)
    1973   *Income Maintenance and Labor Supply.* Academic Press, New York.

Cain, G. G., Nicholson, W., Mallar, C. D., and Woolridge, J.
    1973   "The Labor Supply Response of Married Women, Husband Present, In the Graduated Work Incentive Experiment." *In The Final Report of the New Jersey Graduated Work Incentives Experiment, Vol.* I: *Central Labor Supply Response, Part B.*

Cain, G. G., Nicholson, W., Mallar, C. D. and Woolridge, J.
    1974   "The Labor-Supply Response of Married Women, Husband Present." *The Journal of Human Resources,* **9,** 201–22.

Campbell, D. T.
1963 "From Description to Experimentation: Interpreting Trends as Quasi-Experiments." *In Problems in Measuring Change* (Harris, C. W. ed.) Univ. of Wisconsin Press, Madison.

Cogan, J.
1978 "Negative Income Taxation and Labor Supply—New Evidence from the New Jersey–Pennsylvania Negative Income Tax Experiment." Rand Corp., R-2155, Santa Monica, California.

Cogan, J.
1979 "Review of: The New Jersey Income Maintenance Experiment. Vol. 2: Labor-Supply Response." *Journal of Political Economy* **83**, 436–40.

Conlisk, J.
1973 "Choice of Response Functional Form in Designing Subsidy Experiments." *Econometrica* **41**, 643–56.

Conlisk, J.
1968 "Sample Design for the Negative Income Tax Experiment." Econometrics Society Summer Meeting, Boulder, Colorado. (Unpublished Mimeograph).

Conlisk, J.
1974 "Notes on a Canonical Form Theorem Useful in Regression Designs." *Journal of the American Statistical Association* **69**, 196–98.

Conlisk, J., and Kurz, M.
1972 "The Assignment Model of the Seattle and Denver Income Maintenance Experiments." Research Memorandum 15, Center for the Study of Welfare Policy. Stanford Research Institute, Stanford, California.

Conlisk, J., and Watts, H.
1969 "A Model for Optimizing Experimental Designs for Estimating Response Surfaces." *American Statistical Association Proceedings, Social Statistics Section,* 150–6. (Also reprinted (1970) in *Field Experimentation in Income Maintenance,* Institute for Research on Poverty, University of Wisconsin. Madison Reprint #54).

Crawford, D. L.
1979 "Estimating Models of Earnings from Truncated Samples." Ph.D. Dissertation, University of Wisconsin, Madison, Wisconsin.

Elesh, D., and Lefcowitz, M. J.
1973 "The Effect of Health on the Supply of and Returns to Labor." *The Final Report of the New Jersey Graduated Work Incentives Experiment, Vol.* I: *Central Labor Supply Response, Part* B.

Fedorov, V. V.
1972 "Theory of Optimal Experiments." Academic Press, New York.

Ferber, R., and Hirsch, W. Z.
1978 "Social Experimentation and Economic Policy: A Survey." *Journal of Economic Literature* **16**, 1379–1414.

Ferber, R., and Hirsch, W. Z.
1982 "Social Experimentation and Economic Policy." Cambridge Surveys of Economic Literature. Cambridge University Press, Cambridge.

Friedman, Milton.
1963 *Capitalism and Freedom.* University of Chicago Press, Chicago.

Gallant, A. R., and Fuller, W. A.
1973 "Fitting Segmented Polynomial Regression Models Whose Joint Points Have to Be Estimated." *Journal of the American Statistical Association* **68**, 144–47.

Garfinkel, I.
1973   "The Effects of Welfare on the Labor Supply Response." *The Final Report of the New Jersey Graduates Work Incentives Experiment, Vol.* III: *Responses with Respect to Expenditure, Health, and Social Behavior, Part D.*

Goodwin, L.
1980   "Limitations of the Seattle and Denver Income Maintenance Analysis." *In Evaluation Studies: Review Annual, Vol.* 5, (E. W. Stromsdorfer and G. Farkas eds.) Sage Publications, Beverly Hills, California.

Gottschalk, P. T.
1981   "A Note on Estimating Treatment Effects." *American Economic Review* **71,** 764–69.

Graybill, F. A.
1961   *An Introduction to Linear Statistical Models.* McGraw-Hill, New York.

Greene, W. H.
1981   "Sample Selection Bias as a Specification Error: Comment." *Econometrica,* **49,** 795–98.

Greenless, J. S., Reece, W. S., and Zieschang, K. D.
1982   "Imputation of Missing Values When the Probability of Response Depends on the Variable Being Imputed." *Journal of American Statistics Association,* **77,** 251–61.

Greville, T. N. E.
1968   *Theory and Applications of Spline Functions.* Academic Press, New York.

Hall, R. E.
1975   "Effects of the Experimental Negative Income Tax on Labor Supply." *In Work Incentive and Guarantees: The New Jersey Negative Income Tax Experiment* (J. A. Pechman and P. M. Timpane, eds.) Brookings Studies in Social Experimentation, Brookings Institution, Washington, D.C.

Hall, R. E.
1973   "Wages, Income, and Hours of Work in the U.S. Labor Force." *In Income Maintenance and Labor Supply* (G. G. Cain and H. W. Watts, eds.) Academic Press, New York.

Hannan, M. T., Tuma, N. B., and Groeneveld, L. P.
1980   "Reply to Goodwin." *In Evaluation Studies: Review Annual, Vol.* 5, (E. W. Stromsdorfer, G. Farkas, eds.) Sage Publications, Beverly Hills, California.

Hausman, J. A., and Wise, D. A.
1976   "The Evaluation of Results from Truncated Samples: The New Jersey Income Maintenance Experiment." *Annuals of Economic and Social Measurement* **5,** 421–46.

Hausman, J. A., and Wise, D. A.
1977a "Social Experimentation, Truncated Distributions, and Efficient Estimation." *Econometrica* **45,** 919–38.

Hausman, J., and Wise, D.
1977b "Stratification on Endogenous Variables and Estimation: The Gary Income Maintenance Experiment." Kennedy School Discussion Paper.

Hausman, J. A., and Wise, D. A.
1979   "Attrition Bias in Experimental and Panel Data: The Gary Income Maintenance Experiment." *Econometrica* **47,** 455–73.

Haveman, Robert H., and Watts, Harold W.
1976   "Social Experimentation as Policy Research: A Review of Negative Income Tax Experiments." *In Evaluation Studies, Vol.* 1 (G. V. Glass, ed.) Sage Publications, Beverly Hills, California.

Heckman, J. J.
  1979   "Sample Selection Bias as a Specification Error." *Econometrica* **47,** 153–61.
Heckman, J. J.
  1976   "The Common Structure of Statistical Models of Truncation, Sample Selection and Limited Dependent Variables, and a Simple Estimator for Such Models." *Annual of Economic and Social Measurements* **5,** 475–92.
Heckman, J. J.
  1977   "Sample Selection Bias as a Specification Error (with an Application to the Estimation of Labor Supply Functions)." Report 7720, Center for Mathematical Studies in Business and Economics, University of Chicago Press, Chicago, Illinois.
Heckman, J. J.
  1980   "Addendum to 'Sample Selection Bias as a Specification Error'" *In Evaluation Studies Vol.* 5, (E. Stromsdorfer and G. Farkas eds.), pp. 70–74. Sage Publications, Beverly Hills, California.
Henry, N. W.
  1975   "On the Use of 'The Allocation Model.'" Unpublished memo, the Gary Experiment.
Hildebrand, George H.
  1967   "Second Thoughts on the Negative Income Tax." *Industrial Relations,* **6,** No. 2.
Hitch, Thomas K.
  1966   "Why the Negative Income Tax Won't Work." *Challenge,* **14,** No. 6.
Hollister, R. G.
  1973   "The Labor Supply Response of the Family." *In The Final Report of the New Jersey Graduated Work Incentives Experiment, Vol.* I: *Center Labor Supply Response, Part* B.
Hollister, R. G.
  1974   "The Labor-Supply Response of the Family." *The Journal of Human Resources* **9,** 224–51.
Horner, D.
  1973   "The Impact of Negative Taxes on the Labor Supply of Low Income Male Family Heads." *In The Final Report of the New Jersey Graduated Work Incentives Experiment, Vol.* I: *Central Labor Supply Response, Part* B.
Horner, D. L.
  1977   "A Life Cycle, Human Capital Model of the Labor Supply Response to Negative Income Taxation: Evidence for Black Male Family Heads from the Gary Experiment." Working Paper No. A-24, Mathematica Policy Research, Princeton, New Jersey.
Hum, D., Laub, M., and Powell, B.
  1979a   "The Objectives and Design of the Manitoba Basic Annual Income Experiment." Technical Report No. 1. Mincome Manitoba, Winnipeg, Manitoba.
Hum, D., Laub, M., Metcalf, C., and Sabourin, D.
  1979b   "The Sample Design and Assignment Model of the Manitoba Basic Annual Income Experiment." Technical Report No. 2. Mincome Manitoba, Winnipeg, Manitoba.
Hurd, M.
  1976   "The Estimation of Non-Linear Labor Supply Functions with Taxes from a Truncated Sample." Mimeograph, Stanford University, Stanford, California.
Johnson, N. L., and Kotz, S.
  1972   *Distributions in Statistics: Continuous Multivariate Distributions.* Wiley, New York.

Johnson, T.
 1972 "Qualitative and Limited Dependent Variables in Economic Relationships." *Econometric* **40,** 455–62.
Johnson, W. R.
 1980 "The Effect of a Negative Income Tax on Risk-Taking in the Labor Market." *Economic Inquiry* **18,** 395–407.
Keeley, M. C.
 1981 *Labor Supply and Public Policy: A Critical Review.* Academic Press, New York.
Keeley, M., and Robins, P. K.
 1978 "The Design of Social Experiments: A Critique of the Conlisk–Watts Assignment Model." Research Memorandum 57. Center for the Study of Welfare Policy, Stanford Research Institute, Menlo Park, California.
Keeley, M. C., Robins, P. K., Spiegelman, R. G., and West, R. W.
 1976 "The Estimation of Labor Supply Models Using Experimental Data: Evidence From the Seattle and Denver Income Maintenance Experiments." Research Memorandum 29. Center for the Study of Welfare Policy, Stanford Research Institute, Menlo Park, California.
Keeley, M. C., Robins, P. K., Spiegelman, R. G., and West, R. W.
 1977a "The Labor Supply Effects and Costs of Alternative Negative Income Tax Programs: Evidence from the Seattle and Denver Income Maintenance Experiments, Part I: The Labour Supply Response Function." Research Memorandum 38. Center for the Study of Welfare Policy, Stanford Research Institute, Menlo Park, California.
Keeley, M. C., Robins, P. K., Spiegelman, R. G., and West, R. W.
 1977b "The Labor Supply Effects and Cost of Alternative Negative Income Tax Programs: Evidence from the Seattle and Denver Income Maintenance Experiments, Part II: National Publications Using the Labor Supply Response Function. Research Memorandum 39. Center for the Study of Welfare Policy, Stanford Research Institute, Menlo Park, California.
Keeley, M. C., Robins, P. K., Spiegelman, R. G., and West, R. W.
 1977c "An Interim Report on the World Effort Effects and Costs of a Negative Income Tax Using Results of the Seattle and Denver Income Maintenance Experiments: A Summary." Research Memorandum 41. Center for the Study of Welfare Policy, Stanford Research Institute, Menlo Park, California.
Keeley, M. C., Robins, P.K., Spiegelman, R. G., and West, R. W.
 1978 "The Estimation of Labor Supply Models Using Experimental Data." *The American Economic Review* **68,** 873–87.
Kehrer, K. C.
 1978 "The Gary Income Maintenance Experiment: Summary of Initial Findings." *In Evaluation Studies* (T. Cook and associates, eds.) *Vol.* 3, Sage Publications, Beverly Hills, California.
Kehrer, K. C., Bruml, E. K., Burtless, G. T., and Richardson, D. N.
 1975 "The Gary Income Maintenance Experiment: Design, Administration and Data Files." *In Final Report of the Gary Income Maintenance Experiment.* Mathematica Policy Research, Princeton, New Jersey.
Kehrer, K. C., McDonald, J. F., and Moffitt, R. A.
 1979 *Final Report of the Gary Income Maintenance Experiment: Labor Supply.* Mathematica Policy Research, Princeton, New Jersey.
Kelly, T., and Singer, L.
 1971 "The Gary Income Maintenance Experiment: Plans and Progress," *American Economic Review Proceeding* **61,** May, pp. 30–38.

Kendall, M. G., and Stuart, A.
1968   *The Advanced Theory of Statistics, Vol.* 3.   Charles Griffin and Company, London.
Kershaw, D. N., and Fair, J. (eds.)
1973   "Operations, Surveys, and Administration."   *The Final Report of the New Jersey Graduated Work Incentives Experiment, Vol.* IV.   Mathematica, Inc., Princeton, New Jersey.
Kiefer, J.
1959   "Optimum Experimental Designs."   *Journal of the Royal Statistical Society Series B,* **21,** 272–304.
Knudsen, J. H., Mamer, J., Scott, R. A., and Shore, A. R.
1973a "Information Levels and Labor Response."   *In The Final Report of the New Jersey Graduated Work Incentives Experiment, Vol.* I: *Central Labor Supply Response, Part* B.   Mathematica, Inc., Princeton, New Jersey.
Knudsen, J. H., Scott, R. A., and Shore, A. R.
1973b "Changes in Household Composition."   *In The Final Report of the New Jersey Graduated Work Incentives Experiment, Vol.* III: *Responses with Respect to Expenditure, Health and Social Behavior, Part* D.   Mathematica, Inc., Princeton, New Jersey.
Kurz, M.
1978   "Negative Income Taxation."   *In Federal Tax Reform: Myths and Realities.*   Institute for Contemporary Studies, (M. J. Boskin, ed.)   San Francisco, California.
Kurz, M., and Spiegelman, R.
1971   "The Seattle Experiment: The Combined Effect of Income Maintenance and Manpower Investment," *American Economic Review,* Proceedings, **61,** May, pp. 22–29.
Kurz, M., and Spiegelman, R.
1972   "The Design of the Seattle and Denver Income Maintenance Experiments" Research Memorandum 18, Center for the Study of Welfare Policy.   Stanford Research Institute, Stanford, California.
Ladinsky, J., and Wells, A.
1973   "Social Integration, Leisure Activity, Media Expose, and Life-Style Enhancement."   *In The Final Report of the New Jersey Graduated Work Incentives Experiment, Vol.* III: *Responses with Respect to Expenditure, Health and Social Behavior, Part* D.   Mathematica Inc., Princeton, New Jersey.
Lady Rhys-Williams
1942   *Something to Look Forward to.*   MacDonald, London.
Lady Rhys-Williams
1953   *Taxation and Incentive.*   Oxford University Press, London and New York.
Lampman, R. J.
1965a *Negative Rates Income Taxation.*   Prepared for the Office of Economic Opportunity, unpublished.
Lampman, R. J.
1965b *Preliminary Report on a Plan for Negative Income Taxation.*   Prepared for the Office of Economic Opportunity, unpublished.
Lampman, R. J.
1974   "The Decision to undertake the New Jersey Experiment."   *In Final Report of the New Jersey Experiment, Vol.* IV, mimeograph.   Mathematica, Princeton, New Jersey and Institute for Research on Poverty, Madison, Wisconsin.
Lee, L. F.
1975   *A Note on Two Stage Estimations of Heckman's Model,* University of Rochester Press, Rochester, New York.

Lefcowitz, M. J., and Elesh, D.
1973 "Experimental Effects on Health and Health Care Utilization." *In The Final Report of the New Jersey Graduated Work Incentives Experiment, Vol. III: Responses with Respect to Expenditure, Health and Social Behavior, Part D.* Mathematica Inc., Princeton, New Jersey.

Levine, R. A.
1975 "How and Why the Experiment Came About." *In Work Incentives and Income Guarantees: The New Jersey Negative Income Tax Experiment* (J. A. Pechman and P. M. Timpane, eds.) Brookings Studies in Social Experimentation, Brookings Institution, Washington, D.C.

Little, R. A.
1982 "Models for Non-response in Sample Surveys." *Journal of the American Statistical Association* **77,** 237–250.

McDonald, J. F., and Stephenson, S. P.
1979 "The Effect of Income Maintenance on the School-Enrollment and Labor Supply Decisions of Teenagers." *The Journal of Human Resources,* **14,** 488–495.

Maddala, G. S.
1977 *Econometrics.* McGraw-Hill, New York.

Maddala, G., and Lee, L. F.
1978 "Recursive Models with Qualitative Endogenous Variables." *Annals of Economic and Social Measurement,* **5,** 525–545.

Mahoney, B. S. and Mahoney, W. M.
1975 "Policy Implications: A Skeptical View." *In Work Incentives and Income Guarantees: The New Jersey Negative Income Tax Experiment,* (J. A. Pechman and P. M. Timpane, eds.) Brookings Studies in Social Experimentation, Brookings Institution, Washington, D.C.

Mallar, C.
1973 "School Enrollment and Labor Force Participation Among Young Adults." *In The Final Report of the New Jersey Graduated Work Incentives Experiment, Vol. I: Central Labor Supply Response, Part B.* Mathematica Inc., Princeton, New Jersey.

Metcalf, C. E.
1973a "Consumption Behavior Under a Permanent Negative Income Tax: Preliminary Evidence." *In The Final Report of the New Jersey Graduated Work Incentives Experiment, Vol. III: Responses with Respect to Expenditure, Health and Social Behavior, Part D.* Mathematica Inc., Princeton, New Jersey.

Metcalf, C. E.
1973b "Making Inferences from Controlled Income Maintenance Experiments." *American Economic Review* **63,** 478–83.

Metcalf, C., and Bawden, D. L.
1976 "The Sample Design" Chapter 3, *In RIME Final Report, Vol.* 1.

Middleton, R., and Allen, V.
1973 "Social Psychological Consequences of the Graduated Work Incentive Experiment." *In The Final Report of the New Jersey Graduated Work Incentives Experiment, Vol. III: Responses with Respect to Expenditure, Health and Social Behavior, Part D.* Mathematica Inc., Princeton, New Jersey.

Moffitt, R. A.
1977 *Labor Supply, Kinked Budget Constraints, and the Negative Income Tax.* Working Paper A-19. Mathematica Policy Research, Princeton, New Jersey.

Moffitt, R. A.
1979 "The Labor Supply Response in the Gary Experiment." *The Journal of Human Resources* **14,** 477–87.

Morris, C. N., Newhause, J. P., and Archibald, R. W.
1980   "On the Theory and Practice of Obtaining Unbiased and Efficient Samples in Social Surveys." *In Evaluation Studies, Review Annual, Vol.* 5, (E. W. Stromsdorfer and G. Farkas, eds.) Sage Publ., Beverly Hills, California.

Nelson, F. D.
1977   "Censored Regression Models With Unobserved, Stochastic Censoring Thresholds." *Journal of Econometrics* **6**, 581–92.

Nicholson, W.
1973a   "Relationship of the Female Labor Supply Characteristics of the Experimental Sample to Those of Other Samples." *In The Final Report of the New Jersey Graduated Work Incentive Experiment, Vol.* I: *Central Labor Supply Response, Part* B. Mathematica Inc., Princeton, New Jersey.

Nicholson, W.
1973b   "Expenditure Patterns in the Graduated Work Incentive Experiment: A Descriptive Survey." *The Final Report of the New Jersey Graduated Work Incentives Experiment, Vol.* III: *Responses with Respect to Expenditure, Health and Social Behavior, Part* D. Mathematica Inc., Princeton, New Jersey.

Orcutt, G., and A. Orcutt
1968   "Incentive and Disincentive Experimentation for Income Maintenance Policy Purposes." *American Economic Review* **58**, 754–772.

Palmer, J. L., and Pechman, J. A. (eds.)
1978   *Welfare in Rural Areas: The North Carolina–Iowa Income Maintenance Experiment.* Brookings Institution, Washington, D.C.

Pechman, J. A., and Timpane, P. M.
1975a   "Introduction and Summary." *In* Work Incentives and Income Guarantees: The New Jersey Negative Income Tax Experiment (J. A. Pechman and P. M. Timpane, eds.) Brookings Studies in Social Experimentation, Brookings Institution, Washington, D.C.

Pechman, J. A., and Timpane, P. M. (eds.)
1975b   *Work Incentives and Income Guarantees: The New Jersey Negative Income Tax Experiment.* Brookings Studies in Social Experimentation, Brookings Institution, Washington, D.C.

Podoluk, J.
1968   *Income of Canadians.* Queen's Printer, Ottawa, Ontario.

Poirier, D. J.
1973a   "Technical Notes on Bilinear Splines." *The New Jersey Graduated Work Incentives Experiment, Vol.* III: *Technical Notes, Part* E. Mathematica Inc., Princeton, New Jersey.

Poirier, D. J.
1973b   "Technical Notes on Cubic Splines." *The New Jersey Graduated Work Incentives Experiment, Vol.* III: *Technical Notes, Part* E. Mathematica Inc., Princeton, New Jersey.

Poirier, D. J.
1973c   "Technical Notes on Periodic Cubic Splines." *The Final Report of the New Jersey Graduated Work Incentives Experiment, Vol.* III: *Technical Notes, Part* E. Mathematica Inc., Princeton, New Jersey.

Poirier, D. J.
1976   The Econometrics of Structural Change. North-Holland Publ., Amsterdam.

Poirier, D. J.
1973   "Piecewise Regression Using Cubic Splines." Journal of the American Statistical Association **68**, 515–24.

Poirier, D. J.
1978 "The Use of the Box–Cox Transformation in Limited Dependent Variable Models." *Journal of the American Statistical Association,* **68,** 284–287.

Primus, W. E.
1976a "Impact of Data Errors Upon Treatment Estimates of Farm Population." *In Final Report, Institute for Research on Poverty, Vol.* II, Ch. 3. University of Wisconsin Press, Madison, Wisconsin.

Primus, W. E.
1976b "Rural Income Maintenance Experiment." *In Final Report, Institute for Research on Poverty, Vol.* IV, *Ch.* 1, Univ. of Wisconsin Press, Madison, Wisconsin.

Rees, A.
1973 "An Overview of the Labor Supply Results." *In The Final Report of The New Jersey Graduated Work Incentives Experiment, Vol.* I: *Central Labour Supply Response, Part* A. Mathematica Inc., Princeton, New Jersey.

Rees, A.
1974 "An Overview of the Labor-Supply Results." *The Journal of Human Resources* **9,** 158–80.

Rees, A., and Watts H. W.
1975 "An Overview of the Labor Supply Results." *In Work Incentives and Income Guarantees: The New Jersey Negative Income Tax Experiment,* (J. A. Pechman and P. M. Timpane eds.) Brookings Studies in Social Experimentation; Brookings Institution, Washington, D.C.

Riecken, H., and Boruch, R. (eds.)
1974 *Social Experimentation: A Method for Planning and Evaluating Social Intervention.* Academic Press, New York.

Robins, P., and West, R.
1978 "Participation in the Seattle and Denver Income Maintenance Experiments, and Its Effects on Labor Supply." Research Memoranda No. 53, Center for the Study of Welfare Policy, Stanford Research Institute International, Stanford, California.

Rolph, Earl
1967 "The Case for a Negative Income Tax Device." *Industrial Relations,* **6,** No. 2.

Rosett, R. N., and Nelson, F. D.
1975 "Estimation of the Two-Limit Probit Regression Model." *Econometrica* **4,** 141–46.

Rossi, P. H.
1975 "A Critical Review of the Analysis of Non-Labor Force Responses." *In Work Incentives and Guarantees: The New Jersey Negative Income Tax Experiment,* (J. A. Pechman and P. M. Timpane, eds.) Brookings Studies in Social Experimentation, Brookings Institution, Washington, D.C.

Rossi, P. H., and Lyall, K.
1976 *Reforming Public Welfare: A Critique of the Negative Income Tax Experiment.* Russell Sage Foundation, New York.

Scheffe, H.
1959 *The Analysis of Variance.* Wiley, New York.

Schorr, A.
1966 "Against a Negative Income Tax," *The Public Interest,* No. 5, Fall issue.

Schwartz, E. E.
1964 "A Way to End the Means Test." *Journal of Social Work,* **IX,** July.

Seal, H. L.
1964 *Multivariate Statistical Analysis for Biologists,* Methuen, London.

Searle, S. R.
1971 *"Linear Models."* Wiley, New York.
Sharir, S., and Weiss, Y.
1975 *Two Rules of Aggregation of Work Efforts and Leisure Times.* Research Report 7601, Department of Economics. University of Western Ontario.
Skidmore, F. M.
1974 "Availability of Data From the Graduated Work Incentive Experiment." *The Journal of Human Resources* **9**, 265–89.
Skidmore, F. M.
1975 "Operational Design of the Experiment." *In Work Incentives and Income Guarantees: The New Jersey Negative Income Tax Experiment* (J. A. Pechman and P. M. Timpane, eds.) Brookings Studies in Social Experimentation, Brookings Institution, Washington, D.C.
Sonquist, J. A., Baker, E. L., and Morgan, J. N.
1973 *Searching for Structure.* Survey Research Center, Institute for Social Research, University of Michigan.
Spiegelman, R.G., and West, R. W.
1976 "Feasibility of a Social Experiment and Issues in its Design." *American Statistical Association Proceedings of the Business and Economic Statistical Section.*
Spilerman, S., and Miller, R. E.
1973 "The Effect of Negative Tax Payments on Job Turnover and Job Selection." *In The Final Report of the New Jersey Graduated Work Incentives Experiment, Vol.* I: *Central Labor Supply Response, Part* B.
Swamy, P. A. V. B.
1974 "Linear Model with Random Coefficients" *In Frontiers in Econometrics.* (P. Zarembka, ed.) Academic Press, New York.
Theobald, R.
1963 *Free Men and Free Markets.* Clarkson Potter, Inc., New York.
Tobin, J.
1958 "Estimation of Relationships for Limited Department Variables." *Econometrica* **26**, 24–36.
Tobin, J.
1965 "On Improving the Economic Status of the Negro." *Daedalus,* Fall issue.
Tobin, J.
1966 "The Case for an Income Guarantee." *The Public Interest,* No. 4, Summer issue.
Tobin, J., Pechman, J., and Mieszkowski, P.
1967 "Is a Negative Income Tax Practical?" *Yale Law Journal,* **77**, No. 1.
Tocher, K. D.
1952 "A Note on the Design Problem." *Biometrika* **39**, p. 189.
U.S. Department of Health, Education and Welfare
1973 *Summary Report: New Jersey Graduated Work Incentive Experiment.*
U.S. Department of Health, Education and Welfare
1976 *Summary Report: Rural Income Maintenance Experiment.*
Vadakin, J.
1968 "A Critique of the Guaranteed Annual Income." *The Public Interest,* No. 11, Spring issue.
Wang, M. M., Novick, M. R., Isaacs, G. L., and Ozenne, D.
1977 "A Baysian Data Analysis System for the Evaluation of Social Programs." *Journal of the American Statistical Association* **72**, 711–22.
Watts, H. W.
1973a "Labor Supply Response of Married Men." *In The Final Report of the New Jersey*

Graduated Work Incentives Experiment, Vol. I: *Central Labor Supply Response, Part* B. Mathematica Inc., Princeton, New Jersey.

Watts, H. W.
1973b "Technical Notes on Adaptation of a Variance Components Model to Intermittent Panel Data." *In The Final Report of the New Jersey Graduated Work Incentives Experiment, Vol.* III: *Tehnical Notes, Part* E. Mathematica Inc., Princeton, New Jersey.

Watts, H. W., and Mallar, J.
1973 "Wage Rate Response." *In The Final Report of the New Jersey Graduated Work Incentives Experiment, Vol.* I: *Central Labor Supply Response, Part* B. Mathematica Inc., Princeton, New Jersey.

Watts, H. W., and Rees, A. (eds.)
1977 *The New Jersey Income Maintenance Experiment. Labor-Supply Responses, Vol.* 2, Academic Press, New York.

Watts, H. W., Poirier, D. J., and Mallar, C.
1973 "Concepts Used in the Central Analysis and their Measurement." *In The Final Report of the New Jersey Graduated Work Incentives Experiment, Vol.* I: *Central Labor Supply Response, Part* B. Mathematica Inc., Princeton, New Jersey.

Watts, H. W., Avery, R., Elesh, D., Horner, D., Lefcowitz, M. J., Mamer, J., Poirier, D., Spilerman, S., and Wright, S.
1974 "The Labor-Supply Response of Husbands." *The Journal of Human Resources* **9,** 181–200.

Welch, F.
1978 "The Labor Supply Response of Farmers," *In Welfare in Rural Areas,* (J. Palmer, and J. Pechman, eds.) Brookings Institution, Washington, D.C.

Wolf, D.
1977 *Income Maintenance, Labor Supply and Family Stability: An Empirical Analysis of Marital Dissolution,* Ph.D. dissertation, University of Pennsylvania.

Wooldridge, J.
1973 "Housing Consumption in the New Jersey–Pennsylvania Experiment." *In The Final Report of the New Jersey Graduated Work Incentives Experiment, Vol.* III: *Responses with Respect to Expenditure, Health and Social Behavior, Part* D. Mathematica Inc., Princeton, New Jersey.

Wright, S.
1973 "Social Psychological Characteristics and Labor Force Response of Male Heads." *In The Final Report of the New Jersey Graduated Work Incentives Experiment, Vol.* I: *Central Labor Supply Response, Part* B. Mathematica Inc., Princeton, New Jersey.

Index

QUANTITATIVE STUDIES IN SOCIAL RELATIONS
(*Continued from page ii*)

QUANTITATIVE STUDIES IN SOCIAL RELATIONS